MAY MORRIS DESIGNS

'The Very Soul and Essence of Beautiful Embroidery'

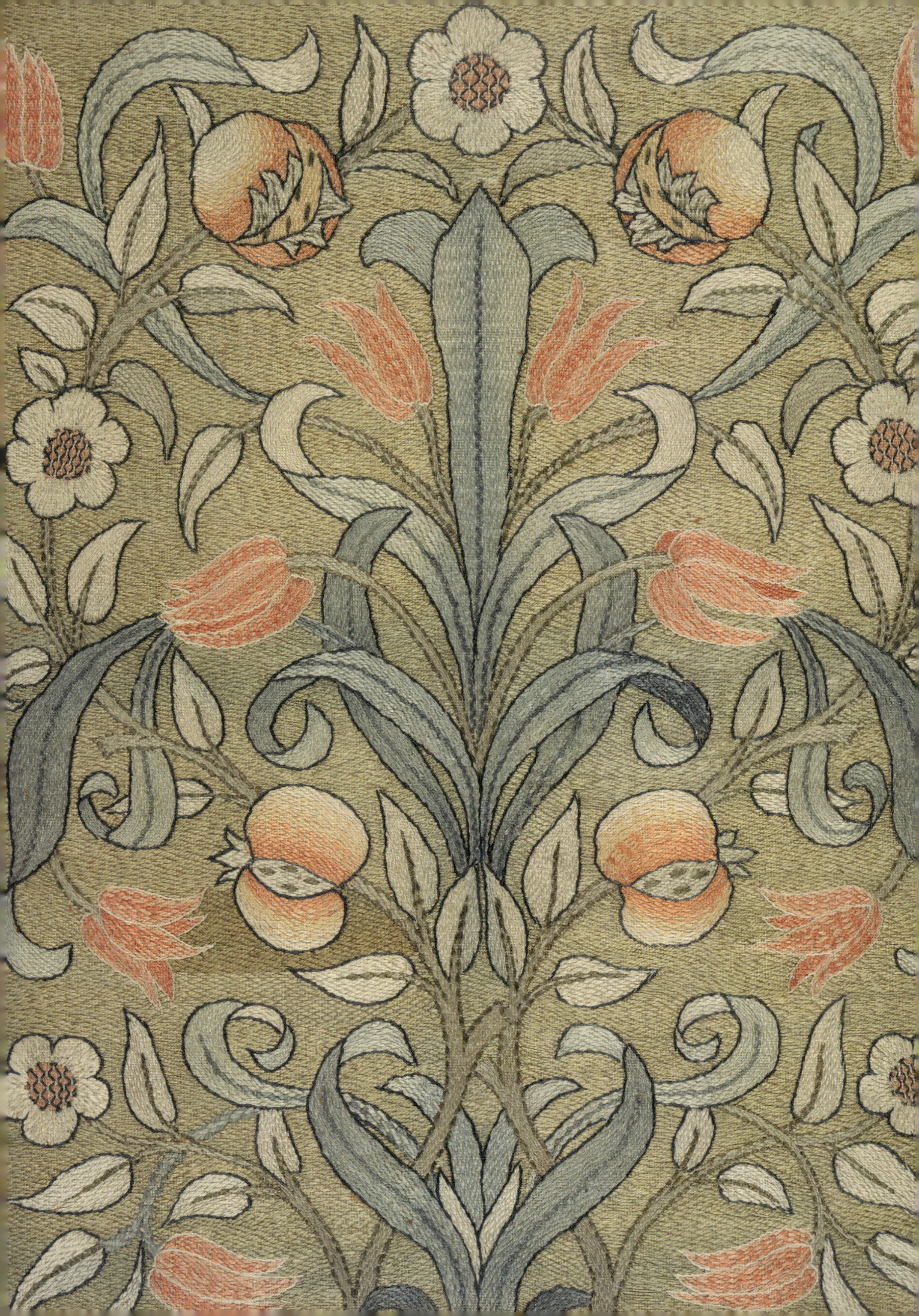

MAY MORRIS DESIGNS

‘The Very Soul and Essence of Beautiful Embroidery’

Lynn Hulse

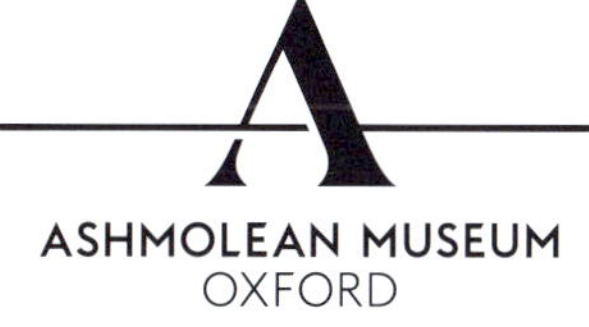

MAY MORRIS DESIGNS:
'THE VERY SOUL AND ESSENCE OF BEAUTIFUL EMBROIDERY'

British Library Cataloguing in Publications Data

A catalogue record for this book is available from the British Library.

ISBN: 978-1-910807-69-9

Design and line drawings by Stephen Hebron

Printed and bound by Gutenberg Press, Malta

Cover: May Morris (1862–1938), *Tulip and acanthus* scrapbook cover, 1890s, polychrome silks on Manchester cloth, 30.8 × 19.5 cm. Private collection

Inside cover: James Pearsall & Co., *Eastern Unfading Dyes*, embroidery silks shade card, 1880s, 18 × 61.7 cm. Private collection

Frontispiece: May Morris (1862–1938), *Tulip and pomegranate* fire screen panel or cushion cover, 1890s, polychrome silks on Manchester cloth, 58.6 × 49 cm. Private collection

For further details of Ashmolean titles please visit:
www.ashmolean.org/shop

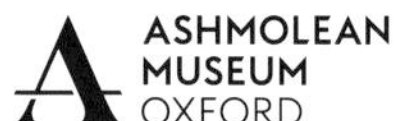

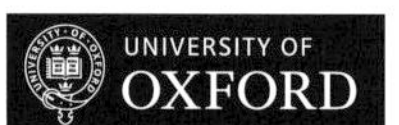

Published with the support of:

The Albert Dawson Educational Trust
Ornamental Embroidery

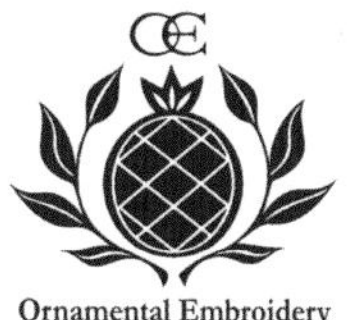

Contents

Acknowledgements

This book would not have been published without the assistance of the staff at the Ashmolean Museum. Sincere thanks go to Declan McCarthy and Carrie Hickman for all their efforts in seeing this book through the press, and to Jude Barrett in the Informal Learning and Public Programmes team for helping to deliver Ornamental Embroidery's programme of workshops and lectures at the Museum since 2010. I owe a special debt of gratitude to Dr Caroline Palmer in the Department of Western Art Print Room for answering my endless enquiries about May Morris's designs with such good grace.

Heartfelt thanks go to my dear friend and fellow May Morris enthusiast Paul Reeves who shared his textile collection and photographed some of the objects illustrated in this book. I would also like to thank the private owners who kindly agreed to their works being included here.

Thanks are due to the following individuals who have granted access to their collections and supplied images: Rowan Bain at the William Morris Gallery; Jenny Lister at the Victoria and Albert Museum; Helen Elletson and Vanessa Manson at The William Morris Society; Dr Kathy Haslam at the Society of Antiquaries of London (Kelmscott Manor); Helen Bratt-Wyton at Wightwick Manor (National Trust); John Mackie at Lyon and Turnbull; Max Clark at Cumbria Archives; Rowan Speakman at the Ruskin Museum; Wellcome Collection; the Library of Congress; and the Metropolitan Museum of Art. I am especially grateful to Anna Mason for passing on her knowledge of May Morris's correspondence.

I would like to thank The Albert Dawson Educational Trust for their generous financial contribution towards this publication.

Finally, the book would not have been written without the support of family and friends. I am particularly indebted to my son Andrew, whose critical and editorial comments have been invaluable. As always, any mistakes that remain are my own.

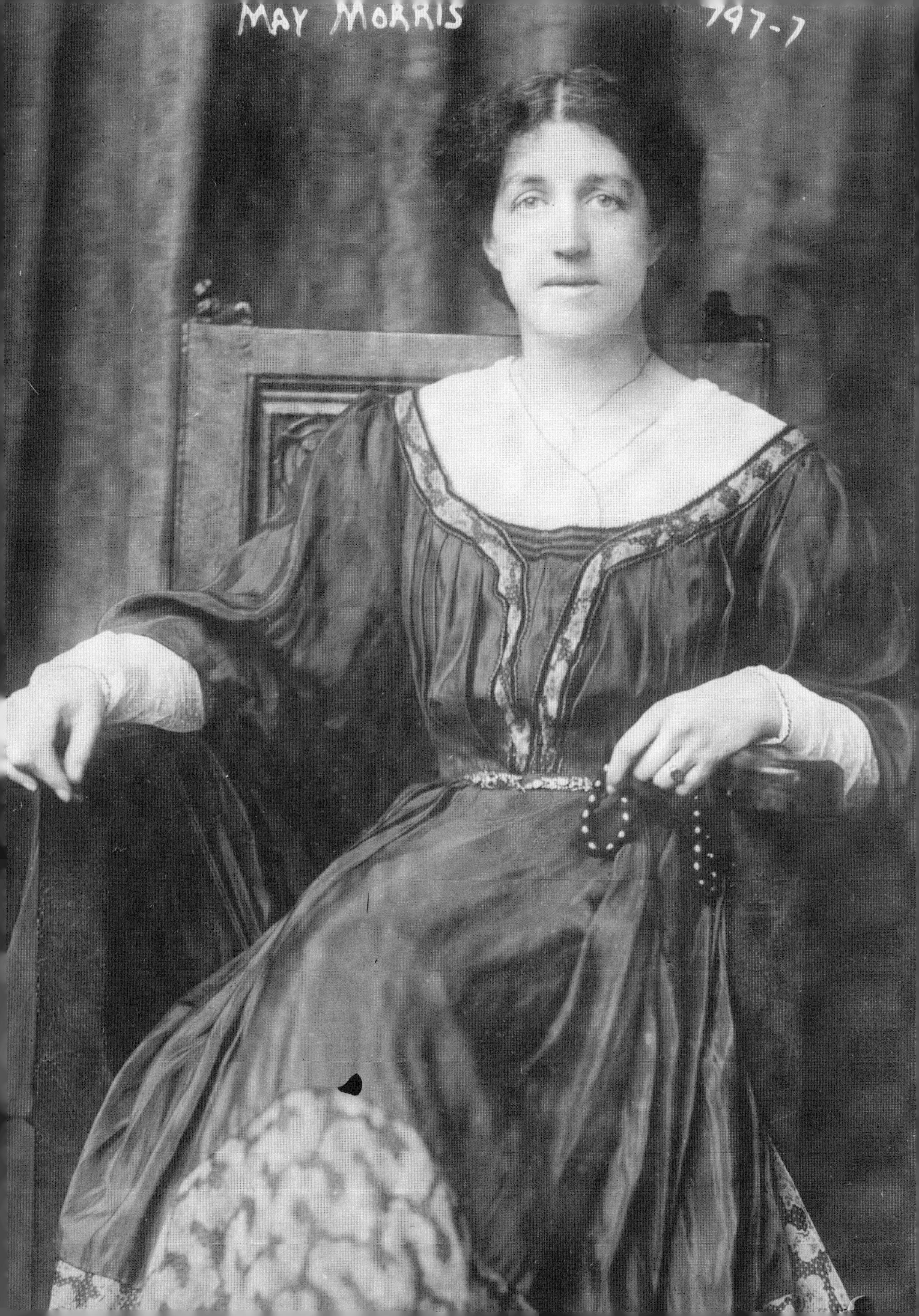
MAY MORRIS
797-7

Introduction

May Morris (1862–1938) is recognised today as one of the leading designer-makers of the Arts and Crafts movement (**fig.1**). She was both a pioneer of decorative needlework and an expert on the history of her craft. May's endeavours were lauded by the press early in her career; one critic commented in his review of the 1890 Arts and Crafts exhibition: 'There are many good contributions of needlework from Miss Morris, who has made herself not a little of an authority on the subject, as writer, designer, and actual worker.'[1] It is this union of art historical knowledge and craft practice in May's work that fascinates twenty-first century designers and embroiderers.

The objectives of this book are threefold: first, to showcase May's substantial corpus of needlework designs in the Ashmolean Museum, of which a selection of 25 are published here for the first time for readers to stitch; second, to illuminate her approach to translating a sketched idea into a finished piece of embroidery; and third, to contextualise her work within the artistic developments of needle-art that were taking place in the years leading up to and during her lifetime.

The book opens with a chapter exploring May's life and the circumstances that gave rise to the resurgence of decorative needlework. It includes a survey of the technical guidebooks and stitch primers published to meet the growing demand for this new style of embroidery, before closing with a summary of May's training in needlework and design. Chapter 2 analyses the four elements that make a piece of embroidery 'artistic' – design, colour, materials and stitch – with reference to May and the work of other late nineteenth- and early twentieth-century commentators. Chapter 3 discusses her working process, from drawing plants and flowers to transferring the finished pattern to the cloth, and gives a detailed description of the 25 botanical designs for domestic furnishings and apparel selected from the Ashmolean's collection. This is followed by stitch patterns for the designs, which embroiderers can use in their own work. The book concludes with a handful of technical samples demonstrating May's approach to stitch.

The synthesis between history and practice espoused by May throughout her life lies at the heart of my own research and teaching as a textile scholar and needleworker specialising in Victorian and Edwardian decorative arts. At Ornamental Embroidery, needlework and design are taught through a programme of lectures, workshops and first-hand study of objects in public and private collections. This book has grown out of a desire to answer the many questions posed by embroiderers in classes dedicated to the work of this remarkable woman.

Fig.1 May Morris (1862–1938), Photograph taken *c.*1909 for her American lecture tour. Library of Congress, Rare Book and Special Collections Division. https://lccn.loc.gov/2014683895

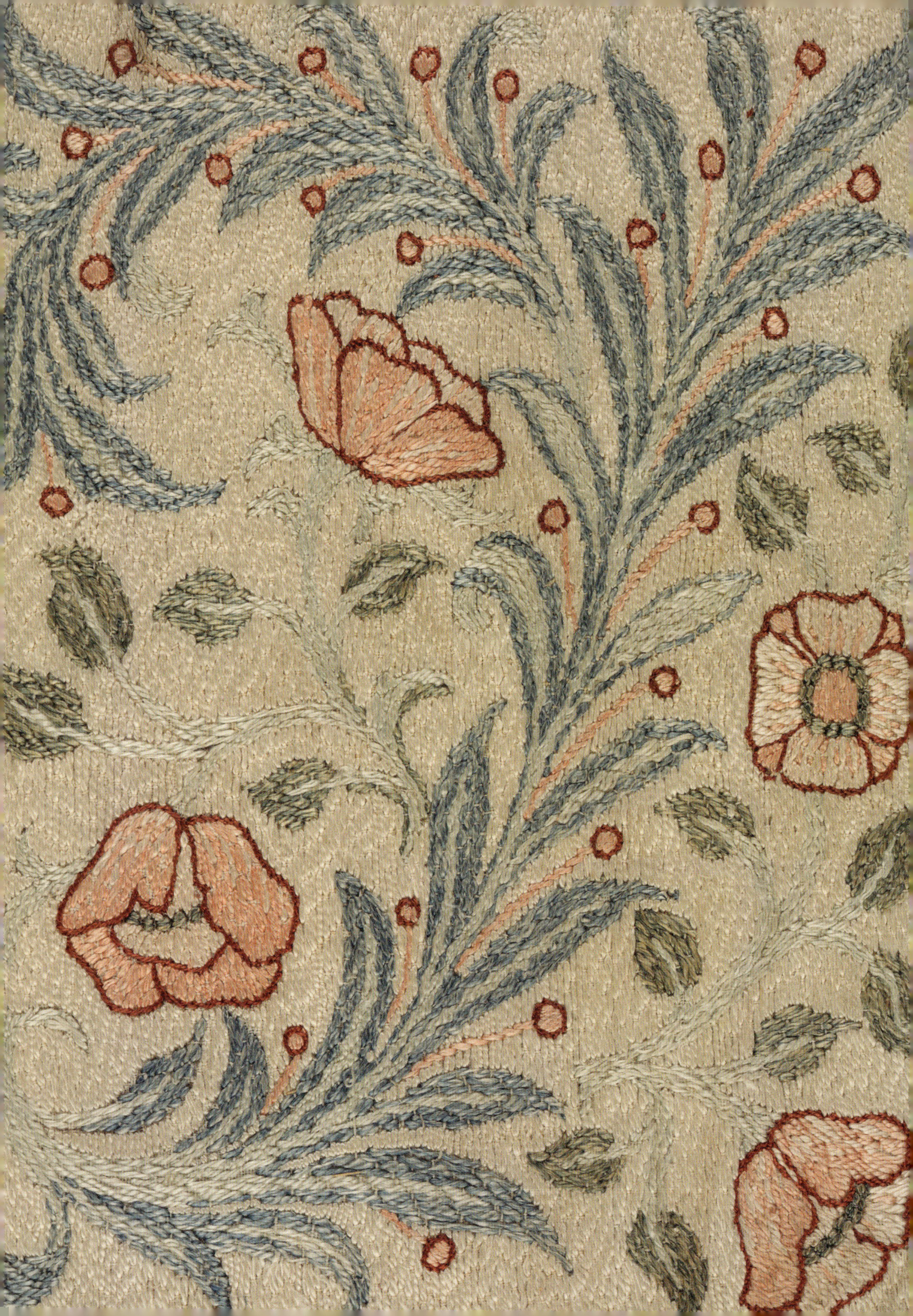

1 May Morris and the Revival of Decorative Needlework

MAY MORRIS WAS the younger daughter of the designer, author and visionary socialist William Morris (1834–1896) and his wife, the embroiderer and artist's model Jane Morris, née Burden (1839–1914). Her formative years were spent living over the shop at 26 Queen Square, London, site of her father's furnishings and decorative arts firm Morris, Marshall, Faulkner & Co., where she began to develop a talent for design, a keen eye for colour and a mastery of stitch.

The Arts and Crafts movement provided new opportunities for women to carve out a professional career in design and making. In 1885, when May was just 23, her father recognised her skill in decorative needlework by appointing her as manageress of the embroidery department of his reorganised and expanded business, Morris & Co. May ran the studio for twelve years (1885–96), designing kits and special commissions for the firm's British and overseas clients while supervising her small team of workers (**fig.2**). At her father's death in 1896, she stepped down from the role to pursue her own career as designer, maker, embroidery tutor, writer and lecturer, travelling around the United States in 1909–10 to deliver an intensive speaking tour and exhibit her work. May was also a vigorous advocate for women artists, co-founding the Women's Guild of Arts in 1907 to provide a forum for her 'sisters' working in the fine and decorative arts who were denied membership of exclusively male organisations like the Art Workers' Guild.

May lectured and published on embroidery for more than 30 years; her publications are listed in **Table 1**. In her earliest printed work, she wrote: 'I am inclined to take needle-art seriously, and regard its simply priceless qualities worth as careful study and appreciation as any other form of art; certainly research into its history and development is as rich and fruitful.'[1] It is evident from her writings and her store of photographs and glass plate negatives that she carried out first-hand study of historic needlework in churches and museum collections across Britain and Europe. She also researched archival records, antiquarian tomes and learned journals, as well as the published works of modern scholars. Finally, she was an avid collector of historic and modern textiles, and used them to inform her practice.

May continued to design for embroidery, fired by her passion for gardening and love of the countryside around Kelmscott Manor, her Oxfordshire home. Her final recorded work, *A Garden Piece* (1938), made for the Manders

Opposite: detail of fig.51

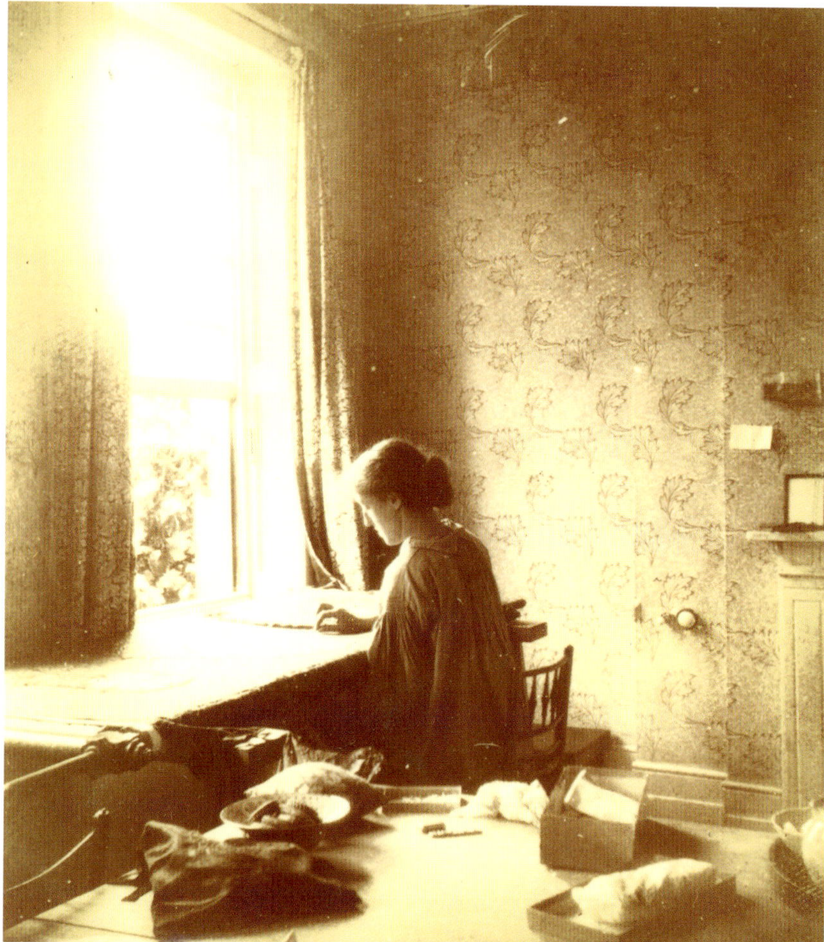

Fig.2 May Morris (1862–1938) sitting at her embroidery frame, 8 Hammersmith Terrace, 1890s, 8 × 7 cm, William Morris Gallery, P710.

of Wightwick Manor in Staffordshire a few months before her death, epitomises her love of English meadow plants and cottage garden flowers.[2]

May was at the forefront of the generation of decorative artists who sought to elevate the embroiderer's craft from a trifling pastime brought into disrepute by the 'uselessness and ugliness' of Berlin wool work, the most popular form of embroidery in the early Victorian period, to a serious art form.[3] Decorative needlework, or art embroidery as it was known from the early 1870s, was defined by Sophia Caulfeild and Blanche Saward as 'a general term for all descriptions of needlework that spring from the application of a knowledge of design and colouring, with skill in fitting and executing'.[4] This new style of textile furnishings for the home had begun to take root in the early 1860s through the work of Morris, Marshall, Faulkner & Co., yet Berlin wool work was to remain the prevailing fashion in middle- and upper-class homes for another decade.

Popular in Britain throughout the mid-nineteenth century, Berlin wool work was a type of canvas work executed primarily in tent or cross stitch

TABLE I: MAY MORRIS'S PUBLISHED WRITINGS ON NEEDLEWORK

1888	'Chain Stitch Embroidery', *The Century Guild Hobby Horse*, 3, pp.24–29
1889, rep.1893	'Of Embroidery', *Arts and Crafts Exhibition Society: Catalogue of the Second Exhibition*, pp.68–74, reprinted in *Arts and Crafts Essays*, pp.212–23
1890, rep.1893	'Of Materials' and 'Of Colours and Colouring', *Arts and Crafts Exhibition Society: Catalogue of the Third Exhibition*, pp.92–107; reprinted in *Arts and Crafts Essays*, pp.212–23, 365–86
1890	'Design in Embroidery', *The Queen, The Lady's Newspaper*, 6 December, p.844
1892	'Embroidery', in A. H. Mackmurdo, *Plain Handicrafts, being Essays by Artists Setting Forth the Principles of Design & Established Methods of Workmanship*, pp.46–56
1892	'Embroidered Sleeves', *The Queen, The Lady's Newspaper*, 3 December, pp.946–47
1893	'Embroidery', *The Decorator and Furnisher*, 21/5 (February) pp.178–79
1893	*Decorative Needlework*
1893–94	'Of Church Embroidery' I–XIII, *The Building News and Engineering Journal*, 65/2023 (13 October 1893) I, pp.465–66; 65/2025 (27 October 1893) II, 'Appliqué', pp.533–34; 65/2027 (10 November 1893) III, 'Couching and Flat Gold-Work', pp.603–04; 65/2029 (24 November 1893) IV, 'Couching and Raised Gold-Work', pp.674–75; 65/2031 (8 December 1893) V, 'Gold Work', pp.744–45; 65/2033 (22 December 1893) VI, 'Figure Work, pp.814–15; 66/2035 (5 January 1894) VII, 'Figure Work', pp.3–4; 66/2037 (19 January 1894) VIII, 'White Linen Work', pp.73–74; 66/2040 (9 February 1894) IX, 'Burses, Shields &c', pp.175–77; 66/2042 (23 February 1894) X, 'Design', pp.245–46; 66/2063 (20 July 1984) XI, 'Animals and Symbols', pp.66–67; 66/2066 (10 August 1894) XII, 'Design', pp.168–69; 66/2069 (31 August 1894) XIII, 'Conclusion', pp.277–78
1895	'Mediæval Embroidery', *Journal of the Society for Arts*, 43/2207 (8 March 1895) pp.384–96
1899	'Coptic Textiles', *The Architectural Review: For the Artist and Craftsman*, 5/30 (May 1899) pp.275–87
1900	'Decorative Needlework', *Women in Professions being the Professional Section of The International Congress of Women, London, July 1899*, ed. The Countess of Aberdeen, pp.191–94
1902	'Line Embroidery', *The Art Workers' Quarterly*, I/4 (October 1902) pp.117–21
1905	'Opus Anglicanum – The Syon Cope', 'II – The Ascoli Cope', 'III – The Pienza Cope' and 'Opus Anglicanum at the Burlington Fine Arts Club', *The Burlington Magazine*, 6/22 (January 1905) pp.278–85; 6/24 (March 1905) pp.440–48; 7/25 (April 1905) pp.54–65; 7/28 (July 1905) pp.302–09
1913–14	'Embroidery' in Board of Trade, *Ghent International Exhibition 1913: Catalogue of the British Arts and Crafts Section*, pp.clxii–clxxvii; Board of Trade, *Arts Décoratifs de Grande-Bretagne et d'Irlande. Exposition Organisée par le Gouvernement Britannique. Palais du Louvre, Pavillon de Marsan. Avril-Octobre* MCMXIV, pp.clxii–clxxvii
1919	'Weaving and Textile Crafts' in *Handicrafts and Reconstruction: Notes by Members of the Arts and Crafts Exhibition Society*, pp.41–52

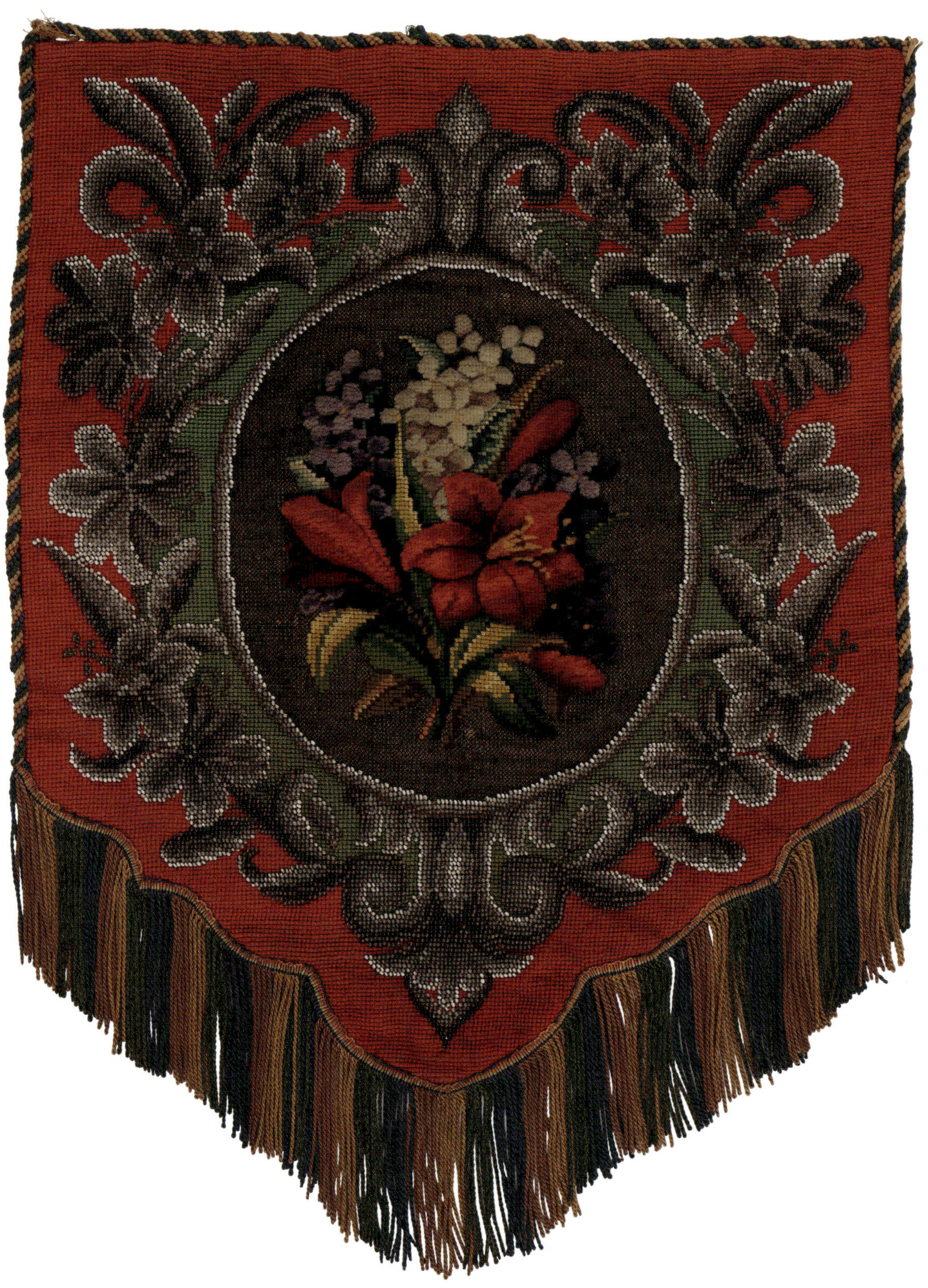

from a pattern printed on squared paper, each square of the printed design representing one square of the canvas. Around 14,000 designs, from flowers to pictorial images based on famous paintings, were sold through Berlin warehouses and fancy repositories across Britain. Patterns were also available in women's magazines like *The Lady's Newspaper*. From the 1850s, upholstered furniture, cushions, carpets, framed pictures, screens, bellpulls and tea cosies were decorated with exotic blooms such as arum lilies, peonies, cabbage roses, gloxinias, fuchsias and amaryllis, stitched in the new, brightly coloured chemical dyes.[5] The banner screen in **fig.3** is a typical example of the work produced in *c.*1860.

Despite its popularity, Berlin wool work had many detractors among exponents of decorative needlework, not least May Morris, who loathed modern canvas work. The architect and designer George Edmund Street (1824–1881) described it as 'that contemptible system of cross-stitch work, which requires no sense, no thought, hardly any manual dexterity on the part of the worker; and which, be the work good, bad, or indifferent, produces the same hard formal absence of good results.'[6] By the mid 1870s, the craze for Berlin wool work had finally been superseded by art embroidery. To place May's work in context, we need to look at the origins of this new style of interior decoration.

THE ORIGINS OF ART EMBROIDERY

The revival of decorative needlework can be traced back to the religious and artistic developments of the 1830s. Many of the restrictions imposed on Roman Catholics during the Reformation, not least the inability to practice their religion freely, were reversed by the Catholic Emancipation Act of 1829. In the early 1830s the founders of the Oxford Movement, which later developed into Anglo-Catholicism, argued for the restoration of High Church ideals within the Protestant liturgy, including the use of lavishly embroidered vestments and church furnishings. The desire to beautify the fabric of the Church in Victorian Britain coincided with the Gothic Revival, a resurgence of interest in late medieval art and architecture.

Around the same time, designers and makers were engaged in an economic and aesthetic debate on British design and industry, claiming that they had failed to keep pace with continental rivals. Among the topics hotly disputed was the use of three-dimensional ornament to create a false impression of depth on a flat surface. This was one of the criticisms levelled against Berlin wool work: 'The flowers appear to stand out from the canvas, so that the cushion or stool seems intended for anything rather than resting a weary head or foot.'[7] To improve the design and quality of manufactured goods, the Government School of Design was established in London in 1837, where students received instruction in drawing and colouring as well as the history and principles of ornamental art in a range of styles, from the antique

Fig.3 Banner screen, *c.*1860, polychrome wools and beads with braided silk fringe on Penelope canvas, 57.4 × 42.8 cm. Private collection

to the modern. By the late 1840s, art schools had been set up in several cities throughout Britain and Ireland.

Despite attempts to promote a balance between beauty and utility, manufacturers continued to reflect consumer taste. The display of British domestic furnishings at the 1851 Great Exhibition in London was criticised by reformers for its low standard of design and excessive use of ornamentation. The designer and educator Henry Cole (1808–1882), the artist Richard Redgrave (1804–1888) and the ornamentalist and theorist Owen Jones (1809–1874) were instrumental in developing formal guidelines for a modern design vocabulary that would give rise to the Aesthetic and Arts and Crafts movements. These principles – known collectively as Design Reform – were codified and expanded in Jones's seminal publication *The Grammar of Ornament* (London, 1856).

Gothic Revival and Design Reform were key to the renaissance of decorative needlework. Chief among the associated factors was a renewed appreciation for the technical mastery and artistic expression found in the work of medieval craftsmen and women. This was manifested in publications like the Reverend Charles Hartshorne's *English Medieval Embroidery* (London, 1848), and in a series of loan exhibitions held in London, Manchester and Leeds during the 1850s and 1860s which featured notable examples of *opus Anglicanum*, or English medieval work, including the Syon and Butler-Bowden copes (Victoria and Albert Museum (V&A), 83-1864 and T.36-1955).

A second factor was the creation of a cultural district of museums and colleges in South Kensington, London, devoted to art and science. The South Kensington Museum (known today as the V&A) was established in 1852 under Cole's direction to educate and inspire designers, manufacturers and consumers in art and design. Historic and contemporary objects from home and abroad were made available to a wider audience and given status as works of art.[8] Cole also took charge of the Government School of Design, renamed the National Art Training School in 1853. (In 1896, it was renamed once again as the Royal College of Art.)

A third factor in the development of art embroidery was the renewed interest in the decorative arts of the Middle East, India and the Far East, stimulated by the advent of international exhibitions showcasing the latest industrial, cultural and technological achievements around the world.

ART EMBROIDERY

The revival of decorative needlework in the 1840s was predominantly ecclesiastical but within a single generation, this new style of church decoration began to influence the development of embroidered furnishings for the domestic interior.

Terminology

The terms 'art embroidery' and 'art needlework' were used interchangeably during the last quarter of the nineteenth century.[9] The description was first coined in August 1872 when Victoria Welby (1837–1912) called her new embroidery society the School of Art Needlework (renamed the Royal School of Art Needlework (RSAN) in 1875). The prefix 'art' gained traction following the success of the School's *Special Loan Exhibition of Decorative Art Needlework,* hosted by the South Kensington Museum in 1873. The display, which featured 630 examples of British, European and Asian embroidery dating from the ninth to the eighteenth centuries, became a turning point in the revival of 'artistic' needlework.[10]

Not everyone used the term 'art embroidery' to described decorative needlework in the later Victorian and Edwardian periods. The art critic Lucy Crane (1842–1882) considered it to be a tautological expression invented by shopkeepers 'to characterise a kind of goods got up in a certain style to please that part of the public that cares for fashion and novelty alone'.[11] Embroidery is an art by its very nature, she reasoned, just as chemistry is a science. Similarly, May Morris described her profession as 'the art **of** embroidery' in the sense of the Greek term 'techne', meaning art, skill or craft employed in creating a work of beauty and utility.[12]

Technical Guidebooks and Stitch Primers

Responding to readers' curiosity, *The Queen,* a newspaper for ladies, published in August 1875 one of the earliest articles on the subject: 'What is Art Needlework?'[13] Commercial publishers soon began to realise the financial potential in printing technical guidebooks and stitch primers to meet the growing demand for this new style of embroidery; all the publications printed prior to the First World War are listed in **Table 2**. Ward, Lock and Tyler paved the way in March 1877 with E. Masé's *Art Needlework,* praised by the critics for its clear and practical instruction in crewel, silk and appliqué.[14] *The Englishwoman's Domestic Magazine* especially hoped that the chapters on design and colour would 'work a reform among the untutored workers of what they fondly imagine to be art needlework'.[15] Around the same time, Mary Ann Turner (fl. 1860–82), who ran a fancy repository at 38 Lamb's Conduit Street in London's West End, published *Practical Hints on the Revived Art of Crewel & Silk Embroidery*. Despite being reprinted at least six times, Turner's booklet was dismissed by *The Queen* for its cursory manner and its failure to use the names given to stitches by experienced embroiderers in art work.[16]

The following year, the Irish firm Marcus Ward & Co. published *Art Embroidery: A Treatise on the Revived Practice of Decorative Needlework.* Co-authored by Elizabeth Glaister (1839–1892) and her cousin Mortimer Sarah Lockwood (1837–1923), the book was commended by one critic as 'a serious and at the same time a successful attempt to raise the art of

TABLE 2: TECHNICAL GUIDEBOOKS AND STITCH PRIMERS, 1877–1914*

Date	Author	Title
1877	E. Masé	*Art Needlework: A Guide to Embroidery in Crewels, Silks, Appliqué, etc.*
1877 (6th edn 1882)	Mary Ann Turner	*Practical Hints on the Revived Art of Crewel & Silk Embroidery*
1878	Mortimer Sarah Lockwood and Elizabeth Glaister	*Art Embroidery: A Treatise on the Revived Practice of Decorative Needlework*
1880	Letitia Higgin, ed. Lady Marian Alford	*Handbook of Embroidery*
1882	No author attributed	*Art Needlework. A Complete Manual of Embroidery in Silks and Crewels, with Full Instructions as to Stitches, Materials, and Implements*
1893	May Morris	*Decorative Needlework*
1899	Ellen T. Masters	*The Book of Stitches*
1899/1907	William George Paulson Townsend	*Embroidery: or The Craft of the Needle*
1900/1901/1907	Lewis Foreman Day and Mary Buckle	*Art in Needlework*
1904	Manchester School of Embroidery†	*The Fourth Book of Hows, or How to Work Embroidery Stitches*
1906	Grace Christie	*Embroidery and Tapestry Weaving*
1909	Mrs Bessie Townend	*Talks on Art Needlework*
1911	Mrs Bessie Townend	*Art Needlework Made Easy*
1900s	Needlecraft Ltd	*Needlecraft Practical Journal* (no.12 'Decorative Needlework', no.55 'The Art of Embroidery Shading', and no.87 'Crewel Wool Embroidery in Early English Designs')
1912	Ada Wentworth Fitzwilliam and A. F. Morris Hands	*Jacobean Embroidery: Its Forms and Fillings Including Late Tudor*

* This list excludes books that deal exclusively with ecclesiastical work, such as Audrey Ridsdale, *Designs for Church Embroidery* (London, 1894); Hilda Hands, *Church Needlework: A Manual of Practical Tuition* (London, 1907); and Alice Dryden, *Church Embroidery* (London, 1911).

† Not to be confused with the Manchester School of Art established in 1838. The Manchester School of Embroidery was the address of Briggs's factory and wholesale warehouse on Cannon Street, in the heart of the city.

Fig.4 Thomas Crane (1843–1903), *Strawberry blossom*, design for a square footstool or cushion, to be worked in silks on silk or satin, or in crewels on woollen cloth, printed in Mortimer Sarah Lockwood (1837–1923) and Elizabeth Glaister (1839–1892), *Art Embroidery: A Treatise on the Revived Practice of Decorative Needlework* (London, 1878) plate 1, 31.2 × 24.5 cm (page). Private collection

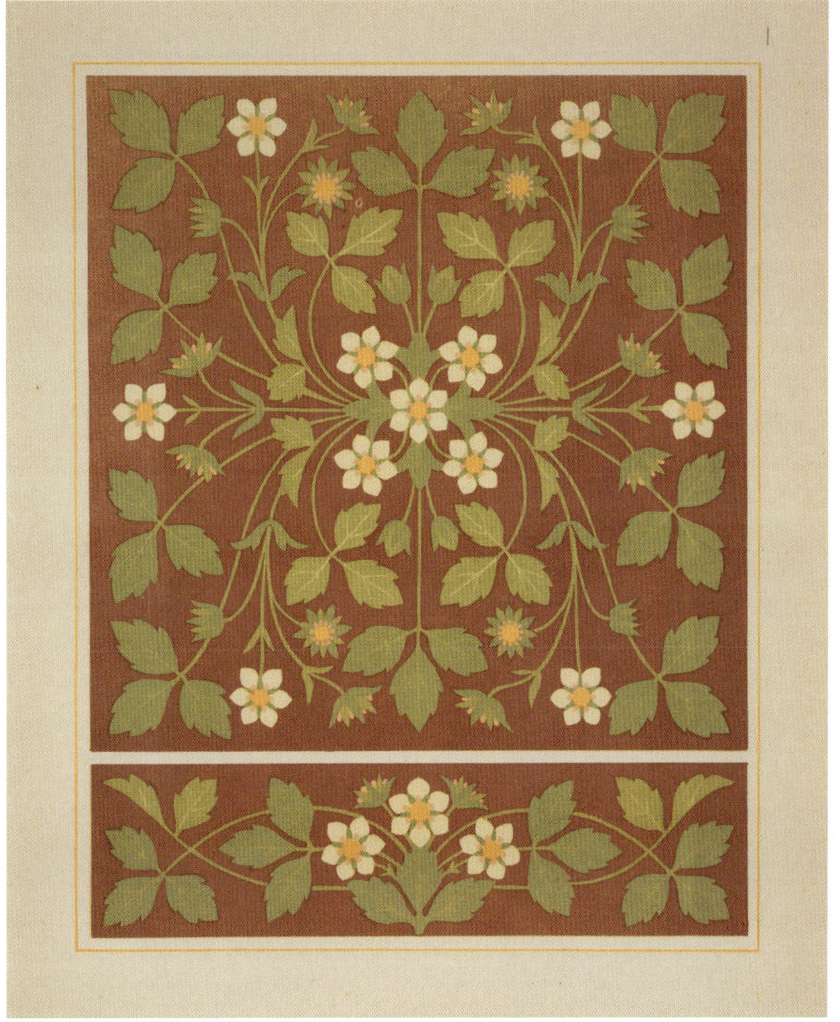

embroidery'.[17] The volume included a detailed analysis of the essential characteristics of decorative needlework along with nineteen patterns (**fig.4**) for home furnishings by Thomas Crane (1843–1903), director of design at the publisher's London office.

Between 1880 and 1914, a further eleven volumes were published by embroiderers and designers working in the decorative arts, including William George Paulson Townsend (1868–1941), design master at the RSAN and editor of *The Art Workers' Quarterly* (1902–1906); the artist and industrial designer Lewis Foreman Day (1845–1910); and Grace Christie (1872–1953), instructor of embroidery and weaving at the Royal College of Art. In 1900, the Manchester needlework manufacturer William Briggs & Co. began publishing the series *Needlecraft Practical Journal* under the imprint Needlecraft Ltd. Issues included 'Decorative Needlework', 'The Art of Embroidery Shading', and 'Crewel Wool Embroidery in Early English Designs' (**fig.5**), no

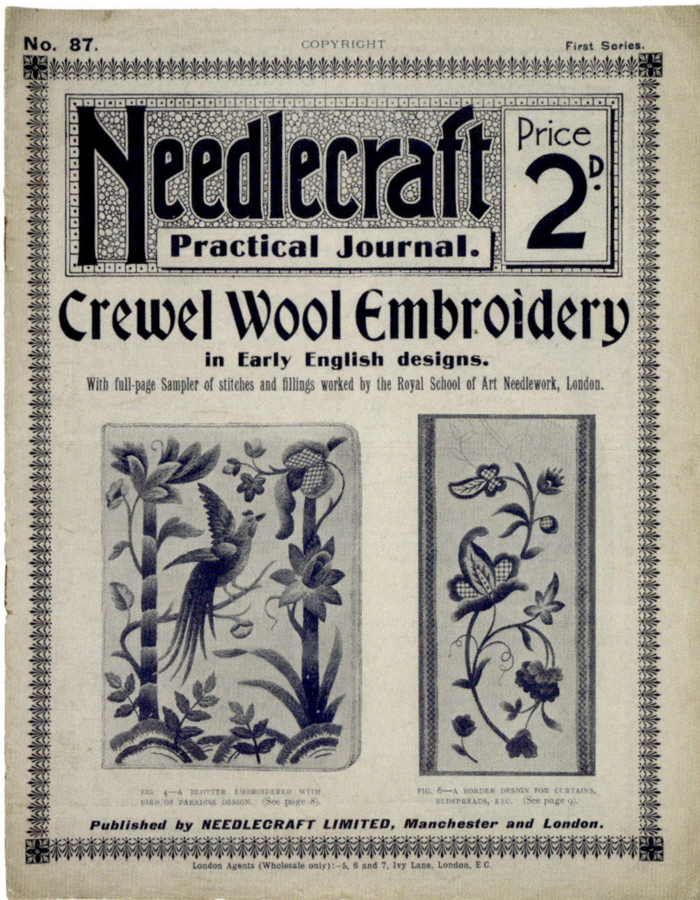

No. 87. COPYRIGHT First Series.

Needlecraft Practical Journal. Price 2D.

Crewel Wool Embroidery in Early English designs.

With full-page Sampler of stitches and fillings worked by the Royal School of Art Needlework, London.

FIG. 4—A BLOTTER EMBROIDERED WITH BIRD OF PARADISE DESIGN. (See page 8).

FIG. 6—A BORDER DESIGN FOR CURTAINS, BEDSPREADS, ETC. (See page 9).

Published by NEEDLECRAFT LIMITED, Manchester and London.

London Agents (Wholesale only):—5, 6 and 7, Ivy Lane, London, E.C.

Fig.5 'Crewel Wool Embroidery in Early English Designs', *Needlecraft Practical Journal*, no.87, 1900s, cover, 31 × 25 cm. Private collection

doubt capitalising on the resurgence of interest among middle- and upper-class women in the use and replication of historic needlework as a furnishing fabric.[18]

The RSAN's *Handbook of Embroidery* (1880), written by Letitia Higgin (1837–1913) and edited by Lady Marian Alford (1817–1888), author of *Needlework as Art* (London, 1886), was widely acclaimed by the Victorian press as 'an authoritative exposition of the mystery of art-needlework' from 'the headquarters of decorative stitchery in Great Britain'.[19] The *Handbook* begins with a survey of the tools and threads commonly employed as well as the materials best suited as grounds for needlework. Chapters follow on the stitches used in hand and frame embroidery. Appended to the volume are 25 designs by leading artists associated with the school, including William Morris, Walter Crane (1845–1915), Edward Burne-Jones (1833–1898) and Selwyn Image (1849–1930), plus some of the female designers from the RSAN's own studio.

By her late twenties, May Morris had established her claim as a leading authority on the history and practice of embroidery. In 1891, she was invited

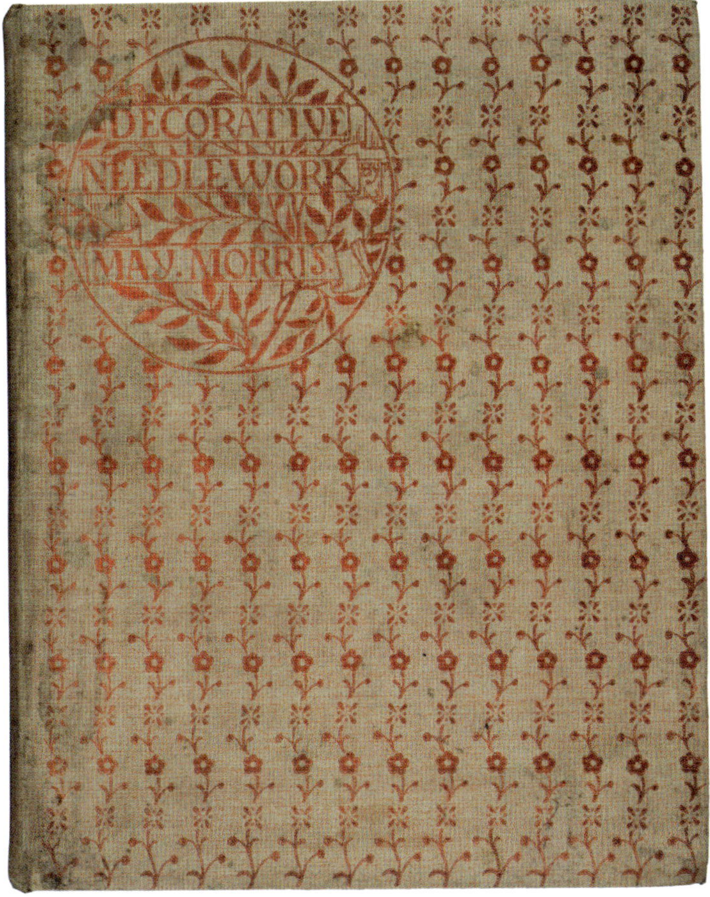

Fig.6 May Morris (1862–1938), *Decorative Needlework* (London, 1893), front cover, printed in red on pink buckram, 22.7 × 18.4 cm. Private collection

by publisher Joseph Hughes to write a chapter on decorating the home for the manual *Domestic Economy*, aimed at trainee teachers and schoolmistresses as well as housewives of limited means.[20] Hughes was renowned for the quality of his instruction books, so it is not surprising that May joined forces with him two years later to publish her own technical guidebook entitled *Decorative Needlework*, described by Joan Edwards as the first 'modern' book on the subject.[21] May designed the cover for the publisher binding, printed in red on pink buckram (**fig.6**), or in gold on the special copies bound in parchment.[22] The volume was issued in very large, uncut paper with wide margins so that, in the words of Hughes's circular, 'There is plenty of room…for notes, if the fair readers should wish to make any.'[23]

Decorative Needlework was singled out by one reviewer from all the other publications on embroidery for being 'extremely simple and in teaching just those simple things which most of the books on art-needlework seem to think unworthy of notice, but which yet are the foundation to all good honest needlework.'[24] Another described it as 'written in the spirit of an artist, and yet is thoroughly practical.'[25] The volume elaborates on May's earlier published writings on the fundamental principles of art embroidery and is liberally peppered with references to historic and non-western practice. *Decorative Needlework* is therefore an indispensable source for understanding May's approach to needlecraft.

THE DESIGNER-MAKER IDEAL

The Queen argued in 1876 that if the revival of art embroidery was to have any real value, and not fall out of fashion like other 'manias', it was incumbent upon teachers and promoters to develop the inventive faculties: 'If women exert their own powers in drawing, designing, and colouring their work, the revival will prove a cultivation of artistic taste.'[26] Nevertheless, opinion was divided amongst designers and practitioners over the notion that art embroidery should be conceived and executed by one person to ensure unity and coherence in the work produced. Lockwood and Glaister, for example, contended that 'division of labour' was 'fatal to distinction and individuality.'[27] While May Morris relished the freedom of thought and execution that such an arrangement allowed, she recognised that most needlewomen struggled with design:

> Designing for embroidery, is, or should be, a serious art, and there is a world of difference between the work produced by an amateur with a pretty taste for drawing, who sits down before a spray of wild flowers, and transfers some ghost of it haphazard to one corner of a cloth, and that which comes from the hand of a practical designer, who, after years of patient training, is qualified to produce a decorative pattern, skilfully filling a given space...[28]

Day and Mary Buckle (fl. 1890–1910) concluded that the Arts and Crafts ideal of the designer-maker was for the most part impossible to fulfil, but like many other writers on decorative needlework, they insisted that the artist must know 'which stitches answer which purpose', while the embroiderer must have 'sympathy enough with a design to choose the stitch or stitches that will best render it.'[29]

MAY MORRIS'S TRAINING IN EMBROIDERY AND DESIGN

May grew up surrounded by craftsmen and women while living over the firm at 26 Queen Square (1865–72). She was fascinated by the processes involved in the production of textiles: the air at home 'saturated with dyeing', and her father's study that 'smelt pleasantly of tracing-paper'.[30] In an interview given in America in January 1910 she recalled: 'Embroidery is the first thing I learned...I sat beside my mother at her embroidery frame and watched the needle come down and begged to be allowed to fasten the thread.'[31] May began to stitch from an early age, making pen wipes and kettle holders as Christmas gifts with the aid of her older sister Jenny (1861–1935). Following a visit to the family home in March 1869, American novelist Henry James (1843–1916) wrote to his sister that William Morris designed all the patterns used in his embroideries and worked them 'stitch by stitch, with his own fingers – aided by those of his wife and little girls'.[32] In March 1878, May sent a birthday gift of a tobacco pouch to her father, who admired the 'pretty' shape and indigo colour, though he asked her to replace the cotton strings with silk, 'as cotton on cotton sets my teeth on edge'.[33]

May was taught to embroider by her mother and her aunt Elizabeth Burden (1841–1924). Like many early Victorian girls, the Burden sisters had stitched samplers in childhood.[34] Shortly after William Morris began experimenting with embroidery he taught Jane 'the first principles of laying the stitches together closely so as to cover the ground smoothly and radiating them properly afterwards'.[35] Georgiana Burne-Jones observed that his instructions 'could not be improved upon and that disaster followed their neglect'.[36] Friends and family members worked for the firm, supplying all kinds of embroidered furnishings for domestic and ecclesiastical purposes. By 1880, Morris & Co. was also employing outworkers under Jane's management.

May described her mother as a 'past-Mistress in her art'.[37] The *Honeysuckle* hanging in **fig.7**, designed by William Morris in 1876, is one of the few works to survive by Jane, assisted by her daughter Jenny. May's opinion of the skills of her aunt Elizabeth is unrecorded, though William Morris deemed her to be a 'first-rate needle-woman' with a 'complete mastery of the theory & practice of all kinds of needlework'.[38] Her expertise in handling silk and gold thread is evident in the medieval-style angel musician in **fig.8**. According to one contemporary source, Burden was such a stickler for excellence that she sometimes required the outworkers to 'practice 2 or 3 weeks at one stitch before they come up to her standard of perfection'.[39]

May also encountered the work of her father's favourite embroiderer Catherine Holiday (1839–1924), the only person he had ever met whose stitching 'was as good as the old'.[40] In a letter addressed to May on her sixteenth birthday in 1878, William Morris described a new piece by Holiday in such glowing terms that he wrote, almost apologetically, 'but I must take care, or I shall rouse jealousy'.[41] Writing to Holiday's daughter Winifred (1866–1949) five decades later, May likened the quality of Catherine's colouring to that of her own 'mammie': 'It was interesting to me to compare the same splendid great design done by their hands – very different in character, and both so beautiful!'[42] May promised Winifred that her gift of Holiday's embroidery silks would be put to good use. In addition, a small selection of threads, together with a parcel of tracings from Holiday's workroom, were labelled and set aside as 'precious relics of the old days' in her plans for Kelmscott as a living memorial dedicated to her father's life and work.[43]

Beyond the confines of the Morris circle, May would have been aware of St Katherine's School of Embroidery, the London workroom of the East

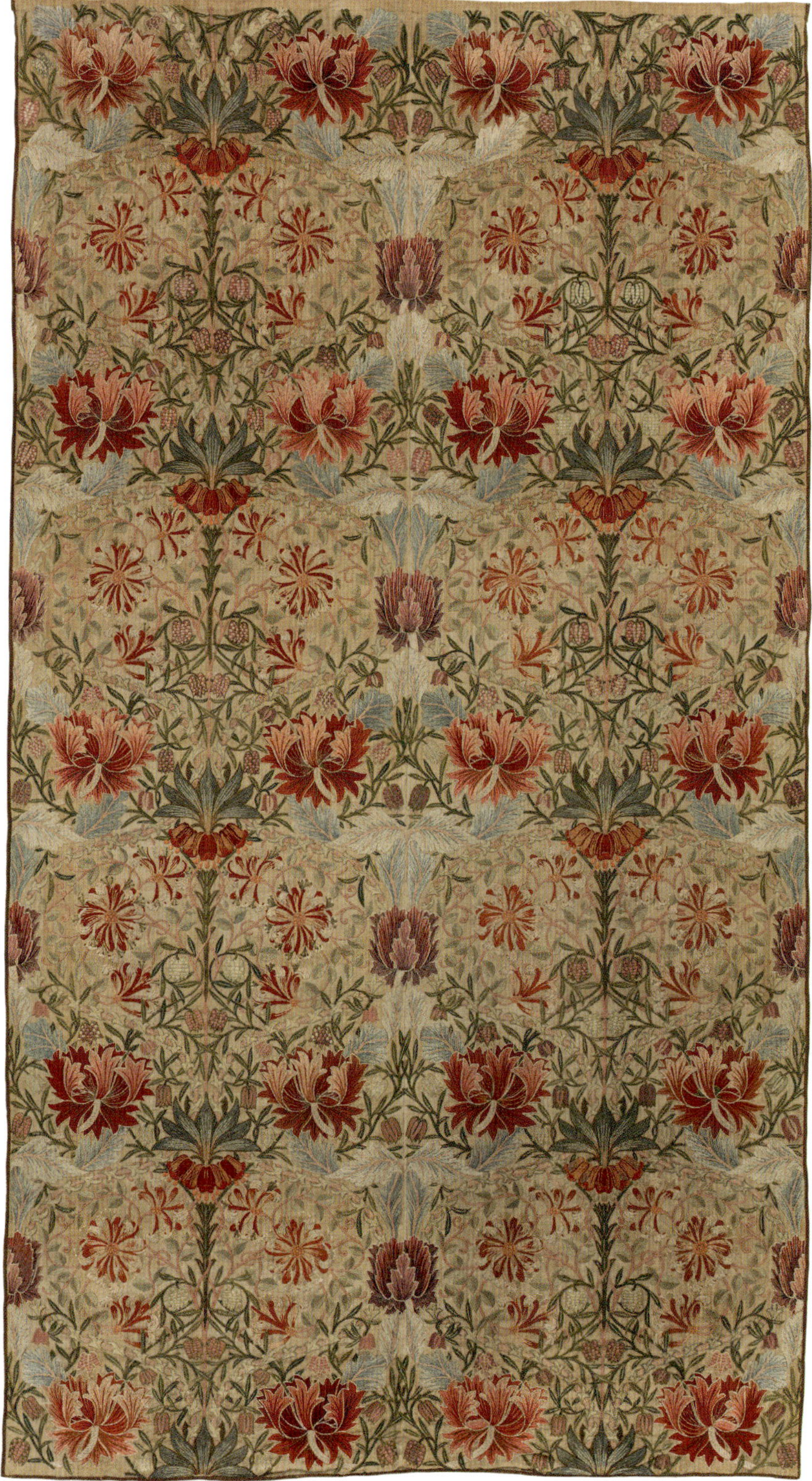

Fig.7 William Morris (1834–1896), *Honeysuckle* wall hanging, designed 1876, stitched by Jane and Jenny Morris, 1880s, polychrome silks on linen, 267 × 150 cm, William Morris Gallery, F434.

Fig.8 Elizabeth Burden (1841–1924), *Angel minstrel* chalice cover, *c.*1885, based on William Morris's *c.*1867 design for stained glass, polychrome silks and gold thread on cotton, 25 × 12.5 cm, William Morris Gallery, F454.

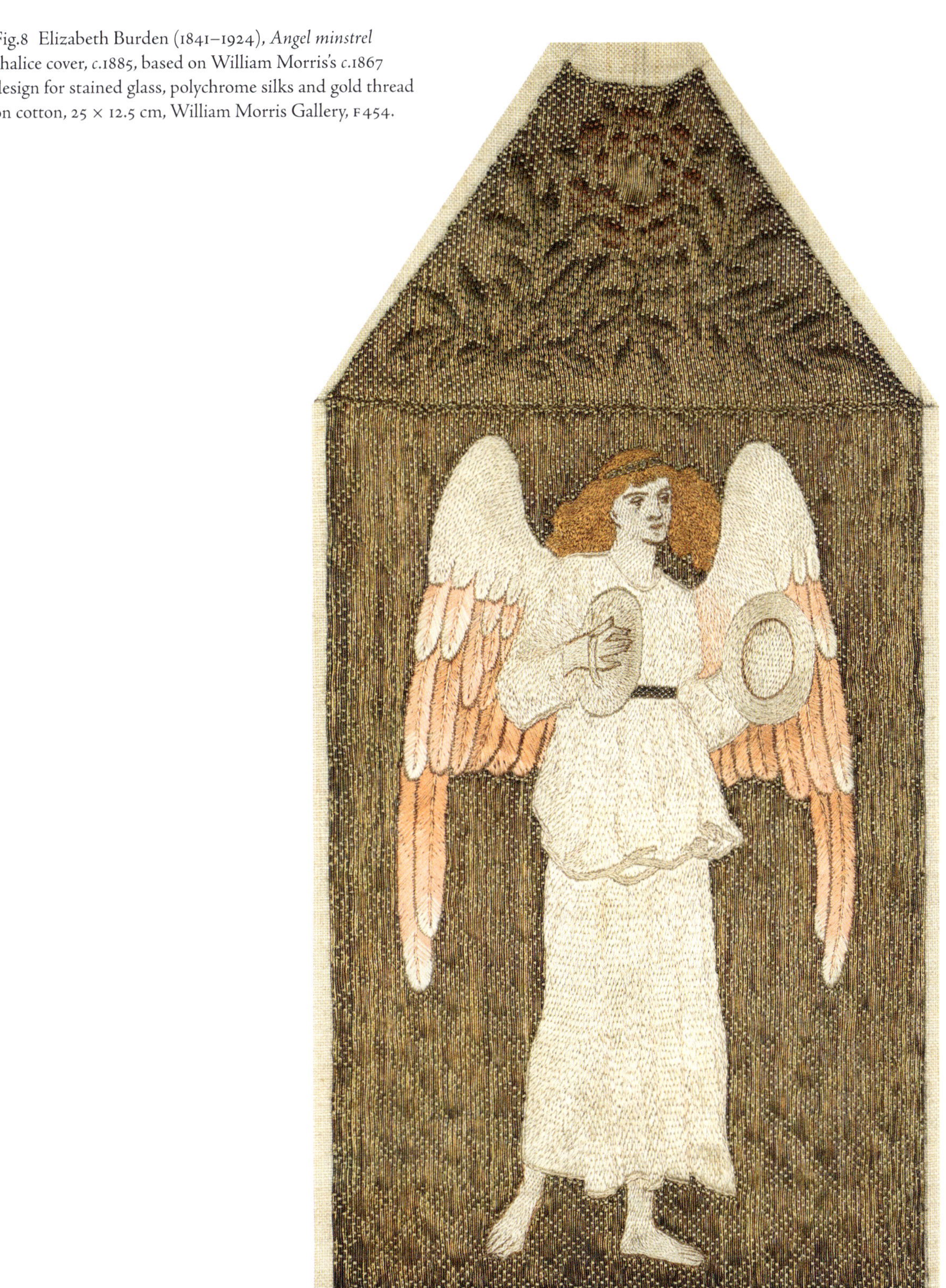

Grinstead-based Society of St Margaret at 32 Queen Square, a few doors away from her home. Under the direction of the talented Sister Winifred (d.1879), pupils and visitors were taught church embroidery.[44] May would also have known about the RSAN, which had just moved into its new premises in South Kensington. Between 1875 and 1877, Elizabeth Burden ran its 'artistic room', specially set aside for working the designs of William Morris, Walter Crane and others in crewels.[45] The RSAN provided training for women who were keen to pursue a career in embroidery and design.[46] Reflecting later on the opportunities available to women, May criticised church workrooms for no longer producing the work they once did, and embroidery societies like the RSAN for employing none but gentlewomen by birth and education which, she believed, 'narrowed the scope of such enterprises'.[47] She described herself as belonging to a 'third class of embroiderer', which numbered:

> ...some few people who, furnished with a historical knowledge of the art, happen to have leisure and opportunity to pursue it experimentally on new and unwonted lines. Their experiments may succeed or fail, but their work has always some note of interest, in so far as it is thoughtful, and embodies the serious effort and training for which all art imperatively calls.[48]

May's aptitude for drawing was encouraged initially by her mother's 'dear friend', the Pre-Raphaelite artist Dante Gabriel Rossetti (1828–1882).[49] During the early years of her adolescence, she favoured art over learning, though as her published writings and research interests later reveal, she had gained a 'good grounding in serious study'.[50] In October 1878, aged sixteen, May enrolled at the National Art Training School before pursuing a career in the decorative arts.[51] She later claimed to have chosen the School specifically for its proximity to the South Kensington Museum, 'one of our city's greatest splendours today'.[52] Her father worked at the Museum as designer, advisor, art referee, lender and donor, and valued the contribution it had made to his own creative practice.[53]

By the 1870s, the National Art Training School had deviated from its original aim, which was the practical application of a knowledge of ornamental art to the improvement of manufacture. Instead, it had become an institution primarily for the training of art teachers. No provision was made for students keen to gain experience in the materials they were designing for. 'If I had not known the requirements of the branch of Art manufacture I am connected with,' wrote one textile artist in the early 1880s, 'my time would have been wasted so far as being taught design in the schools is concerned.'[54] May had already learned her craft at home and within the workshop environment at Queen Square.[55] Her purpose in entering the South Kensington system was to hone her skills as a designer and to learn more about the history of art.

No account has been found of the months that May spent at art school, but she was awarded a paintbox for 'good attendance and diligence'.[56] The course of instruction comprised two terms of five months each at a cost £10 a year, plus an entrance fee of 10s.[57] Students were granted admission to the South Kensington Museum and the National Art Library for the purposes of consultation and copying. The Museum was known for its diverse collection of European and non-western textiles that included specimens of ecclesiastical and secular embroidery dating from the early Middle Ages to the present. The Library also contained a wide range of historic and modern books on needlework published in England and mainland Europe.[58]

May presumably followed the course of instruction that had been developed in the late 1850s by Richard Redgrave. This comprised 23 stages, taken concurrently, in any order, and included a drawing course in ornament, anatomy and flowers; a painting course in ornament and flowers from flat examples and from nature; a modelling course; and composition in design. A series of 40 lectures on the historical development of western and non-western ornamental art, from pre-historic to modern, was also given each year.[59]

Students were required to pass tests and examinations at each stage, ranging from historic ornament, botany and geometry to the principles and practical application of ornament. The extant art examination papers dating from the period of May's enrolment indicate the range of topics covered. Candidates were tested on geometric drawing; historical knowledge of period styles, construction and colour; and the scientific study of plants and flowers, and their use in decorative art.[60] They were also expected to produce course work. For example, the second certificate included a group of flowers painted from nature in watercolour or tempera; a set of at least fifteen studies of ornamental design showing treatment of arabesques, diapers, or other ornament in colour or relief illustrative of the decoration of some leading feature of architectural or industrial art from original examples in the South Kensington Museum, or elsewhere; and design embodying the principles outlined in the course.[61]

According to her companion Mary Frances Vivian Lobb (1878–1939), May no longer worked under her father's direction in design from the age of twenty.[62] Within three years, she was entrusted with running the embroidery department at Morris & Co. William Morris wrote to his mother on 27 December 1885:

> May has taken to do a good deal of the designs and superintendence of the embroidery at Oxford Street. This is a good thing, as she does them very nicely and is always ready to design a piece of work that may be wanted; so that people are likely to come for things more, as she does what is wanted at once: also I think it amuses her.[63]

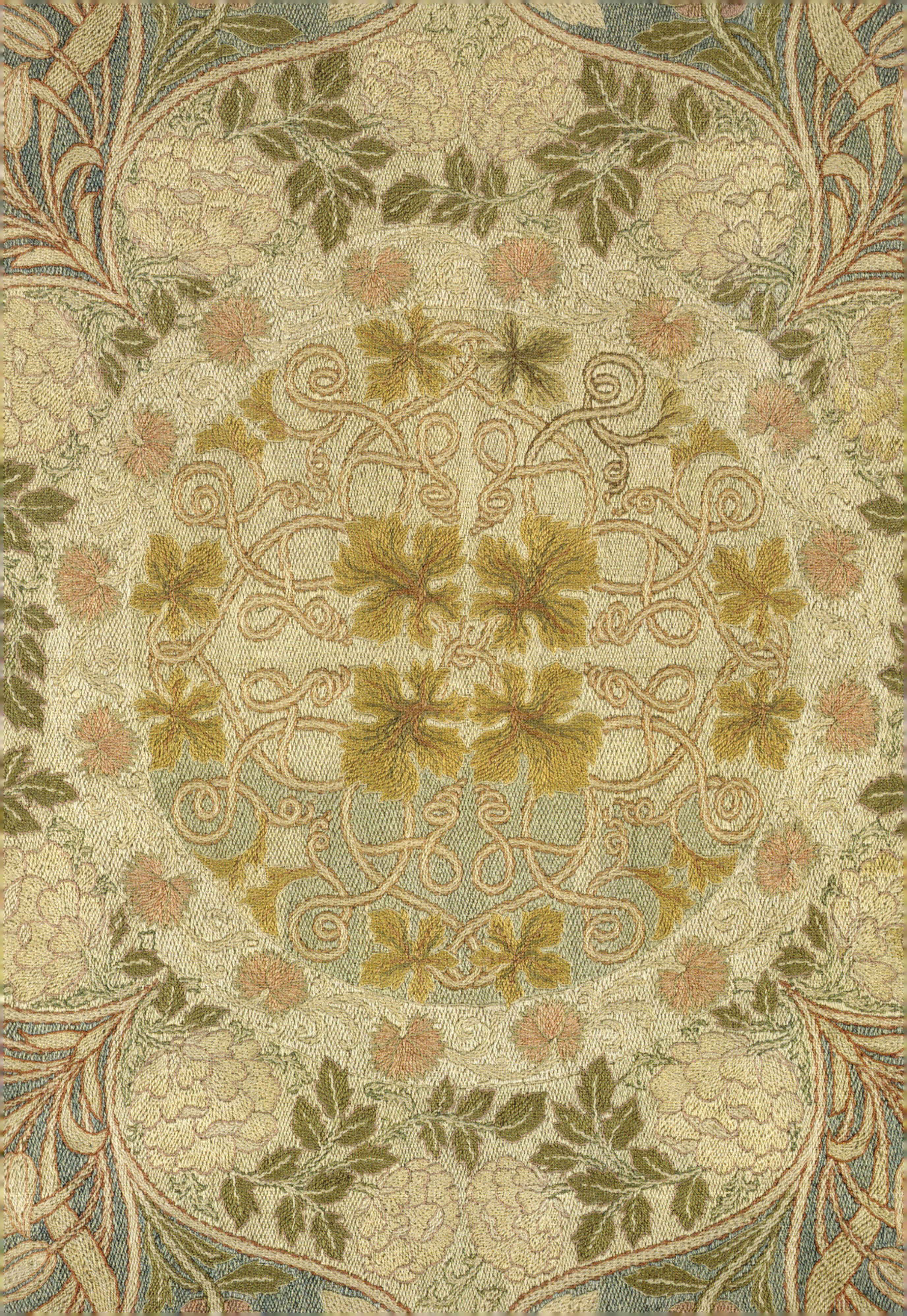

2 The Elements of Art Embroidery

May Morris believed that for a piece of needlework to be 'artistic', it required expertise in the selection and arrangement of colours; skill and invention in the stitches utilised; choice of suitable materials; and, above all, good design derived from historical and non-western ornament, as well as plant and animal sources. Together, these four elements guaranteed that a work of embroidery 'shall not be meaningless, but rather a thing of use and individual interest'.[1] Each of the elements is discussed below, with reference to May's extant embroideries, published writings and teaching notes, as well as the work of other late nineteenth- and early twentieth-century commentators on needle art.

DESIGN

May contended that the key to successful work lay in the choice of design. Inferior work was acceptable provided the design was good, but excellent work on a mediocre pattern was a waste of labour, 'so that, you see, design is the very soul and essence of beautiful embroidery'.[2] Walter Crane argued that the ideal in needlework design was 'something distinctive and inseparable from the characteristics and conditions of the craft...If embroidery is to be a living art, it must, like the other arts, find its own distinctive forms of expression, gathered from many sources...and having roots in the traditions of the past, but belonging to the present'.[3]

Historical Ornament

Most writers on decorative needlework suggested drawing inspiration from the borders of illuminated manuscripts, herbals and woodcuts, or old textiles depicted in medieval and Renaissance painting. May believed that the work of the thirteenth and fourteenth centuries offered the greatest reward to the aspiring designer or practitioner:

> In always recommending ancient rather than modern work for study, I do so with intent; for, in mediæval ornament, whether in an illuminated manuscript or figured stuff, or embroidered cloth, one is always sure that though the interest of detail and beauty of form may vary very much, the work is not lacking in the essential qualities of good design, and is thorough in its way, and executed with due knowledge of material and with due skill of hand.[4]

Opposite: detail of fig.13

The architect John Dando Sedding (1838–1891) advised unskilled artists to consult an old herbal, 'for in all old drawing of nature there is a large element of design'.[5] Woodcut illustrations drawn to fit the engraver's block were well-planned and balanced with no extraneous mark making. For the professional embroiderer, Sedding concluded that an hour spent dipping into an old herbal or a few 'carefully drawn cribs' from *Curtis's Botanical Magazine* 'will do more to revive the original instincts of a true designer than a month of sixpenny days at a stuffy museum'.[6]

For her twentieth birthday, May was gifted the 1633 edition of John Gerard's *The Herball or Generall Historie of Plantes* (**fig.9**), inscribed: 'May Morris with her father's love March 25th 1882'. Eight years later, William Morris also gave her his copy of Leonhart Fuchs's *De historia stirpium commentarii insignes* (Basel, 1542), having replaced it with one in a 'very handsome

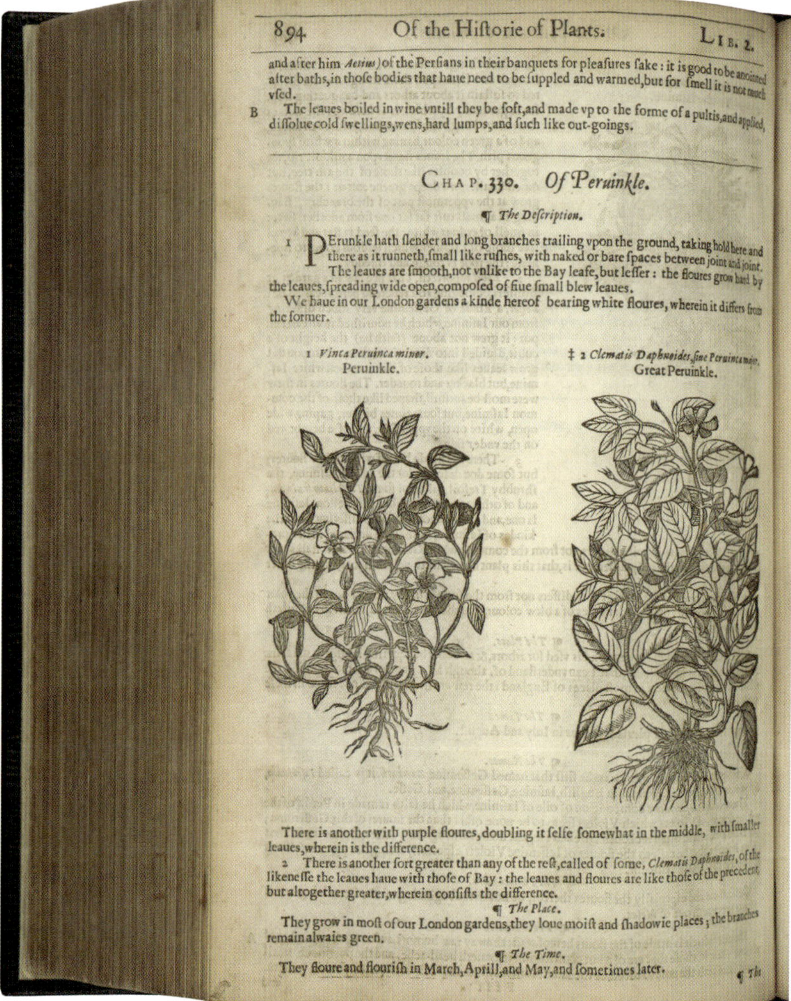

894 Of the Hiſtorie of Plants. LIB. 2.

and after him *Aetius*) of the Perſians in their banquets for pleaſures ſake: it is good to be anointed after baths, in thoſe bodies that haue need to be ſuppled and warmed, but for ſmell it is not much vſed.

B The leaues boiled in wine vntill they be ſoft, and made vp to the forme of a pultis, and applied, diſſolue cold ſwellings, wens, hard lumps, and ſuch like out-goings.

CHAP. 330. *Of Peruinkle.*

¶ *The Deſcription.*

1 PERunkle hath ſlender and long branches trailing vpon the ground, taking hold here and there as it runneth, ſmall like ruſhes, with naked or bare ſpaces between joint and joint. The leaues are ſmooth, not vnlike to the Bay leafe, but leſſer: the floures grow hard by the leaues, ſpreading wide open, compoſed of fiue ſmall blew leaues.

We haue in our London gardens a kinde hereof bearing white floures, wherein it differs from the former.

1 *Vinca Peruinca minor.* Peruinkle.

‡ 2 *Clematis Daphnoides, ſiue Peruinca maior.* Great Peruinkle.

There is another with purple floures, doubling it ſelfe ſomewhat in the middle, with ſmaller leaues, wherein is the difference.

2 There is another ſort greater than any of the reſt, called of ſome, *Clematis Daphnoides*, of the likeneſſe the leaues haue with thoſe of Bay: the leaues and floures are like thoſe of the precedent, but altogether greater, wherein conſiſts the difference.

¶ *The Place.*

They grow in moſt of our London gardens, they loue moiſt and ſhadowie places; the branches remain alwaies green.

¶ *The Time.*

They floure and flouriſh in March, Aprill, and May, and ſometimes later.

Fig.9 Gerard, J., Davyes, R., Johnson, T., Priest, R., Dodoens, R. & Katherine Golden Bitting Collection On Gastronomy. (1633) *The herball: or, Generall historie of plantes*. Chap. 330, p. 894 'Of Periwinkle'.

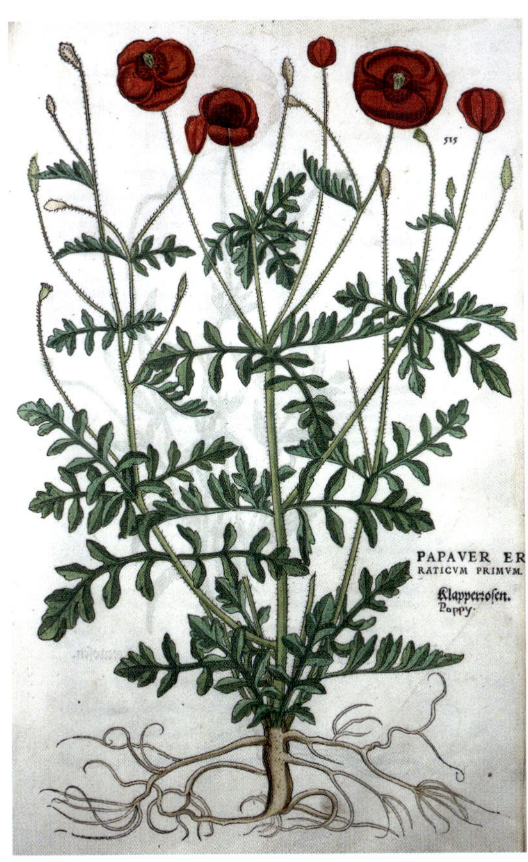

Fig.10 Leonhart Fuchs, *De historia stirpium commentarii insignes* (Basel, 1542) p.515, 'Papaver', 30.48 × 20.32 cm.

contemporary binding'. Tipped in to the volume is a sheet of headed notepaper from 26 Queen Square with a graphite sketch of flowers and leaves drawn from nature. May later referred to both publications in her work. For example, in 'Pattern-Designing', written for her American lecture tour, she cited Fuchs's *De historia* in relation to translating nature into ornament (**fig.10**): 'Fuscius in his "Herbal" shall be a guide to you in this. Note how he simplifies, expressing all that line can express of the tender loveliness of his subject.'[7]

William Morris owned several other English and continental herbals as well as books on botany, four of which passed to May on his death: the 1815 reprint of Nicholas Culpeper's *Complete herbal* (London, 1653); a late sixteenth-century edition of Pietro Andrea Mattioli's *Commentarii in VI libros Pedacii Dioscoridis Anarzabei de medica materia* (Venice, 1583) together with Georg Handsch's German translation of the work, entitled *New Kreüterbuch* (Prague, 1563); and William Baxter's six-volume set, *British Phænogamus Botany, or, Figures and Descriptions of the Genera of British Flowering Plants* (Oxford, 1834–43).[8]

Art embroiderers were also encouraged to study specimens of historic needlework in museums and private collections, with the aim of applying the lessons learned to modern practice.[9] May proposed walking through the South Kensington Museum, 'carefully noting and comparing the fine examples of early work displayed there'.[10] Yet, both Sedding and Selwyn Image noted the propensity among embroiderers to seek inspiration in museums rather than in nature.[11] In his 1890 essay on designing for embroidery, Image wrote:

> The study of old work...is essential...But for what? To learn principles and methods, to secure a sound foundation for oneself; not to slavishly imitate results, and live on bound hand and foot in the swaddling clothes of precedent. Learn your business in the schools but go out to nature for your inspirations.[12]

When it came to finding designs for the workroom, the RSAN was not averse to copying old embroideries belonging to clients and members of its Council. For instance, the *rinceau* pattern on a Jacobean blackwork waistcoat (V&A, T.4–1935), which was lent by Sir Charles Isham (1819–1903) to the *Special Loan Exhibition of Decorative Art Needlework* in 1873, was soon being

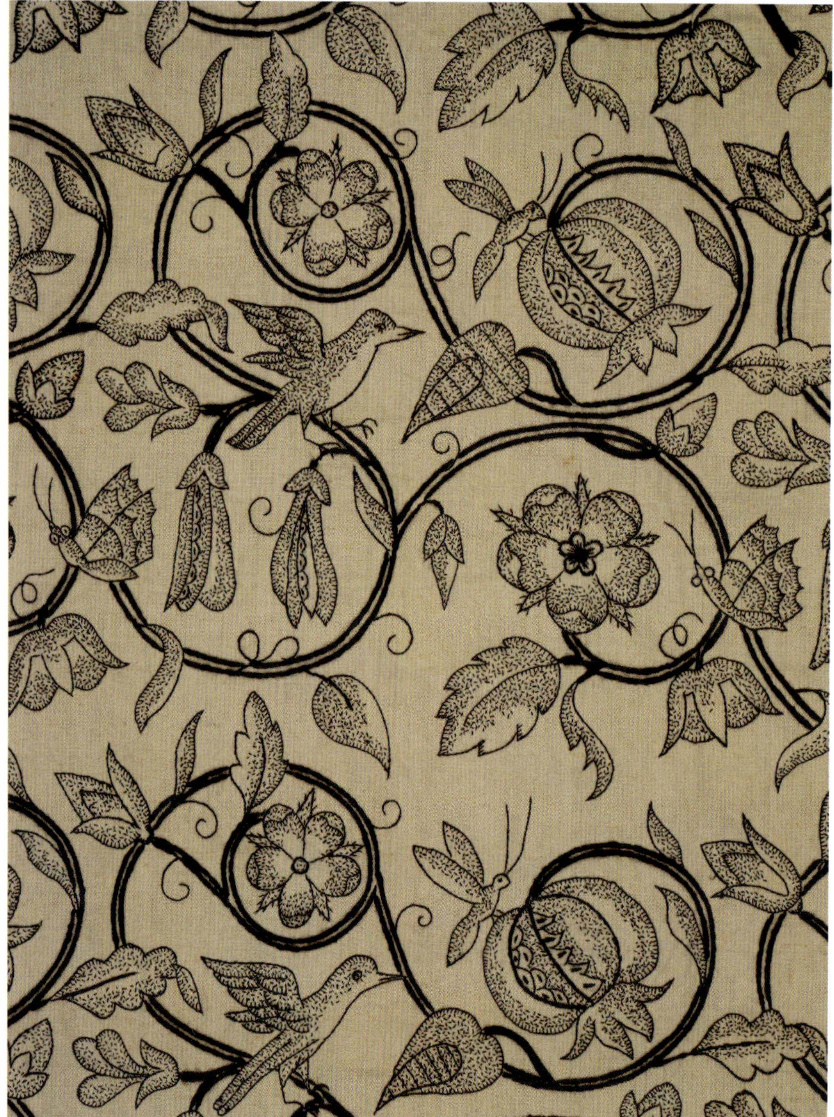

Fig.11 Royal School of Art Needlework, Portière, late nineteenth century, based on a blackwork waistcoat, *c.*1620s, V&A, T.4–1935, black silk on linen, 219 × 177 cm. Private collection

reproduced as a portière and cushion cover (**fig.11**).[13] The design proved so popular with customers that it remained in circulation until at least the 1930s. Sedding railed against this practice: 'The flowers we embroider were not plucked from field and garden, but from the camphor-scented preserves at Kensington…drop this wearisome translation of old styles and translate Nature instead.'[14]

Non-Western Ornament

Equally, designers and practitioners of decorative needlework drew inspiration from Middle Eastern and Asian art. Japan's re-emergence in 1854, after more than two centuries of self-imposed seclusion from the West, was a watershed moment in British art and design. The artistic community was astounded by the range and quality of ornamental decoration displayed in the Japanese Court at the 1862 London International Exhibition of Industry and Art, and was soon buying up Japanese *objets d'art*. The architect and designer William Burges (1827–1881) described Japanese design as the perfect form of medieval art.[15] Produced under similar conditions to *opus Anglicanum*, 'oriental' work served as a model for art embroidery.[16] British designers were inspired to use Japanese motifs in their work. Wall hangings and panels set within ebonised frames decorated with cranes, peacocks, carp, sunflowers, lilies, chrysanthemums, cherry blossom, bamboo, fans and Japanese *mon*, or emblems in the Anglo-Japanese style, found their way into the 'artistic' home; one of the finest examples is the *Vain Jackdaw* four-panel screen designed by Walter Crane for the RSAN in 1875 (**fig.12**). Elements of May's designs recall Japanese ornament. Examples include the *mon*-like patterns in the border of the *Vine leaf* table cover (1896) in **fig.13** and the sunflower motif in the design for a book cover (**fig.70**).

The Morris family home was furnished with textiles from Turkey and Iran, including embroidered Ottoman towels and quilt facings. 'To us pattern-drawers,' wrote William Morris, 'Persia has become a holy land, for there in the process of time our art was perfected, and thence above all places it spread to cover for a while the world, east and west.'[17] He was captivated by

Fig.12 Walter Crane (1845–1915), *Vain Jackdaw* four-panel screen, 1875, stitched by the Royal School of Art Needlework in the late nineteenth century, polychrome silks on silk, 151.5 × 59 cm (each panel). Private collection.

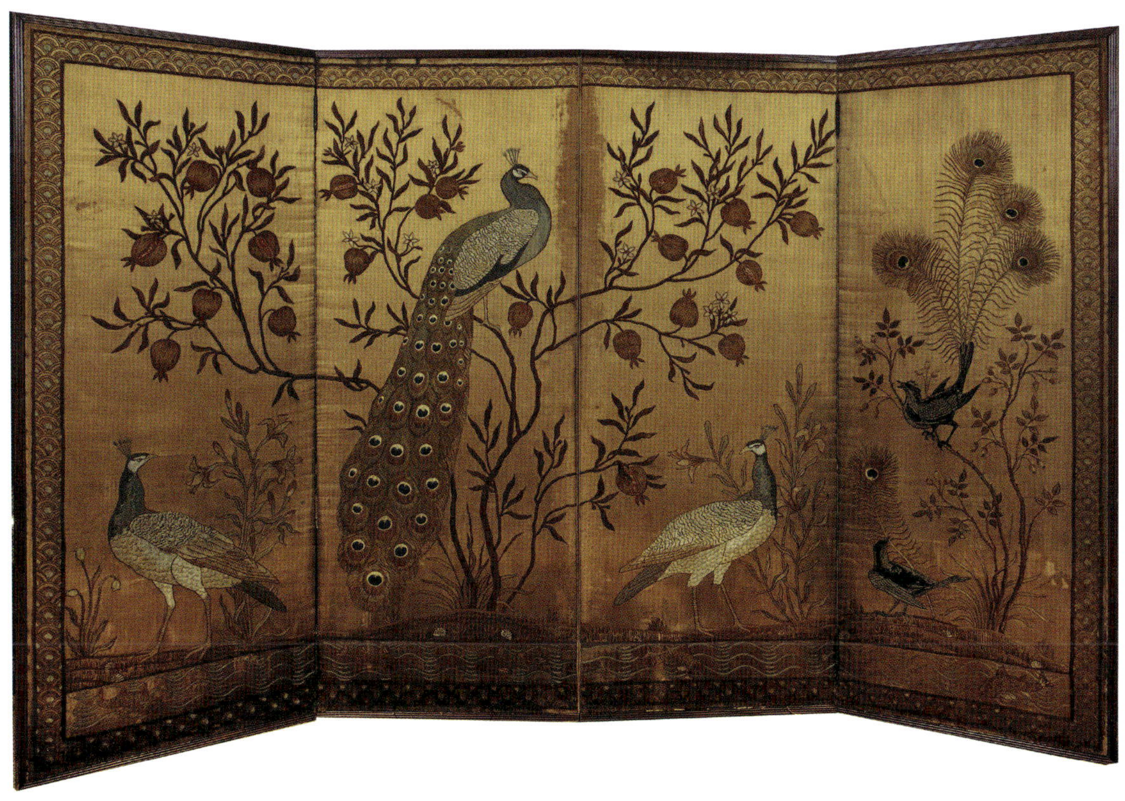

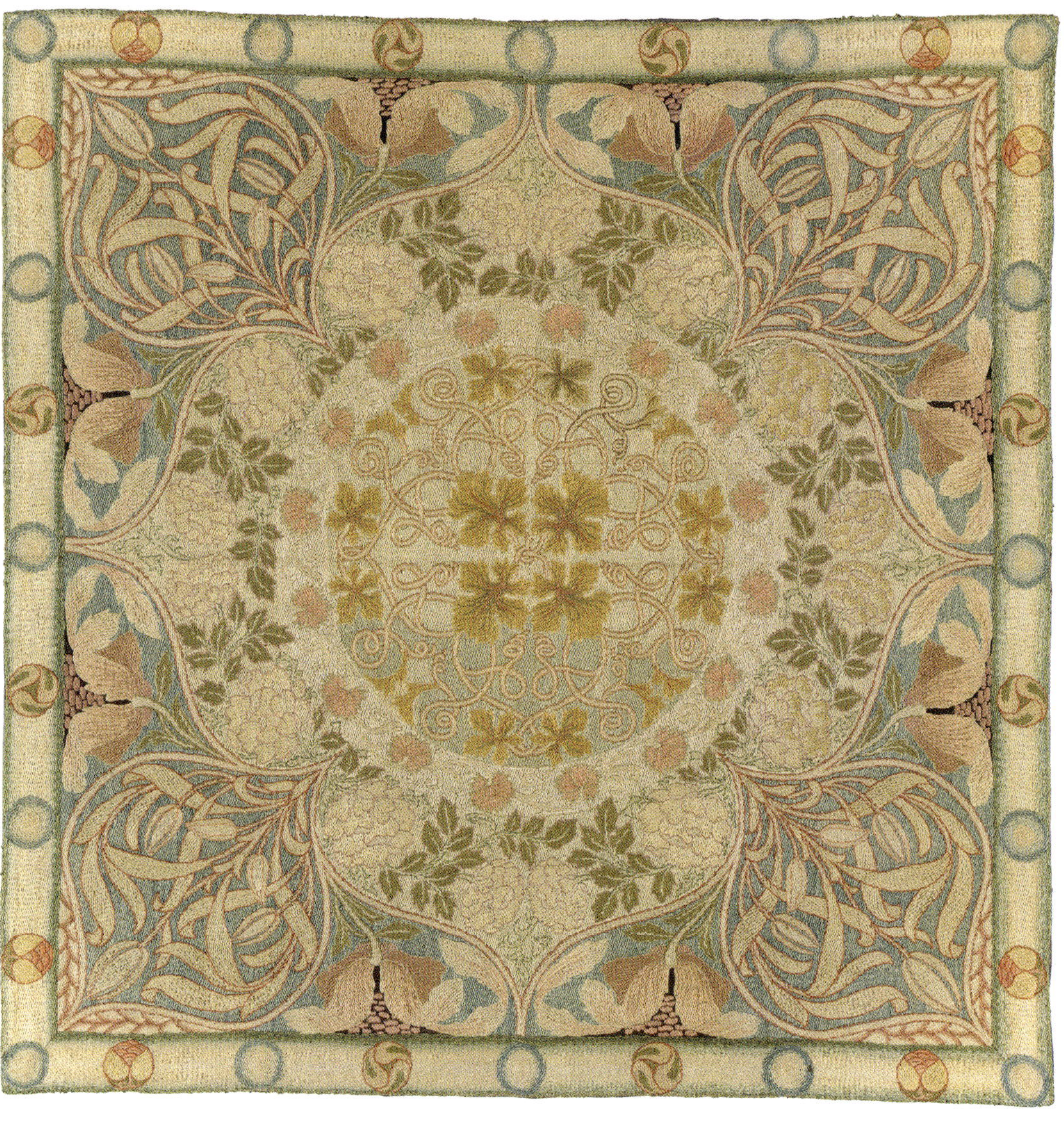

Fig.13 May Morris (1862–1938), *Vine leaf* table cover, 1896, possibly stitched by Mary Hodson, *c.*1896, polychrome silks on linen, 108 × 108 cm, V&A, T.426–1993.

the natural forms and the single and interlocking motifs found in sixteenth- and seventeenth-century Turkish and Persian woven silks and velvets, incorporating them into his needlework designs in the mid-1870s. *Artichoke* (1877), for example, consists of alternating rows of stylised tulips and artichoke heads set on an arabesque pattern of stems, flowers and leaves (V&A, T.166–1978). Morris's embroidered hangings from the 1880s contain more complex patterns, reflecting his interest in Middle Eastern carpets. *Acanthus*, which became one of the firm's most popular designs during May's tenure in charge of the embroidery department, combines a central pattern of interlocking leaves and flowers surrounded by a decorative border (V&A, T.66–1939).

May shared her father's passion for Islamic decorative arts. Islamic textiles, like the panel of Persian Resht embroidery illustrated in **fig.14**, are frequently

Fig.14 Patchwork tent panel, Resht, Iran, *c.*1800–50, polychrome silks on woollen cloth, 131 × 73.5 cm, BMT:1939M268. Birmingham Museums Trust

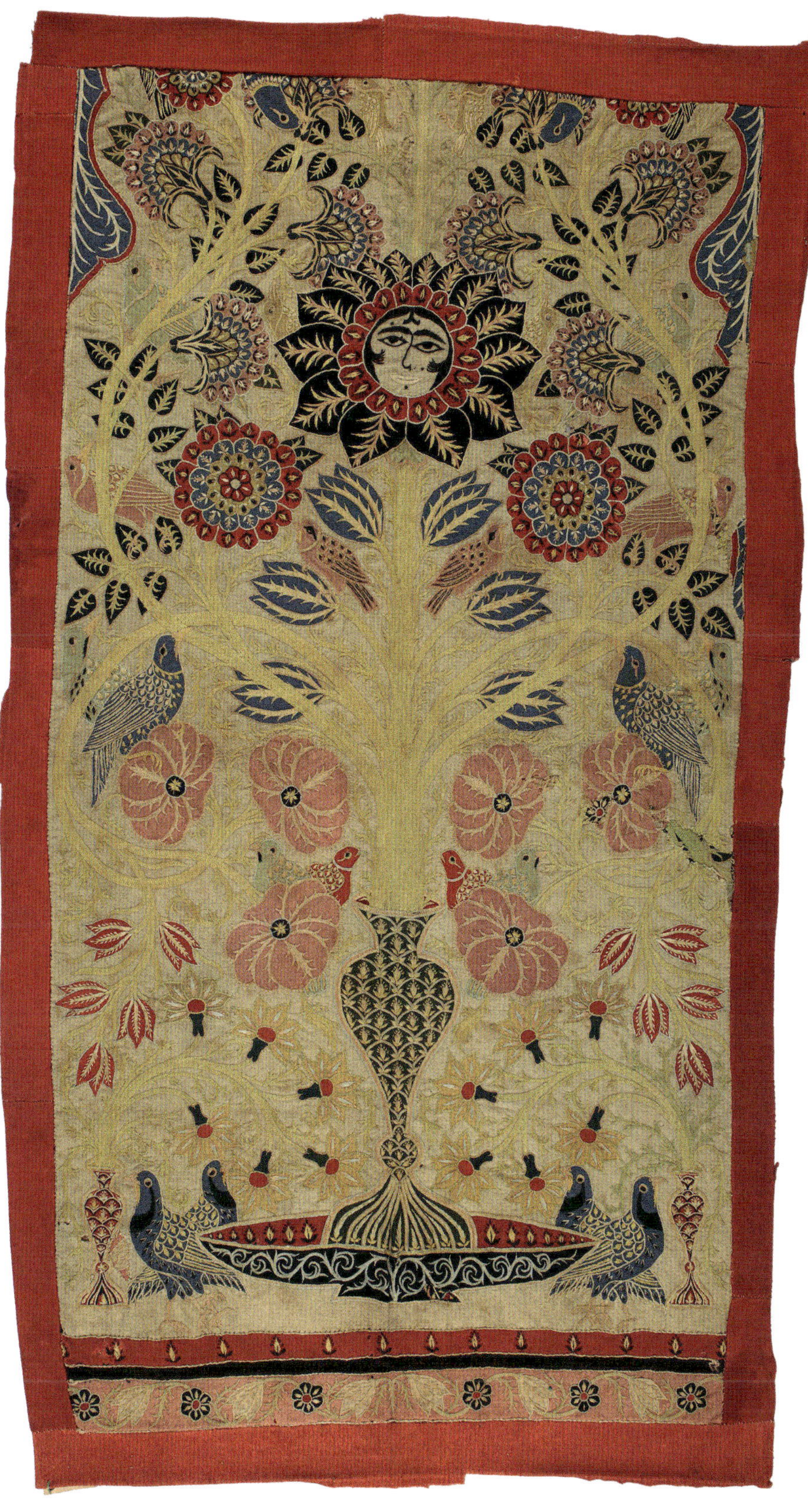

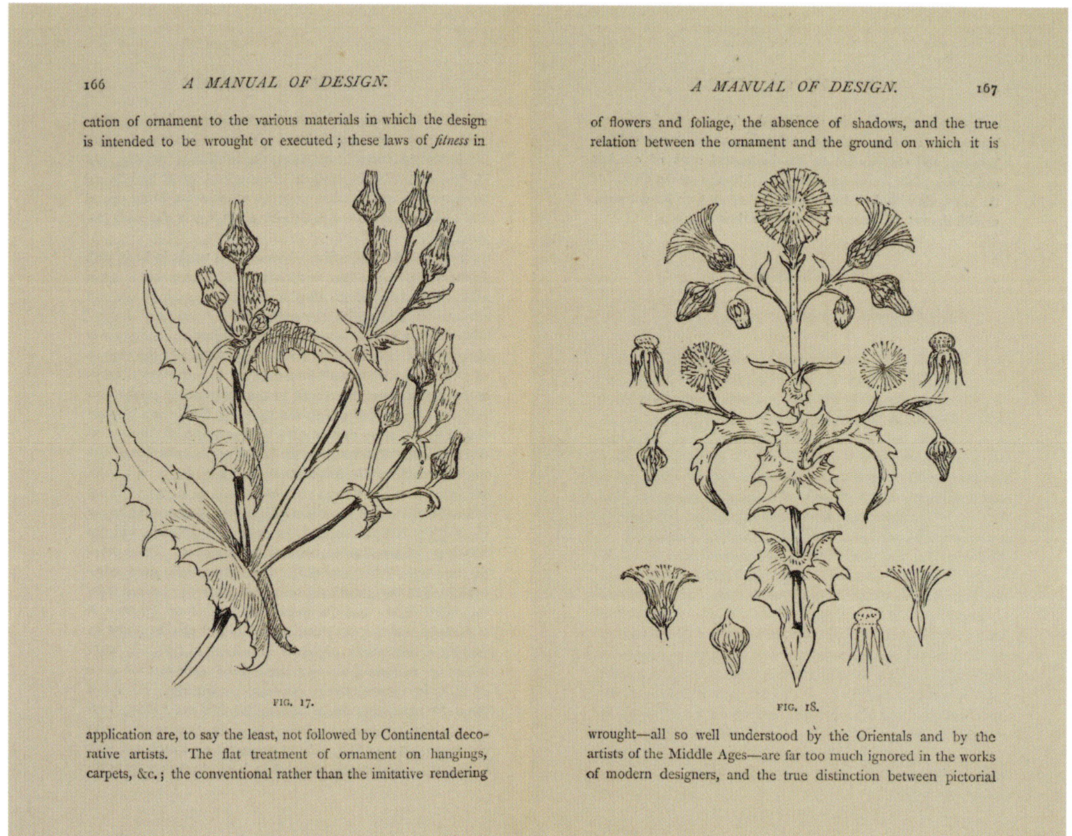

166 *A MANUAL OF DESIGN.*

cation of ornament to the various materials in which the design is intended to be wrought or executed; these laws of *fitness* in

FIG. 17.

application are, to say the least, not followed by Continental decorative artists. The flat treatment of ornament on hangings, carpets, &c.; the conventional rather than the imitative rendering

A MANUAL OF DESIGN. 167

of flowers and foliage, the absence of shadows, and the true relation between the ornament and the ground on which it is

FIG. 18.

wrought—all so well understood by the Orientals and by the artists of the Middle Ages—are far too much ignored in the works of modern designers, and the true distinction between pictorial

Fig.15 Richard Redgrave (1804–1888), Two sketches of a common sow thistle from his *Manual of Design* (London, 1876), pp.166–67, 19.6 × 13 cm (page). Private collection

mentioned in May's published writings and formed part of her own collection of historic and modern needlework, now in the Birmingham Museum and Art Gallery.[18] The blend of naturalism and formalism in the treatment of floral design is present in many of the 25 designs printed in this book, including the choice of botanical subjects (tulip, carnation, rose, peony and pomegranate), and the use of curving lines, ogival patterns and interwoven plants and leaves.

Naturalism vs. Conventionalism

Commentators on decorative needlework agreed that a good knowledge of plants and flowers was necessary, but there was a danger, wrote Sedding, that the untrained designer working directly from nature might fall into the trap of copying outright, 'to give us pure crude fact and not to *design* at all'.[19] William Morris touched on this issue in his lecture on pattern-designing, exhorting embroidery designers to avoid 'cheap and commonplace naturalism':

> ...it is a delightful idea to cover a piece of linen cloth with roses and jonquils and tulips, done quite natural with the needle...we can't

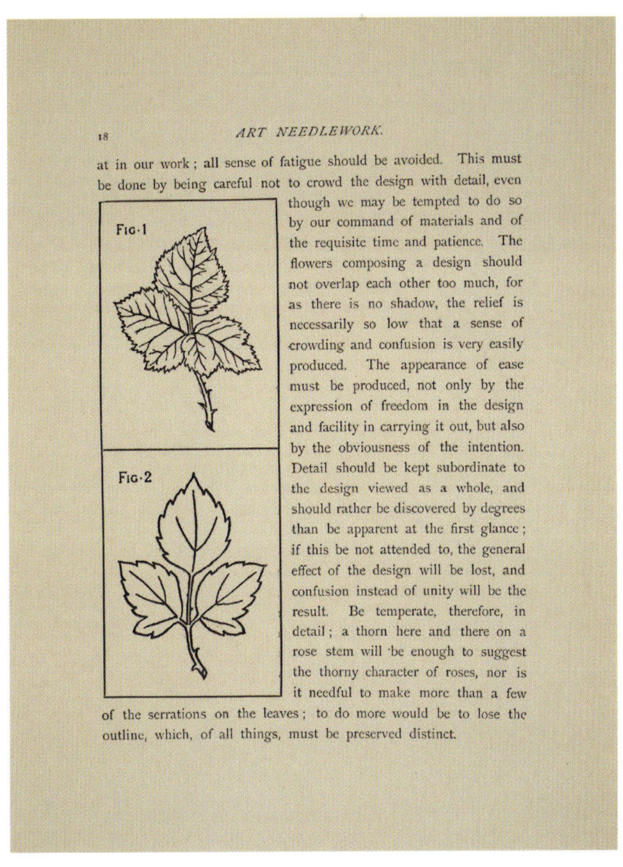

18 *ART NEEDLEWORK.*

FIG·1

FIG·2

at in our work; all sense of fatigue should be avoided. This must be done by being careful not to crowd the design with detail, even though we may be tempted to do so by our command of materials and of the requisite time and patience. The flowers composing a design should not overlap each other too much, for as there is no shadow, the relief is necessarily so low that a sense of crowding and confusion is very easily produced. The appearance of ease must be produced, not only by the expression of freedom in the design and facility in carrying it out, but also by the obviousness of the intention. Detail should be kept subordinate to the design viewed as a whole, and should rather be discovered by degrees than be apparent at the first glance; if this be not attended to, the general effect of the design will be lost, and confusion instead of unity will be the result. Be temperate, therefore, in detail; a thorn here and there on a rose stem will be enough to suggest the thorny character of roses, nor is it needful to make more than a few of the serrations on the leaves; to do more would be to lose the outline, which, of all things, must be preserved distinct.

Fig.16 Mortimer Sarah Lockwood (1837–1923) and Elizabeth Glaister (1839–1892), *Art Embroidery: A Treatise on the Revived Practice of Decorative Needlework* (London, 1878) p.18, figs.1–2, 31.2 × 24.5 cm (page). Private collection

> go too far in that direction if we only remember the needs of our material and the nature of our craft in general: these demand that our roses and the like, however unmistakenly roses, shall be quaint and naïve to the last degree, and also, since we are using specially beautiful materials, that we shall make the most of them, and not forget that we are gardening with silk and gold…[20]

At the National Art Training School students were taught to imitate foliage, fruits and flowers; to investigate the laws of their growth and development; and lastly, as 'a step to invention', to arrange the forms and colours in nature according to 'geometrical laws and principles'.[21] Redgrave's sketches of a common sow thistle in **fig.15** demonstrate this transformation from natural growth to symmetrical ornament.[22] When it came to the issue of detail, writers on art embroidery insisted on moderation: a thorn here or there, and only a few serrations on the leaves to suggest a rose **(fig.16)**.

May made detailed studies of plants throughout her life, to familiarise herself 'with all the possible peculiarities and diversities of such things'.[23] Writing to her American friend Margaret Peirce (1886–1969) in December 1931, she noted: 'The garden wall outside is gay with winter jessamine. I have

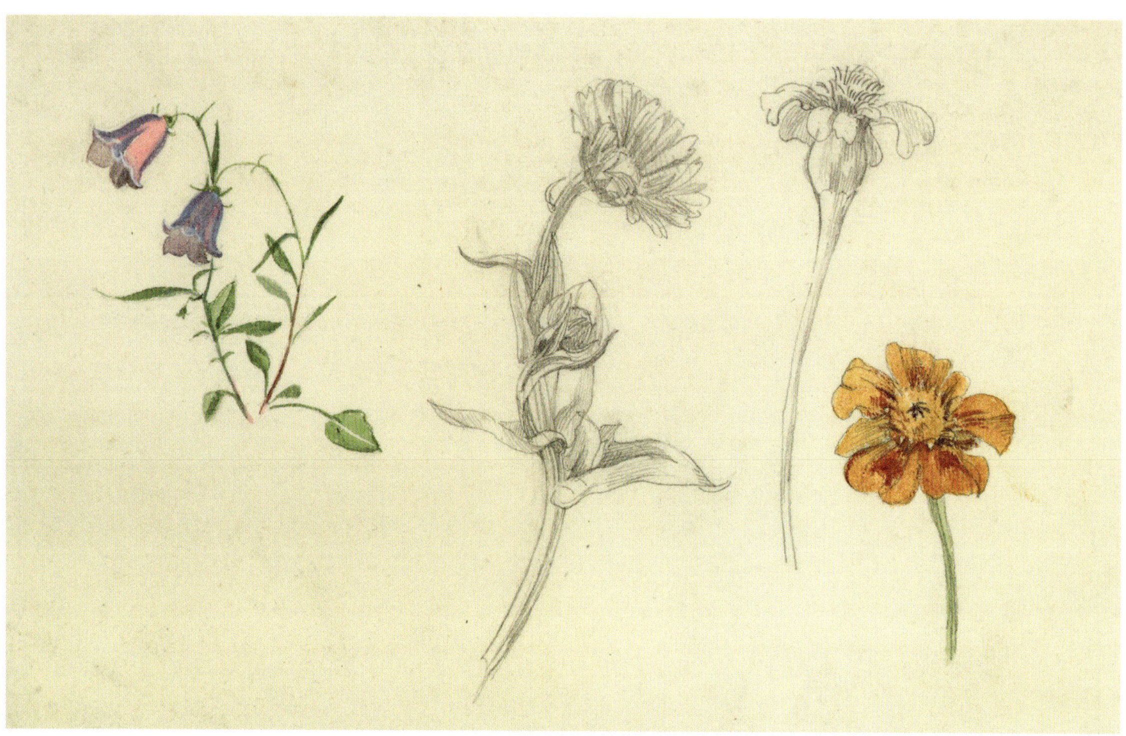

Above: fig.17 May Morris (1862–1938), Studies of harebell and marigold, 1880–1905, watercolour over graphite on cream paper, 14.8 × 24.2 cm. Ashmolean Museum (WA1941.108.166)

Opposite: fig.18 Christopher Dresser (1834–1904), 'Leaves and Flowers from Nature, no. 8' in Owen Jones, *The Grammar of Ornament* (London, 1868), plate XCVIII, 33.2 × 22.7 cm. Private collection

been drawing it to bring it into an embroidery.'[24] Several of May's botanical drawings are preserved in the Ashmolean Museum, including the graphite and watercolour studies of harebell and marigold in **fig.17**. The scrapbook cover and fire screen panel in **figs 82 and 90** exemplify her skill in translating the necessary forms and details of these flowers into embroidery design, thereby producing patterns that 'merely recall nature, not absolutely copy it'.[25]

The Queen argued in 1875 in its column 'What is Art Needlework?' that conventionalism was imperative.[26] Owen Jones had highlighted this point almost two decades earlier in *The Grammar of Ornament*:

> ...in the best periods of art, all ornament was rather based upon an observation of the principles which regulate the arrangement of form in nature, than on an attempt to imitate the absolute forms of those works; and that whenever this limit was exceeded in any art, it was one of the strongest symptoms of decline: true art consisting in idealizing, and not copying, the forms of nature...The more closely nature is copied, the further we are removed from producing a work of art.[27]

To illustrate the underlying geometry of plants, Jones included a watercolour drawing by the design theorist and botanist Christopher Dresser (1834–1904). Most of the flowers are represented from the side, above, in bud, and full bloom, in a flat, abstracted, and symmetrical arrangement using basic colours (**fig.18**).[28]

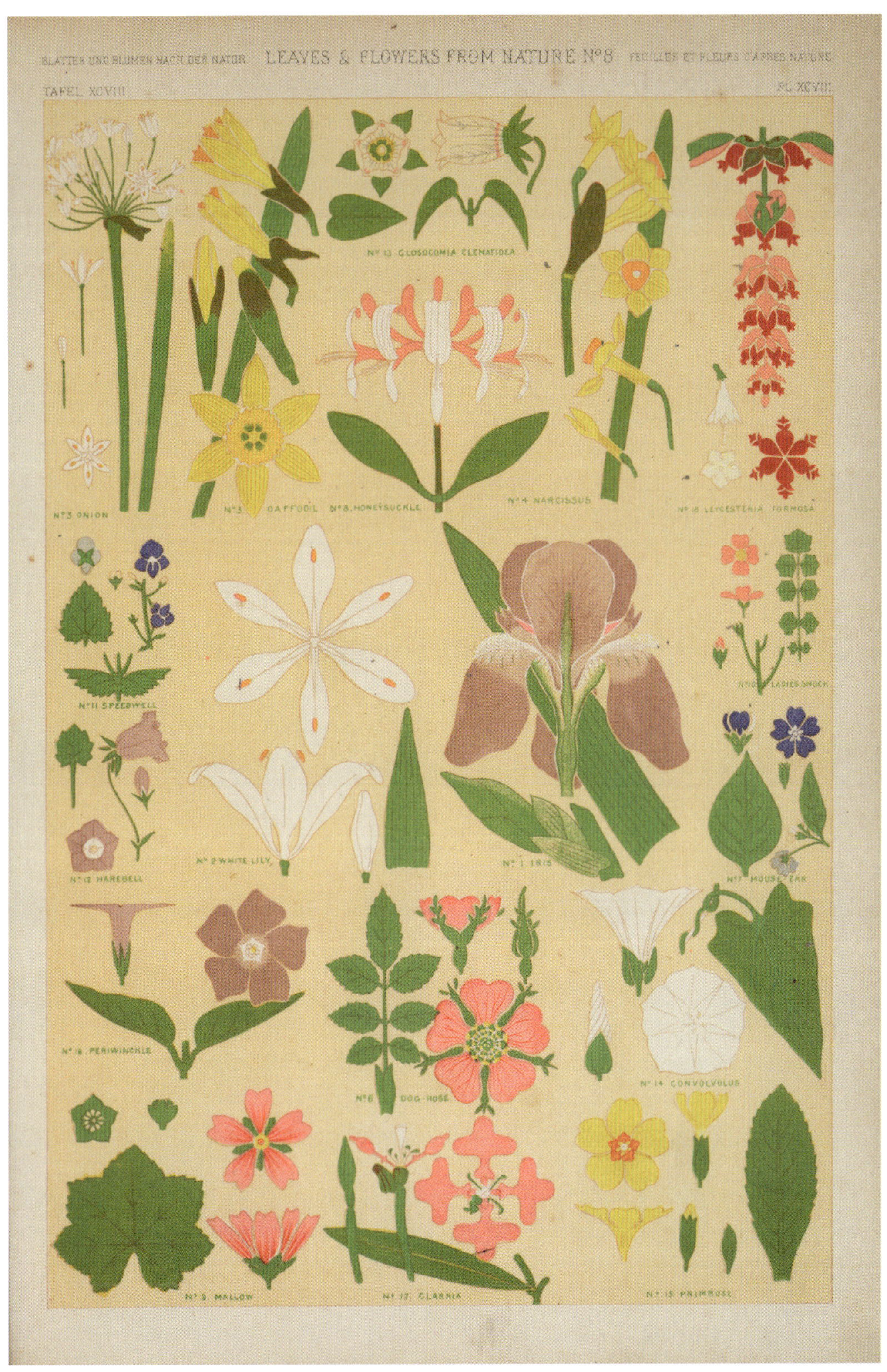
BLATTER UND BLUMEN NACH DER NATUR
LEAVES & FLOWERS FROM NATURE Nº8
FEUILLES ET FLEURS D'APRES NATURE
TAFEL XCVIII
PL. XCVIII
Nº 13 GLOSOCOMIA CLEMATIDEA
Nº 3 ONION
Nº 5 DAFFODIL
Nº 8 HONEYSUCKLE
Nº 4 NARCISSUS
Nº 18 LEYCESTERIA FORMOSA
Nº 11 SPEEDWELL
Nº 10 LADIES SMOCK
Nº 12 HAREBELL
Nº 2 WHITE LILY
Nº 1 IRIS
Nº 7 MOUSE EAR
Nº 16 PERIWINCKLE
Nº 6 DOG-ROSE
Nº 14 CONVOLVULUS
Nº 9 MALLOW
Nº 17 CLARKIA
Nº 15 PRIMROSE

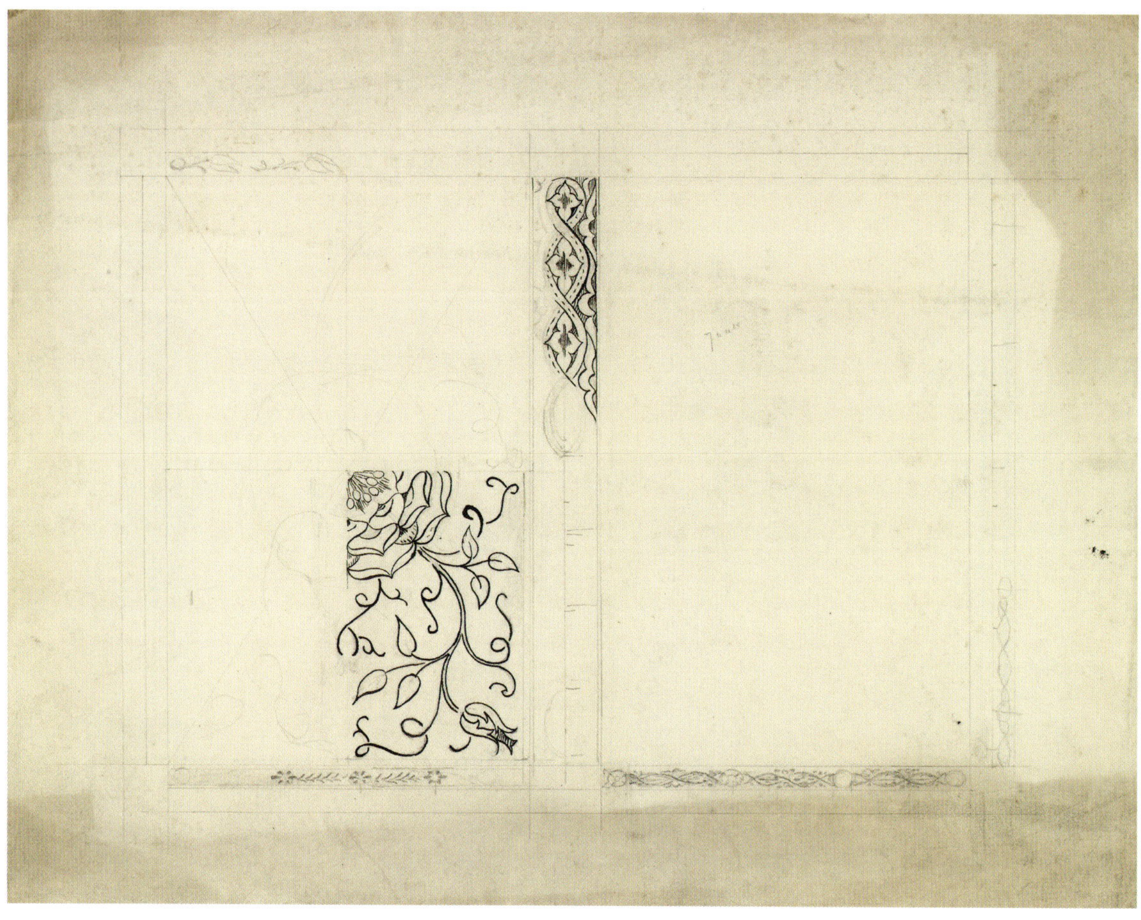

Fig.19 May Morris (1862–1938), Design for a book cover for William Morris's masque *Love is Enough*, 1888, pen and black ink and graphite on off-white woven paper, 38.7 × 50.2 cm (sheet). Ashmolean Museum (WA1941.108.26)

May criticised the modern tendency to 'copy some spray or bough directly from nature and to lay it down haphazard on the surface to be ornamented; a few stray petals or a broken leaf and a caterpillar being peppered about elsewhere without rhyme or reason: this is then called a "quaint" design'. The given space, she argued, should be filled by forms 'in certain rhythmical sequence' to create symmetry, order and balance.[29] Grace Christie advised spacing out the required surface before commencing to draw a pattern.[30] There is evidence of drafting marks in some of May's designs in the Ashmolean collection. For example, in two of the book covers – the pomegranate tree in **fig.69** and the design for the back of *Love is Enough* (1888) in **fig.19** – circles and straight edge lines are used to control the placing of motifs.

May also used mathematical shapes as a design feature in her work. In the panel *Maids of Honour* (*c*.1880–92), the first verse of Robert Herrick's 'To Violets' is set within an annular motif that frames the damask rose and violets mentioned in the poem (**fig.20**); similarly, in the *Vine leaf* table cover, a quatrefoil motif is set within a square.

A second expedient recommended by Christie was the introduction of a main central form, with secondary forms branching out on either side, balancing each other; this device occurs in May's cushion cover or fire screen designs included here. But, as Christie noted, symmetry did not always have to be absolute.[31] For example, in May's *Hazelnut tree* panel (1890s), the pruned branches do not mirror each other, while the squirrel on the right turns away from its companion, as if disturbed by a noise (**fig.21**).

In her series of articles on church embroidery, May referred to use of 'the net', found in both *opus Anglicanum* and Persian ornament, describing

Fig.20 May Morris (1862–1938), *Maids of Honour* fire screen panel or cushion cover, *c.*1890, polychrome silks on silk, 55 × 56 cm. Paul Reeves collection

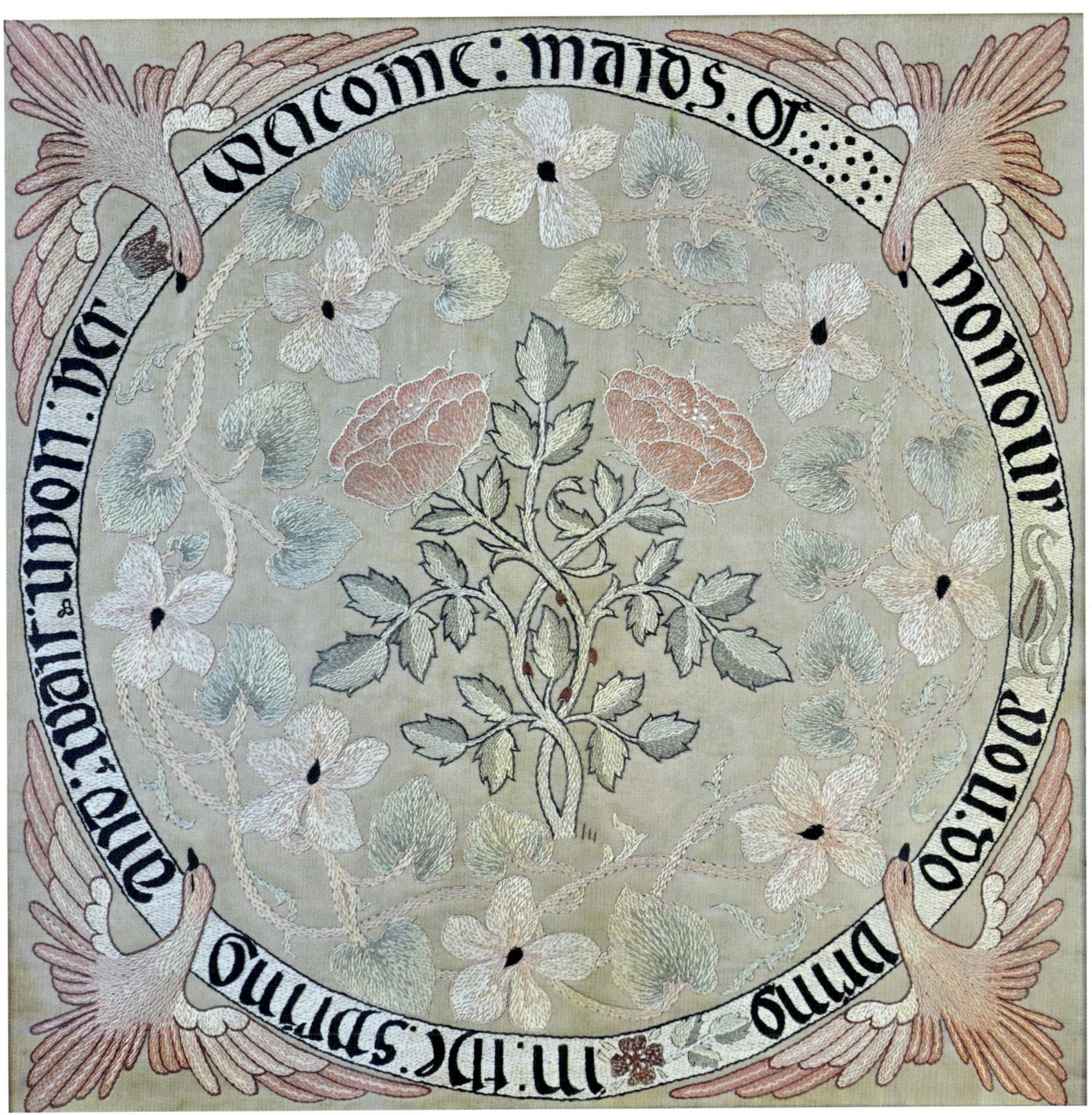

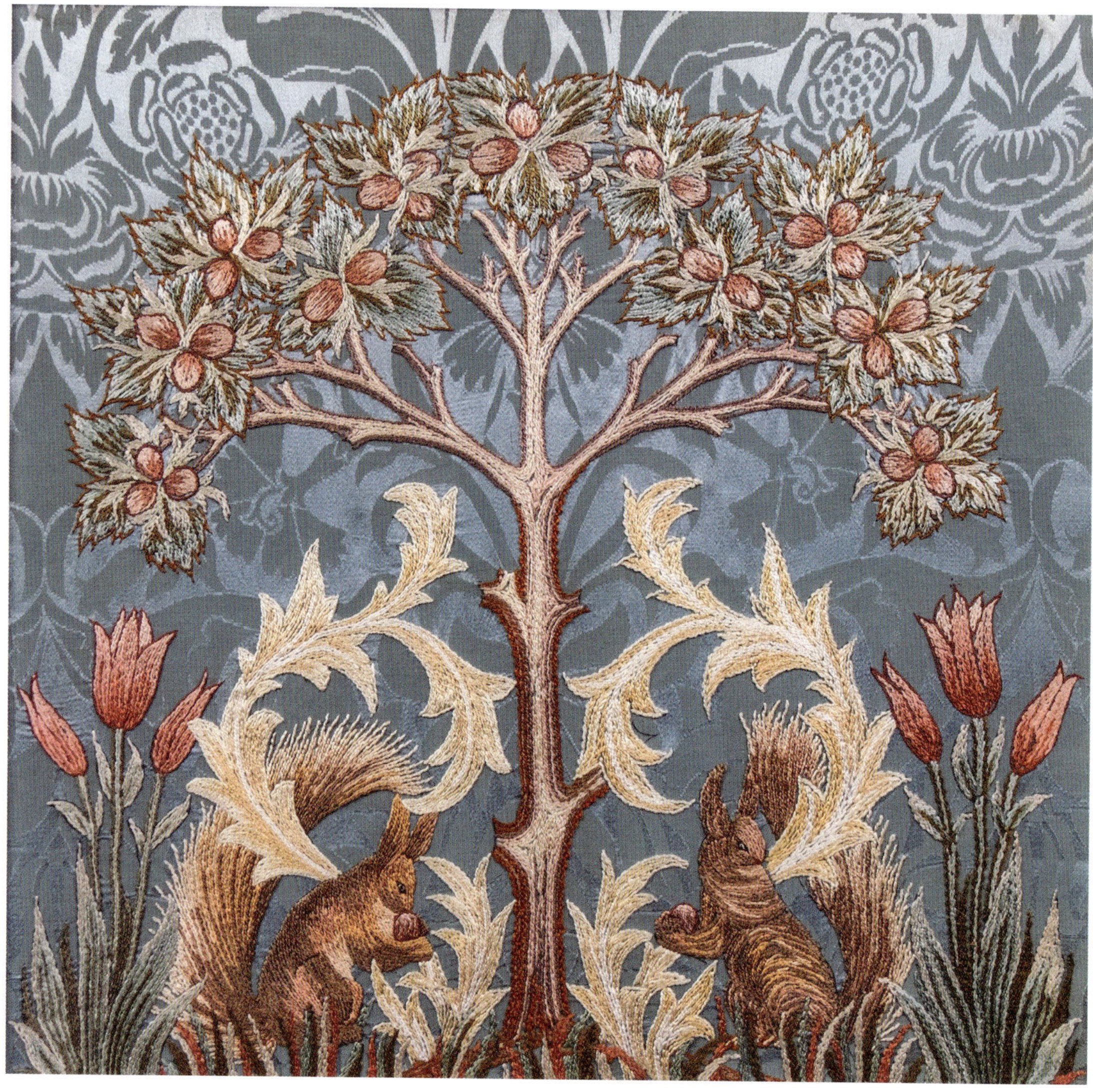

Fig.21 May Morris (1862–1938), *Hazelnut tree* fire screen panel or cushion cover, polychrome silks on Morris & Co. *St James* silk, 1890s, 54 × 57 cm, William Morris Gallery, F461.

it as 'a harmonious and pleasing scaffold or framework on which to build'.[32] This device was utilised to good effect in her own work. In the *Seasons* panels (*c.*1894), birds and flowers are set within a scrolling vine (**fig.22**), recalling the figures of Christ's ancestry depicted in the *Tree of Jesse* cope (1310–25). Notably, May used a monochrome image of this vestment, acquired by the South Kensington Museum in 1889 (V&A, 175–1889), as the frontispiece to *Decorative Needlework* (**fig.23**). Similarly, the individual floral motifs on the Kelmscott bed cover (*c.*1910) are linked together by a Celtic knot design that recalls the diaper pattern found on the Syon cope (1310–20), which is covered with quatrefoils knotted together, each filled with a single figure or group of figures (V&A, 83–1864).[33] In May's opinion, the Syon cope was one of the finest pieces of English medieval work in the Museum.[34]

Fig.22 May Morris (1862–1938), *Autumn and Winter* panel, *c.*1894, polychrome silks on Morris & Co. *Oak* silk damask, 130.8 × 71.8 cm. Private collection.

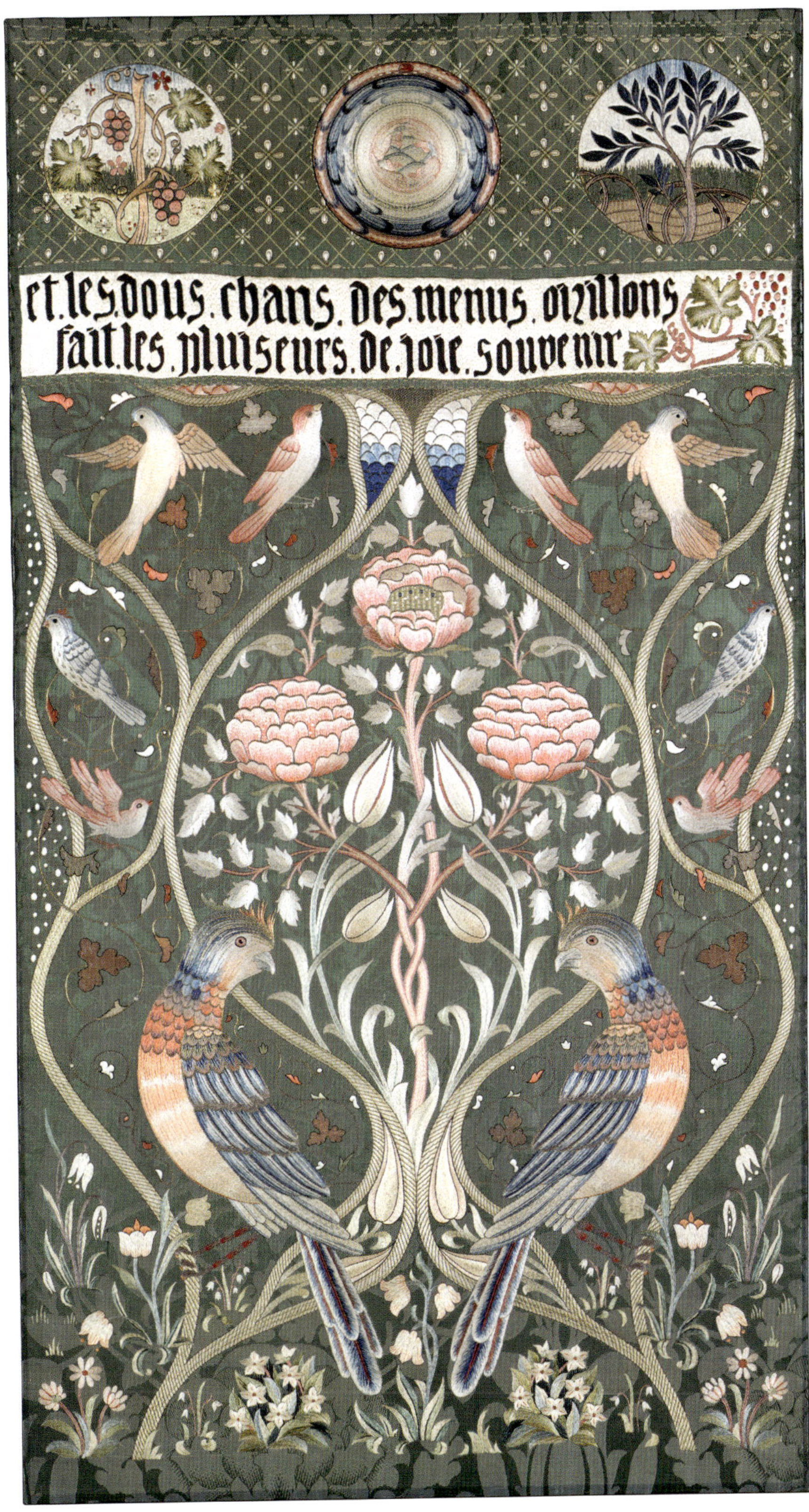

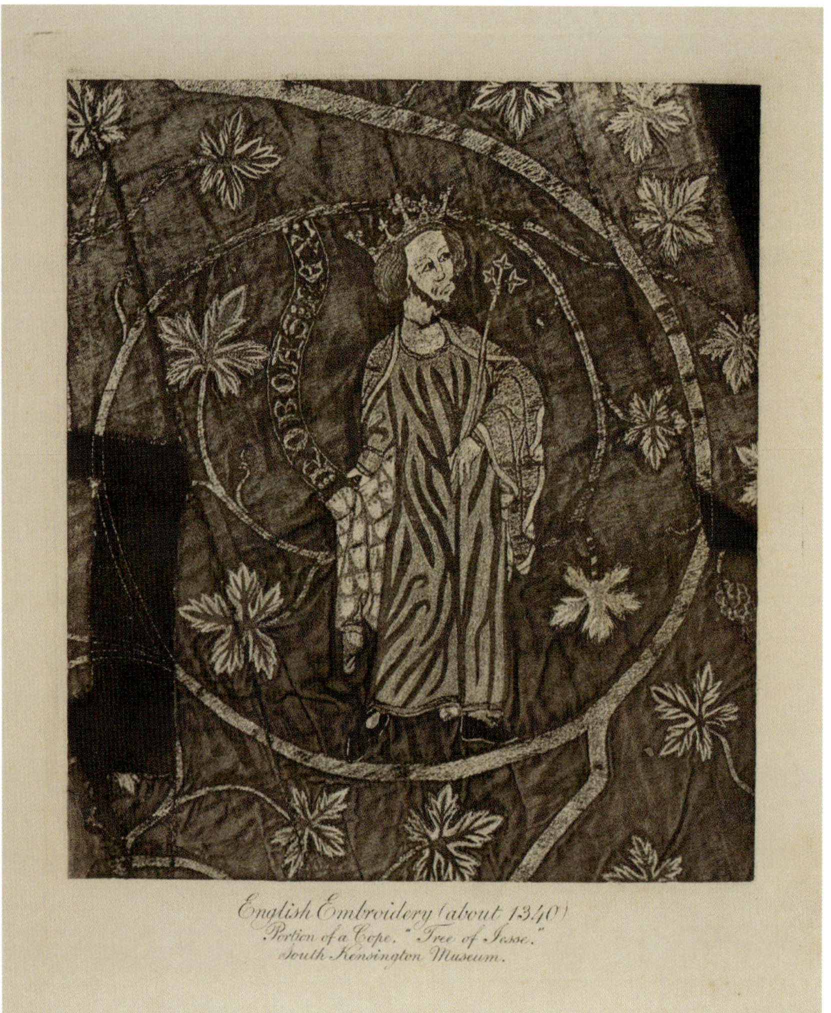

Fig.23 May Morris (1862–1938), *Decorative Needlework* (London, 1893), frontispiece: *Tree of Jesse* cope, 1310–25, V&A, 175–1889, 21.4 × 16.5 cm. Private collection

Art embroiderers were advised to aim at simplicity. William George Paulson Townsend, in his technical guidebook, encouraged readers to place a piece of tracing paper over their design, to trace the best parts and see how much could be done without.[35] Knowing the value of space was also desirable. May found 'too much effort' exerted by inexperienced designers, and urged her students to 'make your <u>spaces</u> interesting[,] for restraint tells as much as profusion – more'.[36] There was also a temptation to place one element of the design behind another, so that a flower or leaf was partly obscured. Lady Alford in *Needlework as Art* recommended adopting the 'wonderful flatness' found in Indian design, in which flowers were laid on the ground and pegged down with care 'to eliminate every variety of surface', and the stems arranged so as not to cross or touch each other.[37] May admired the medieval convention that compelled natural objects 'into a certain subjection without losing sight of their character, and without robbing them of their grace'.[38]

Floral Imagery

Cabbage roses, double dahlias, and other exotic blooms so much admired by lovers of Berlin wool work were banished in decorative needlework for being too complex in form. Art embroiderers turned instead to what Lockwood and Glaister described as 'old-fashioned flowers', rendered with the fewest lines if in outline or the fewest shades if in colour, such as tulip, dianthus, wild rose, honeysuckle, daisy, crocus, periwinkle, columbine, poppy, or fritillary (**fig.24**).[39] This trend towards simplicity coincided with developments in horticulture championed by Irish gardener and journalist William Robinson (1838–1935), author of *The Wild Garden* (London, 1870) and *The English Flowered Garden* (London, 1883). Robinson rejected the artificiality and formality of high Victorian pattern gardening in favour of a more relaxed style, using naturalised plantings of perennial shrubs and climbers. His

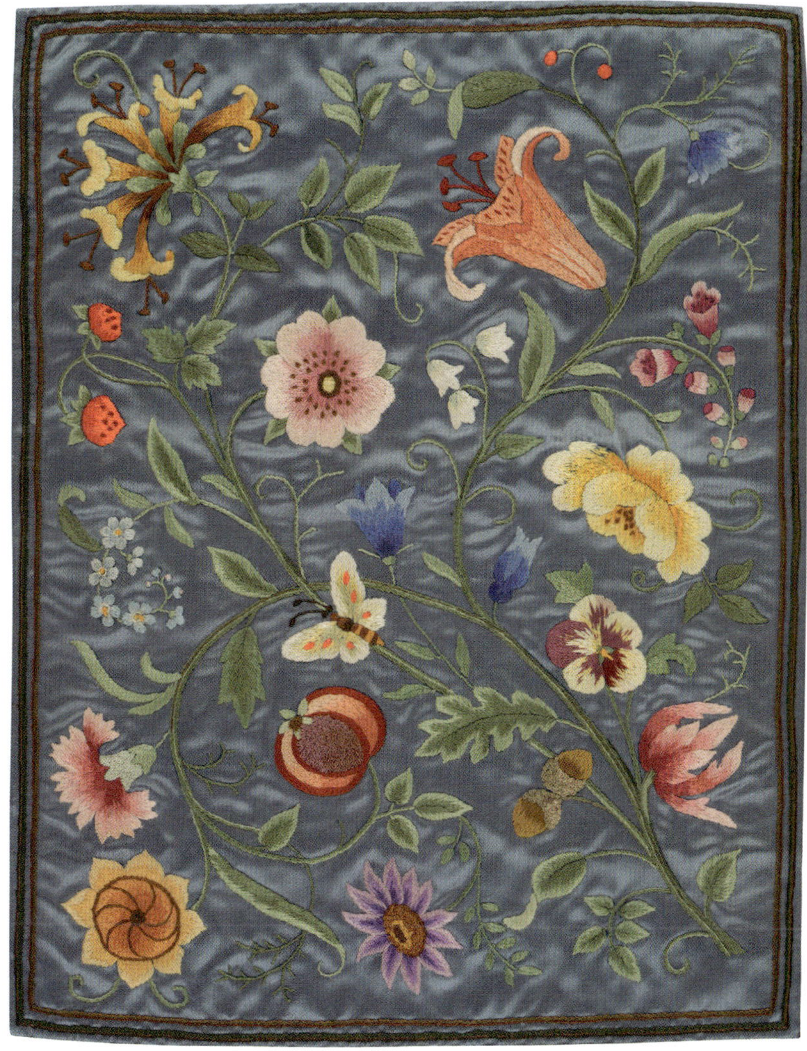

Fig.24 Floral sampler, late nineteenth century, polychrome silks on silk, 34.2 × 26.8 cm. Private collection

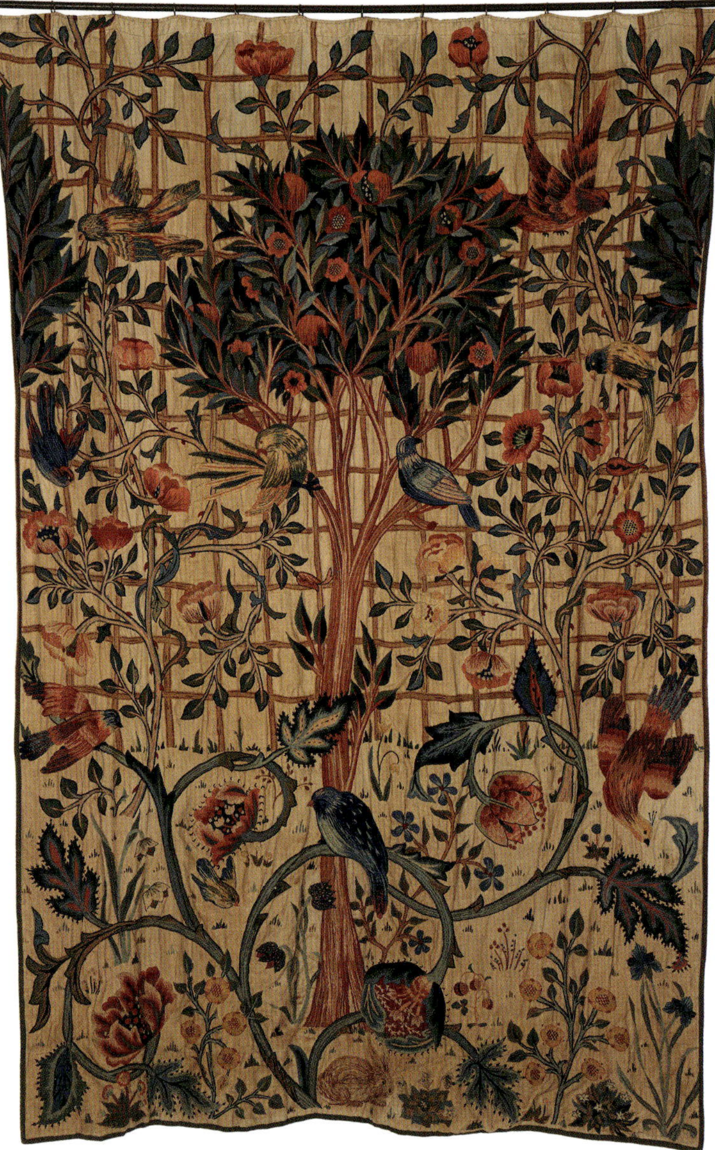

Fig.25 May Morris (1862–1938), Bed hanging, *c.*1893, embroidered by May Morris and her assistants, including Maude Deason, Ellen Wright and Lily Yeats, polychrome crewels on linen, 192 × 122 cm, Society of Antiquaries of London: Kelmscott Manor, KM231.

revolutionary approach was reflected in the choice of botanical subjects in the work of designers and embroiderers associated with the Arts and Crafts movement.[40] For example, in May's bed hangings designed for Kelmscott (*c.*1893), the foreground is sprinkled with meadow flowers in the style of a medieval tapestry. Winding stems of stylised roses cling to the trellis work, while in the background stands a pomegranate tree (**fig.25**) reminiscent of the fruit trees in the wall hangings designed by William Morris *c.*1860 for the dining room at Red House, Bexleyheath, May's childhood home (**fig.26**). Her love of English meadow plants and cottage garden flowers is readily apparent in the designs featured in Chapter 3.

Fig.26 William Morris (1834–1896), *Pomegranate tree* wall panel, unfinished, *c.*1860, wools on Holland cloth, 160.5 × 69.8 cm, V&A, T.124-1985.

COLOUR

Lockwood and Glaister asserted in their 1878 treatise on decorative needlework: 'After good design, good colouring comes next in importance, and is so essential to a piece of embroidery, that while harmonious colouring may atone even for a faulty design, a good design will certainly be spoiled by vulgar colouring.'[41] Design and colour were subject to the same rules of decorative treatment: conventionalism, harmony, contrast and repetition.

From the outset, the pioneers of art embroidery warned against replicating in stitch the 'soft and subtle changes of colour' attainable with a paintbrush, 'for what is legitimate in one art may be a sign of debasement in another'.[42] *The Queen* discouraged its readers from attempting to copy in their own stitching the perfection of an early eighteenth-century Dutch still life by Jan van Huysum (1682–1749).[43] May abhorred the art of needle painting, deriding attempts to recreate in stitch every nuance and shade 'till a libellous caricature of natural growth is achieved'.[44] She advised readers to use a limited palette of flat, simple colours: at the most two shades for a leaf, one side dark, the other light, or both sides shaded up from dark to light; and to treat flower petals in the same way. Both methods can be seen in the violet and rose leaves in the panel *Maids of Honour* (**fig.20**). A firm outline, typical in medieval and non-western ornamentation, was added to make the pattern clear. May instructed beginners to keep it simple at first by choosing one predominant colour plus a few touches of another for light relief. With experience came the introduction of contrasting tones.[45]

Chemical vs. Natural Dyes

Art embroiderers were exhorted to avoid chemical dyes 'as you would poison'.[46] Whilst the intensity of their colour appealed to the manufacturers of Berlin wool work, the new aniline dyes 'offend[ed] against every principle of harmony'.[47] Their harshness and unpredictability led many producers of decorative needlework, including Morris & Co. and the RSAN, to continue using threads coloured with insect and vegetable dyestuffs, which they believed gave 'the only really pure and permanent colours known'.[48]

William Morris had developed a working relationship in the mid-1870s with the Staffordshire dye chemist Thomas Wardle (1831–1909). At the time, Wardle was undertaking a lengthy scientific study of the properties of India's wild silks and indigenous dyes, and was experimenting at his dye works in Leek with mordants that would help fix dye in a fibre, making the colours permanent. In a lecture delivered to the Indian section of the Society of Arts in 1879, he demonstrated the application of tussar embroidery silks on cloths of various designs stitched by his wife Elizabeth (1834–1902).[49] The couple went on to establish the Leek Embroidery Society to execute ecclesiastical and domestic work using the materials produced in the town. Letitia Higgin

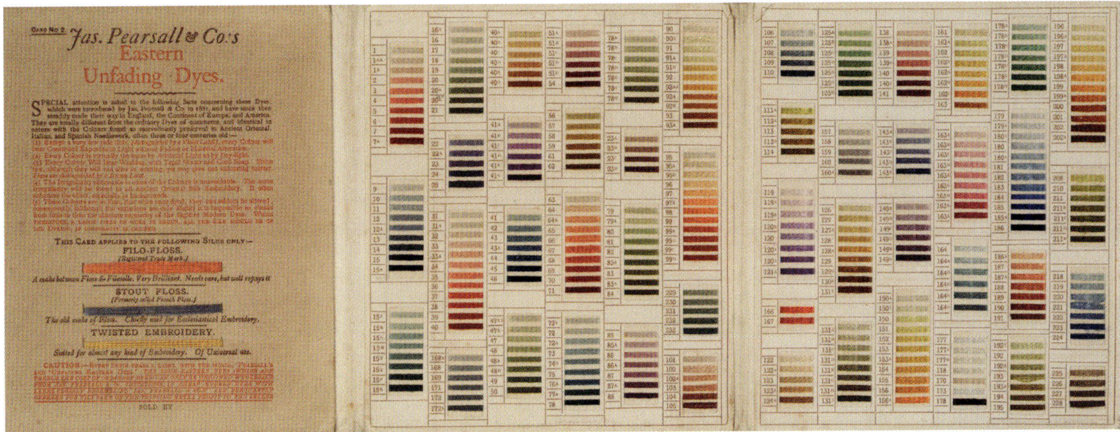

Fig.27 James Pearsall & Co., *Eastern Unfading Dyes*, embroidery silks shade card, 1880s, 18 × 61.7 cm. Private collection

predicted that tussar embroidery yarns would transform decorative needlework, observing that the threads took 'the most delicate dyes with a softness that gives a peculiarly charming effect'.[50] Embroidery outlets were soon using James Pearsall & Co.'s range of tussar silks, first dyed in 1881 with Wardle's 'Eastern Unfading Dyes'.[51] The threads were advertised as being 'totally different from the ordinary Dyes of commerce, and identical in nature with the Colours found so marvellously preserved in Ancient Oriental, Italian, and Spanish Needlework, often three or four centuries old'. More than 340 colours are listed in the shade card in **fig.27**.[52]

William Morris set up his own dye shop in the basement at Queen Square. May later recounted:

> ...bits of madder and indigo lay about, papers of the kermes insect brought home and its habits and customs explained; dye-stuffs of the home-country would be inquired into, Pliny and dear old Gerard read out of an evening to an interested family – no source of information being passed over. Even we children were presented with a set of dyestuffs – how well I remember the look of the broad-stoppered bottles filled with queer powders and lumps and grains that stood in an inviting row on a shelf in the schoolroom, and what distressing messes we made with them![53]

May's essay 'Of Colours & Colouring' summarises her views on natural dyeing. Readers were directed to use the clear blue of indigo, 'perfect in all its tones'; weld or wild mignonette, 'the best and most permanent yellow dye'; yellow- grey- and blue-greens obtained from the indigo dye vat through the modification of weld; the 'endless varieties' of useful reds – from salmon pink through orange to deep purple-red – obtained from kermes, cochineal and madder; and the rich browns from walnut and catechu (an extract of acacia).[54] Her essay also contains advice on the colour combinations to be avoided and which colours to use sparingly. For example, she disliked the mixture of brown and yellow 'often seen in Art Depôts, but not in nature', contrasting this with the combination of yellow, pink and green, which made a 'delightfully fresh and joyous show'.[55]

Reacting to the backlash against gaudy, synthetic dyes, thread suppliers began to advertise 'quaint and artistic colours' for use in decorative needlework: the earthy browns, yellows and greens associated with the Aesthetic movement.[56] Not everyone appreciated these 'dowdy colours', which Glaister scornfully remarked 'pass under the sacred name of Art'.[57] 'Old-fashioned' hues were the best; part of the embroiderer's art was the skilful handling of the shades found in historic textiles.[58] May vigorously defended the use of strong, bright colours, which if harmonised well, produced repose. She gave the example of an old Persian rug decorated with light and dark blue flowers and orange leaves outlined with turquoise blue on a strong red ground, 'a combination that sounds daring, and yet nothing could be more peaceful in tone than the beautiful and complicated group of colours here displayed'.[59] Ellen Masters (1837–1919), who was an authority on decorative needlework, was so taken with the 'artistic scheme of colouring' chosen by May for her *Rose and lattice* screen panel (*c.*1890) – grey green, blue green, peacock blue, indigo, deep purple, dark red, dusky pink, rose, yellow, apricot and white – that she published a four-page account of it, describing the piece as 'a veritable poem embodied in needlework'.[60] A variant of the panel lent to Masters is illustrated in **fig.28**.

MATERIALS

Art embroidery was stitched in wool, silk, metal and flax threads on a variety of cloths, using freestyle or surface embroidery techniques dating from the Middle Ages to the end of the eighteenth century. Given the time and labour required, practitioners were encouraged to utilise materials of the best quality that replicated the fabrics and threads of old to ensure their work was long lasting. Christie argued that the use of such materials had a 'moral effect' upon the worker, 'inciting her to put forth her best efforts in using them'.[61] Moreover, it was important not only to consider the suitability of the materials to the purpose for which the work was intended, but also to remember that every surface required 'its peculiar treatment'. For example, flax threads or crewel wools were to be worked on unbleached linen and never on a silk ground. 'To place the poorer on the richer material,' noted May Morris, 'would be an error in taste.'[62]

Fabric Grounds

Tussar silk, silk damask, Utrecht velvet, Manchester cotton, worsted serge, felted cloth, and machine-made and handwoven linens were all used as grounds for decorative needlework.

Fig.28 May Morris (1862–1938), *Rose and lattice* screen panel, *c.*1890, polychrome silks on Manchester cloth, 137.2 × 57 cm. Ashton Beer collection.

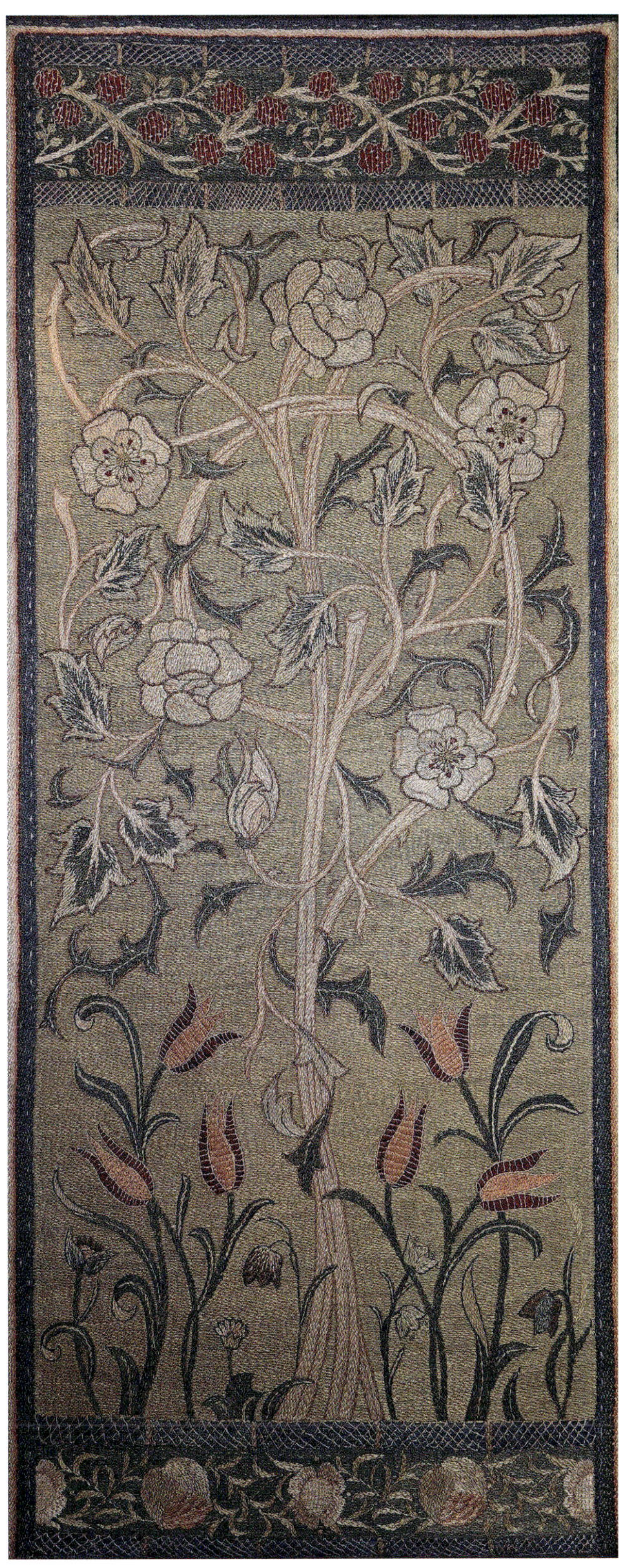

Linens and Cottons

Linen – the most versatile of all stuffs – was rated by Masters 'first rank' as a foundation for art embroidery since it improved with handling, took any thread and could be worked in the hand or frame.[63] Several kinds were available during the second half of the nineteenth century, from sailcloth (a stout linen suitable for screen panels) and Kirriemuir twill (a fine twilled cloth similar to the material found in old embroidered curtains), to a very expensive, fine linen resembling Egyptian mummy cloth. The Decorative Needlework Society, established in 1877, also sold a very soft material known as 'Early English linen' for working heavy designs in wool.[64]

May described linen as 'by far the most pleasing and enduring web' for ordinary use, and confessed in her series of articles on church embroidery that 'one would commit a crime to become possessed of a few rolls of the linen of silky thread' used in the later Middle Ages.[65] She disliked the hard, paper-like surface of very fine, machine-woven linen, 'smooth as glass & cold to the touch as ice', and the thick, home-spun linens made from rough, uneven thread, known as 'Russian crash'.[66] Most art embroiderers favoured handwoven linens specially made for artistic purposes. May drew her readers' attention to the 'charming' linen woven at Langdale in the Lake District, where Albert Fleming (1845–1923), with the support of art historian and critic John Ruskin (1819–1900), had set up a cottage industry in 1883.[67] Both men were members of the Guild of St George, whose aim was to further country life in the best tradition of art, education and handicraft. Fleming sought out local craftsmen and women to assist with the revival of hand-spinning and hand-weaving in Westmoreland (**fig.29**). Within a few years, Langdale linen had won 'an unequalled reputation'.[68] Seventeen different types of bleached and unbleached linens, comparable to sixteenth- and seventeenth-century cloths, were produced in widths of 19 to 42 inches, priced at 2s 6d to 5s 6d per yard.[69] Orders were soon placed by Morris & Co. Between March and October 1889, for example, the firm purchased more than 50 yards of Langdale linen of varying quality.[70]

Several of May's special commissions and works for family and friends were stitched in wools on linen, including the Kelmscott bed hangings and bed cover, *The heavens declare* panel (*c.*1909–10), and the *June* frieze (probably 1910s). The handspun and hand-woven linen used for the Melsetter hangings, embroidered by May and her friend and client Theodosia Middlemore (1861–1944) in *c.*1900, was probably produced on the Middlemore estate on the Orkney island of Hoy.[71]

By the end of the nineteenth century, the Old Bleach Linen Company in Randalstown, Co. Antrim, Ireland had begun to corner the market; among its major clients was the RSAN. Art embroidery linens were a speciality of the Ulster firm, since the warp and weft were of equal strength. Advertisements describe the cloth as 'a delight to work upon. The needle slips through with

Fig.29 'A Revived Cottage Industry – Old Women Spinning Linen in Langdale, Westmoreland', *The Graphic*, 10 January 1885, p.45, 40 × 30 cm. Private collection

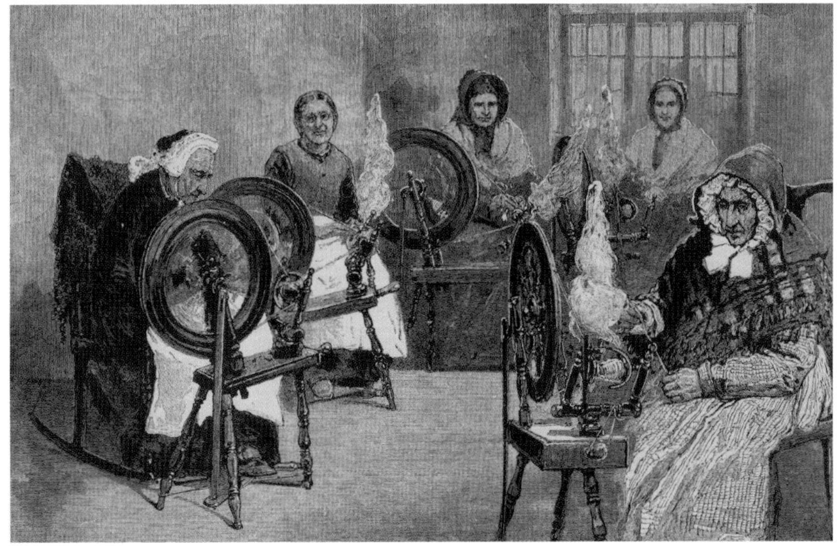

rapidity and ease, and the threads draw without trouble or puckering'.[72] Old Bleach astutely teamed up with James Pearsall and Co. to run art embroidery competitions and jointly advertise their wares. *The Embroideress* magazine, containing articles by leading teachers on historic and contemporary needlework from across the globe, as well as designs and embroidery techniques, was published jointly by Old Bleach and Pearsall between 1922 and 1939.

Masé and Higgin also recommended using Bolton or workhouse sheeting, an inexpensive, coarse-twilled fabric produced in Lancashire's cotton mills, for embroidering curtains, counterpanes and chair coverings.[73] May admired the white cotton ground found in Persian work, 'neither very fine nor very coarse', stitched entirely in floss silks. She used the cloth for a bedcover worked in ivory silk (*c*.1930), though she preferred the 'cool silky surface' of linen.[74] In her essay 'Of Materials', both fabrics are described as being 'good grounds for wool-work, of which the most satisfactory kind is that done on a large scale, with a variety of close and curious stitches with curves and outlines'.[75] Most of the kits produced by Morris & Co. were worked on Manchester cloth, a soft, loosely woven cotton material that was ideal for darning in silks.

Woollens

Serge, a twilled woollen cloth, was regarded as one of the very best materials for needlework.[76] Mrs Lucy Orrinsmith (1839–1910), who had been a manager of Morris, Marshall, Faulkner & Co., wrote in her book on drawing room decoration that 'Portières look well made of serge...in soft greens and peacock blues'. She also suggested that 'heavy patterns worked upon holland, cut out and sewn on serge and cloth, with an edging of filoselle or twisted silk make decorations suitable for portières'.[77] The female figures and fruit trees in William Morris's decorative series based on Chaucer's medieval poem

The Legend of Good Women, designed for the dining room at Red House (*c.*1860), was worked using this technique. May recommended rough serge for wall hangings, stitched in large open wool work, reminiscent of the *Daisy* hangings made for Red House (*c.*1860), and referred readers to entries in the late medieval inventories of Sir John Fastolf (1380–1459), which she had read in the notes to the Paston letters:

> ...the description of green and blue worsted hangings and bankers [cushion seats] worked over with roses and boughs, and hunting scenes, make one long to emulate the rich fancies of forgotten arts, and try to plan out similar work, much of which was quite unambitious and simple, both in design and execution.[78]

May described cloth as the 'king' of woollen fabrics, though as a ground for embroidery it had its limitations.[79] Not to be confused with the generic term, cloth was the name for a closely woven fabric with a short nap that was fulled after weaving to give it a velvety felt surface.[80] Cloth came in all colours and was 'well adapted' for appliqué and silk work.[81] May embroidered two of her father's iconic designs on felted wool: the *Acanthus* bedcover, *c.*1900–10 (V&A, T.66–1939) and *Flowerpot*, 1890–1900 (V&A, T.68–1939).[82]

Silks

Nearly all silk grounds were suitable for decorative needlework. Artistic fabrics used for 'light embroidering' in floss silk or filoselle were available from silk mercers like Liberty & Co., Frank Brunton Goodyer, and A. Stephens & Co. in London's West End. 'A worker must be hard indeed to please,' wrote Masters, 'if she cannot find something to satisfy her both in tint and texture.'[83] The RSAN particularly admired Wardle's tussar silks, which reproduced the exact shades in the 'old Oriental embroideries...with the additional advantage of being perfectly fast in colour.'[84] The designs used by the Leek Embroidery Society were block-printed in a single colour on silk and velveteen at Wardle's print works, ready for stitching in tussar silks and Japanese gold.

Morris & Co. embroideries were worked on various shades of pure dyed twill silk, manufactured on handlooms at the firm's Merton Abbey works.[85] May advised 'rather open' work, 'light in character' when stitching directly on the silk ground.[86] Silk damasks were sometimes used for bedspreads or large portières. Mrs Bessie Townend, who wrote two books on art embroidery, recommended choosing a damask with a large, flat design so that the pattern 'does not show itself too much.'[87] May thought the broken surface of a good damask had the potential to enrich and help out the design.[88] The pair of *Fruit garden* hangings commissioned by her American client Mrs Mary Monro Longyear (1851–1931) in 1892, are worked on the firm's *Oak* silk damask (1881). May also used Morris & Co.'s *St James* silk damask (1881) for her *Hazelnut tree* panel (**fig.21**).

According to Clive Edwards, the use of silk gauze was no longer fashionable as a furnishing fabric in the nineteenth century, though there are at least two instances of May using it as the ground for *Maids of Honour*: one sold by her to the Manchester School of Art in 1909 (Manchester Metropolitan University, MANMU:1907.7), and the other listed in the Kelmscott sale in 1939.[89] The work reveals her technical skill in deftly handling the silk floss threads on this open weave, semi-transparent cloth.

Threads

Mary Elizabeth Turner (1854–1907), who founded the Women's Guild of Arts with May, commented in her essay on modern embroidery that the thread used in decorative needlework should be 'pure, and as well made as it can be, and if dyed, dyed with colours that will stand light and washing'.[90] Thread manufacturers were encouraged to work alongside art embroiderers to produce high-quality, long-lasting materials that replicated the yarns of old.

Crewels

Several of the advances made in the production of woollen threads can be attributed to the tenacity of the RSAN in reviving the art of decorative needlework through the study of antique textiles. Initially, the School had used carpet thrums or waste worsteds left over from weaving Brussels carpets for its crewel work, but found the threads coarse and uneven and the colours limited. As the RSAN's reputation for conserving and copying seventeenth-century embroideries increased, thread manufacturers like Appleton Brothers began to experiment with reproducing crewels (a loosely twisted yarn) based on old specimens found in country houses. Crewels came in three sizes – coarse for large designs, medium for ordinary use and fine for the most delicate work – and were widely available by the late 1870s. The RSAN advised against using inferior threads dyed with aniline dyes that did not wash or clean well, preferring to stitch with crewels of the best quality that allowed the colours, dyed with vegetable dyes that were 'perfectly fast' and bore repeated washing, to blend harmoniously together.[91] In the early 1900s, Briggs & Co., under the brand name Penelope, produced a range of 'old English crewel wool' to replicate the shades found in early English work. Morris & Co. supplied its own tapestry wools 'in a great range of colours', used by May in her special commissions and work for family and friends.[92]

Silks

Art embroiderers used four kinds of silk thread: untwisted floss; embroidery or bobbin silk; fine and thick silk twist; and filoselle. May admired the floss silks found in *opus Anglicanum*, describing the thread as 'quite the foremost of embroidery silks'.[93] The soft, lustrous yarns produced at Wardle's dye works in Leek for less than half the price of the cultivated silks from Italy, China or Japan, became an important element in decorative needlework. Floss silk was ideally suited for laid work, in which threads are laid across the surface of the fabric and secured with stitches, long & short, and satin stitch (a long, straight stitch used for filling shapes), but its delicate texture required 'skilful handling' and was susceptible to fraying.[94] Workers accustomed to pricking their fingers over plain sewing were urged by Masters to avoid floss silk embroidery altogether.[95] May took a different tack: 'If the old workers could use a pure untwisted floss, surely we can take the trouble to conquer the difficulty and do the same.'[96]

Embroidery or bobbin silk was sold as 'rope' (twelve strands to the skein) or fine silk (single strand), which had a slight twist to prevent it from fraying. According to Higgin, silk manufacturers intended dispensing with this distinction, making skeins of uniform thickness comprising eight strands.[97]

Liberty & Co. sold more than 260 shades of art embroidery silks that were specially matched to their art fabrics. The range included tussar, filo floss, twisted silk, rope and filoselle, priced between 2d and 4½d per skein (2s to 4s per dozen).[98] Audrey Ridsdale's 1894 book of designs for church embroidery was supplied with a copy of the Liberty & Co. shade card: 'Many of the colours are perfect; and this verdict is made after comparing them with many original pictures of the old masters in Italy and elsewhere – the shades of red, green blue, and browns being spoken of with special praise.'[99]

In the late 1870s, William Morris experimented with various types of silk thread, including twisted, floss, spun and filoselle. He wrote to Catherine Holiday with advice on how best to use the yarns provided:

> The new silk would not be fit for anything but the darning, or some analogous method: for regular embroidery nothing will do but floss...If it is wanted more durable the thing is either to work it finer & closer, or to quilt [i.e. couch] over long stitches with hair-fine silk[,] for chain-stitch the only thing is twist: only they usually twist our silks over-much: which makes the work look hard: the best thing with the stock of filosel [*sic*] will be to use it in coarse work done with long stitches quilted down with ordinary floss...Meantime I will order some silk of 2 or 3 quality nearly half as thick again & with a little more twist: if too much twisted it will cover badly...[100]

By the mid-1880s, Morris & Co. had perfected its own range of dyed silks, 'renowned for their rare gloss and the beauty of their colours'.[101] Shade cards were available on application from the Oxford Street shop. Thick and fine twist yarns like those in **fig.30** were sold mainly for darning work, and floss silk for working in a frame.[102] Thick twist and floss silk cost 6d per skein (5s 6d per ounce (twelve skeins), or £5 for 1lb); thin twist was slightly cheaper at

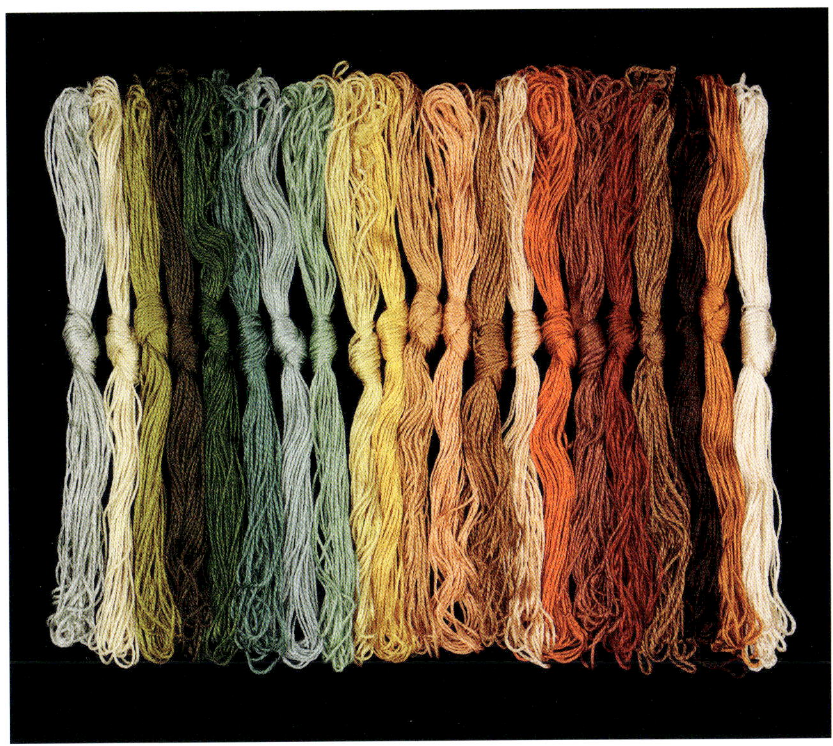

Fig.30 Morris & Co., thick silk twist skeins, V&A, T.183–2016.

4d per skein (6s per ounce (20 skeins), or £5 6s for 1lb). May recommended using fine twist on silk cloth as the thick twist 'stands out in relief against the ground and gives a hard and ropy appearance'.[103] Both versions of the *Lotus* portière, designed by May in 1888, are worked mainly in darning stitch using fine twist (V&A, T.364–1976 and Art Institute of Chicago, 1918.298).[104]

The Embroidery Day Book, a folio size, leather-bound ledger of the business undertaken by the firm between May 1892 and November 1896, contains a handful of orders for kits worked in filoselle.[105] Made from waste cocoons, filoselle was cheaper and easier to use than floss, and was suitable for fine embroidery on silk. Mary Ann Turner described it as 'a most useful article on account of its durability, and the facility with which the twelve threads may be divided'.[106] In 1875, the London silk manufacturers Adams & Co. advertised 140 colours: 'The shades of greens, purples, mauves, and blue, so difficult to meet with in filoselle, and so often required in the new embroidery work, are very good.'[107] James Pearsall & Co., who was regarded as the best manufacturer of embroidery silks, also stocked a thread known as 'filo-floss', a cross between floss silk and filoselle, which needed care 'but well repays it'.[108] The RSAN occasionally used filoselle or embroidery silk to highlight flowers and leaves when working in crewels, as in the reflex rose petals in **fig.31**. There is no evidence of May adopting this technique for her embroideries worked in wool.

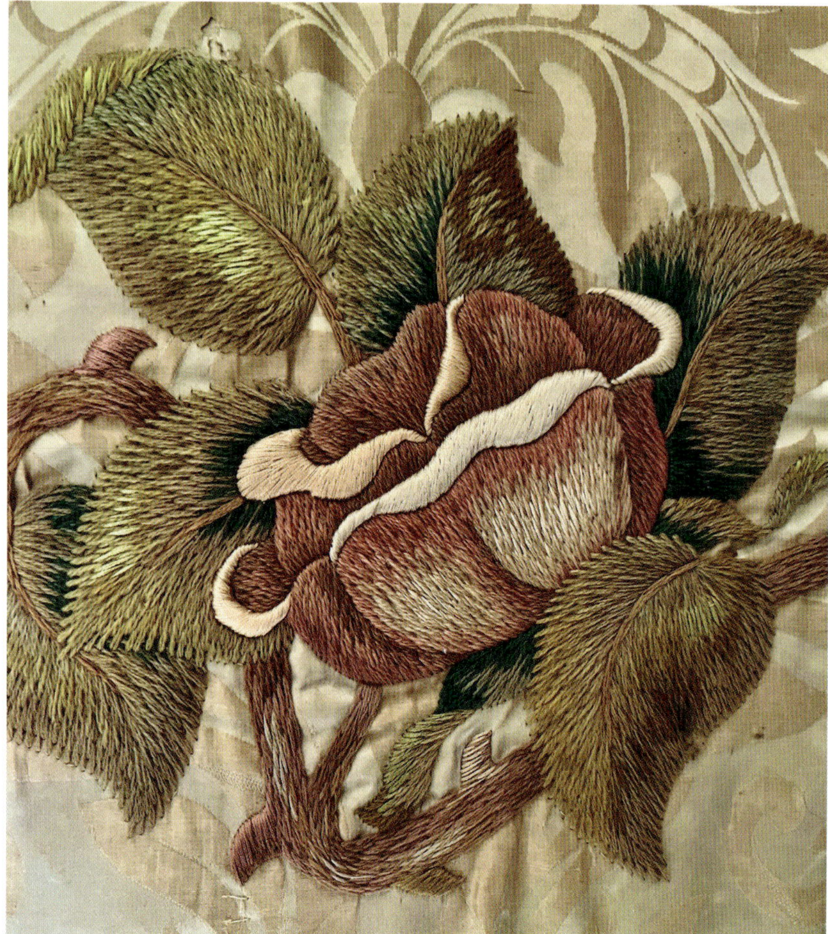

Fig.31 Alexander Fisher (1864–1936), *Rose tree* wall hanging, 1904, detail from a textile fragment stitched by the RSAN, 1904, polychrome crewels and filoselles on silk damask, 74 × 95 cm. Private collection

Metal Threads

Victoria Welby was responsible for introducing Japanese gold into embroidery workrooms in Britain in 1874.[109] Made of gilt paper twisted round a cotton core, it never tarnished compared to the cheaper English and French gold threads used for needlework, which tended to oxidise in the damp and coal smoked atmosphere of London.[110] Jane Morris commented to her daughter on the difficulty of finding gold thread in the 1860s that did not tarnish: 'We adopted a plan of lacquering it afterwards which gave it a beautiful rich tone.'[111] By the 1880s, it was possible to buy Japanese gold 'of the highest quality and warranted not to tarnish' from outlets like Liberty & Co.[112]

May admired the clever use of flat gold tinsel in modern Eastern towels and commended the quality of Japanese gold, though in some ways she found it more troublesome to manage than the gold that could be threaded in a needle and passed through the material.[113] She discussed the treatment of gold in her 1895 lecture to the Royal Society of Arts, noting that the best medieval artists viewed it as one of the colours in their palette, making the most of it as 'a material of decorative value' (compared with the glitter of modern work). In the embroidered bag designed for her father's medieval psalter, the stylised pomegranate and accompanying flowers are outlined in Japanese gold (**fig.32**). The handling of the thread reflects 'the dignity of reticence' that May so admired in the work of medieval embroiderers.[114]

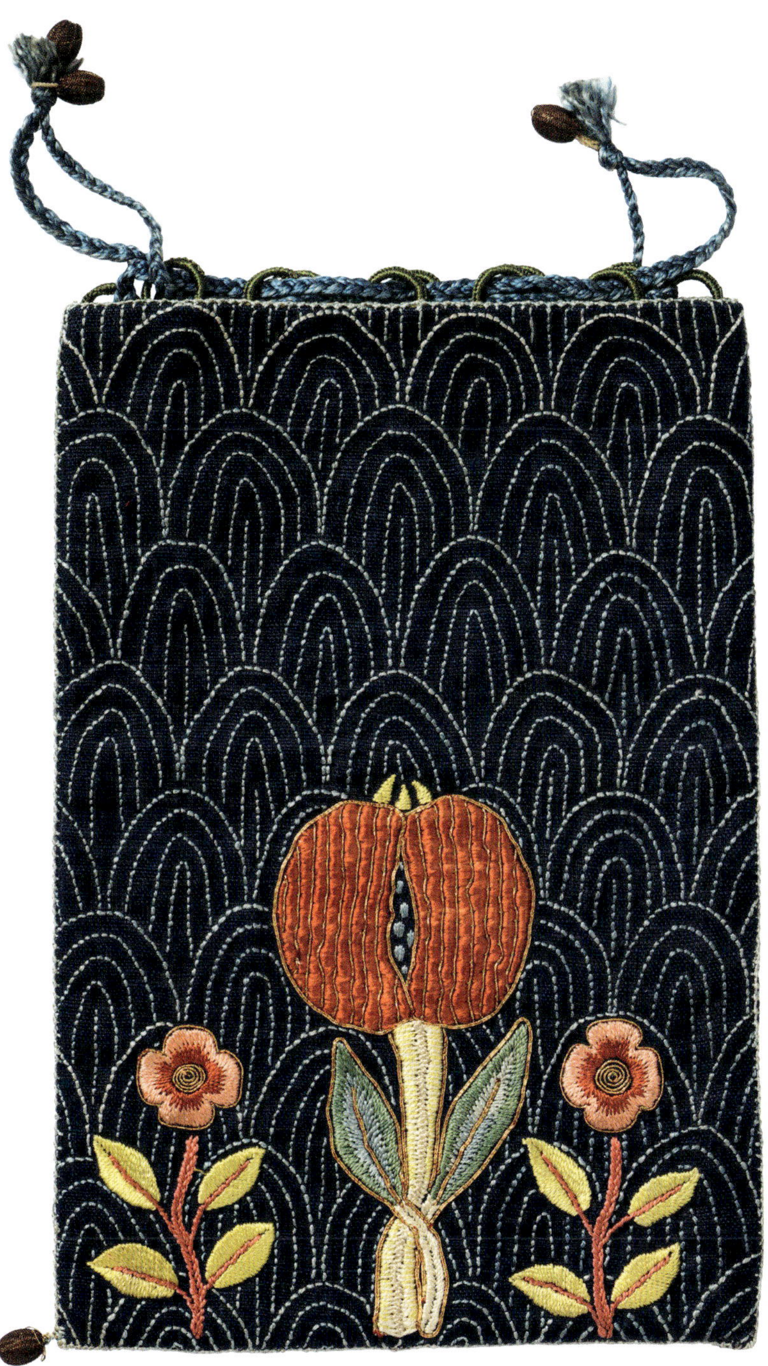

Fig.32 May Morris (1862–1938), Book bag for William Morris's medieval psalter, 1890s, stitched by May and her sister Jenny, polychrome silks and Japanese gold thread on indigo-dyed linen, 22.8 × 15.4 cm, William Morris Gallery, F337.

Flax Threads

According to Masters, many practitioners objected to using flax threads because of their rough and unequal appearance.[115] By the 1890s, the Harris mill in Cockermouth, Cumbria had perfected a range of pure flax embroidery threads capable of taking on the lustre and tone of filoselle at a third of the price. Harris threads were used by several art embroidery outlets in Britain and were exported all over the world. Whilst May recommended linen yarn for embossing and stuffing padded satin stitch, she seldom utilised the thread for surface decoration.[116] The pair of vine-patterned linen napkins stitched in white flax thread illustrated in **fig.33** are a rare example.[117]

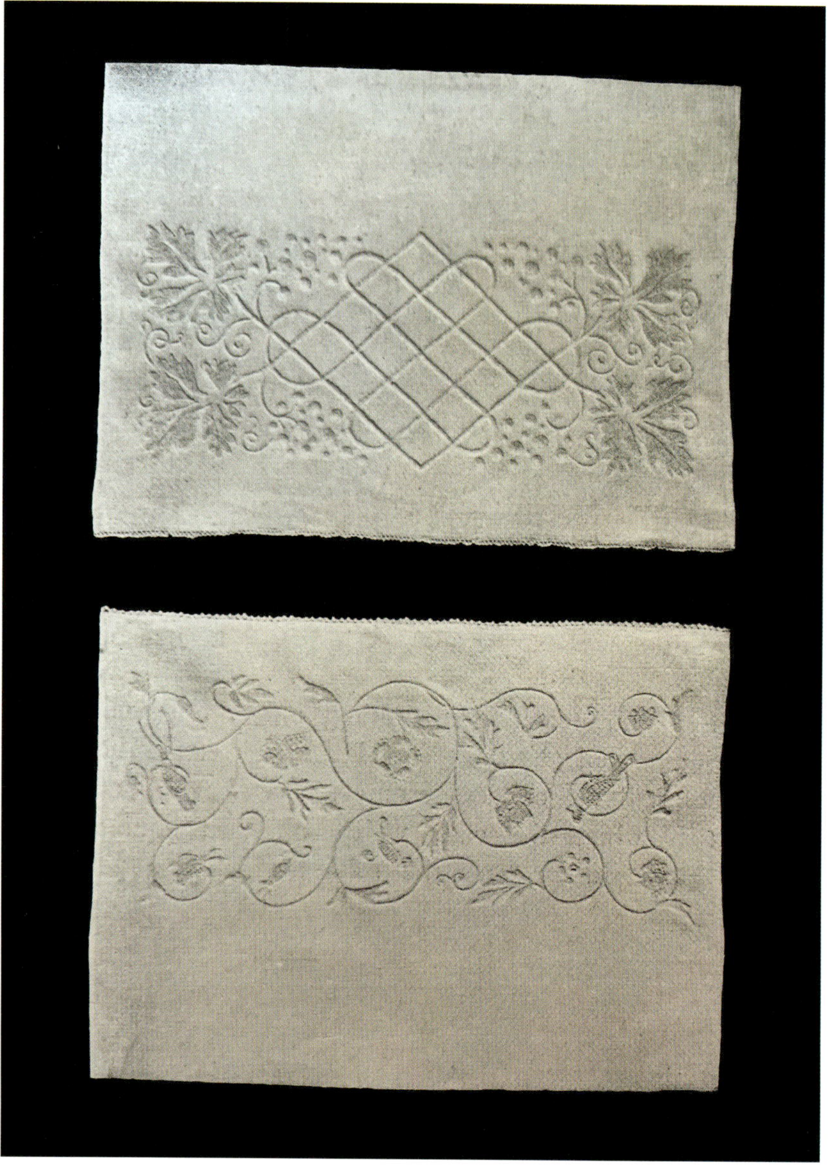

Fig.33 May Morris (1862–1938), Pair of napkins, *c.*1907, flax thread on linen, 31.9 × 23.7 cm (page), illustrated in *The Art Journal* (1907), p.323. Private collection

STITCHES

Sedding claimed in his 1890 essay on design: 'Every ingenious stitch of old humanity has been mastered, and a descriptive name given to it of our own devising.'[118] Convent workrooms, including St Margaret's, East Grinstead, run by Sedding's younger sibling Sister Isa (1841–1906), and embroidery societies like the RSAN, superintended by Anastasia Dolby (1823/4–1873), author of *Church Embroidery Ancient and Modern* (London, 1867), were instrumental in reviving the 'old' stitches found in ecclesiastical work.[119] The Morris family was equally committed to this undertaking. Jane recounted in a letter addressed to May in *c.*1909 that she and William had 'studied old pieces and by unpicking &c: we learnt much.'[120]

Ostensibly, the technical guidebooks and stitch primers listed in **Table 2** furnished embroiderers with a comprehensive list of the 'old' stitches. Nonetheless, when viewed from a modern perspective, Sedding's claim requires qualification. For instance, it was not until after the publication of Louis de Farcy's *La Broderie du Xie siècle jusqu'à nos jours d'après des spécimens authentiques et les anciens inventaires* in 1890 that textile scholars and practitioners first began to decode the medieval technique of underside couching, an inherent feature of *opus Anglicanum*.

When it came to giving descriptive names to the 'old' stitches, the antiquarian and ecclesiologist Dr Daniel Rock (1799–1871) adopted the following set of medieval Latin terms for the 1870 catalogue of the South Kensington Museum's textile collection:[121]

- *opus plumarium*, defined as flat stitches that overlap and blend together like the plumage of a bird, such as long & short, stem, split and satin[122]
- *opus consutum*, translated as 'cut work'. This category comprised patchwork, and inlaid and onlaid appliqué
- *opus pluvinarium*, classified as canvas work. Also known as 'cushion style' because of its use on seat cushions and hassocks
- *opus pectineum*, a form of embroidery akin to woven work, such as couched or laid work
- *opus Anglicum* or *Anglicanum*, embroidery after the English manner. Scholars and practitioners writing in the 1870s and 1880s mistakenly thought that *opus Anglicanum* was worked in chain stitch (for more on this subject, see below).

Rock's classification was swiftly adopted by nineteenth-century textile scholars, including Alan Summerly Cole (1846–1934), curator of the *Special Loan Exhibition of Decorative Art Needlework*, and Lady Alford in her tome *Needlework as Art*. However, Masters derided the use of Latin terms in her stitch primer: 'It is evident that the average woman feels no interest in knowing that when she is working an *appliqué* panel for a screen she is executing the classical *opus consutum*, or that her favourite "long and short" stitch is the same as the *opus plumarium* of the ancients.'[123] Lewis Forman Day and Mary Buckle likewise observed that the 'quasi-learned descriptions' of old stitches were not much help as the authorities did not always agree on their meaning.[124] Even Cole had rejected them by 1886, commenting in a lecture to the Society of Arts: 'Closer scrutiny of the precise meaning of these Latin titles seems to me to have demonstrated their comparative uselessness in conveying definite technical information.' He chose instead to divide embroidery stitches into two classes: the first, made for display on one side of the material, including long & short, stem and chain stitch; the second, for work that is equally finished on both sides, like satin stitch.[125] Masters disputed Cole's system of classification, citing the examples of Holbein embroidery and certain kinds of cross stitch.[126] In many of the publications listed in **Table 2**, the stitches are grouped according to those best suited for working in the hand or on a frame, or by their several uses in embroidery: outline (stem, split, chain), looped (chain, buttonhole, French knot), flat (laid, satin), shading (long & short), and so on.

Paulson Townsend's 1899 manual *Embroidery: or The Craft of the Needle*, written in response to repeated enquiries from students, contains instructions for 70 stitches in 'general use or recognized as good from much experience'. Readers were advised to persist in 'puzzling out' some of the volume's more intricate stitches taken from old work in the South Kensington Museum, such as a sixteenth-century Portuguese linen coverlet (V&A, 326–1898) worked in 'elaborate fancy stitches' that were 'exceedingly effective in use'.[127] For the most part, professional art embroiderers used the simplest and most common stitches, believing that 'Excellence of workmanship does not lie in many curious and difficult varieties of stitch but in the expressive use of a few ordinary ones.'[128] May Morris argued that the finest work, whether old or modern, was notable for its restraint and simplicity, and advised the learner to confine herself to the use of one or two: 'Variety and effect are more honestly produced by good design and careful colouring than by the skilfullest admixture of stitches.'[129] Christie, who had studied embroidery under May at the Central School of Arts and Crafts, suggested that work carried out entirely in a single stitch, like the outline version of Image's figure of *Juno* in **fig.34**, executed in stem stitch, had 'a certain unity and character that is very pleasing'.[130]

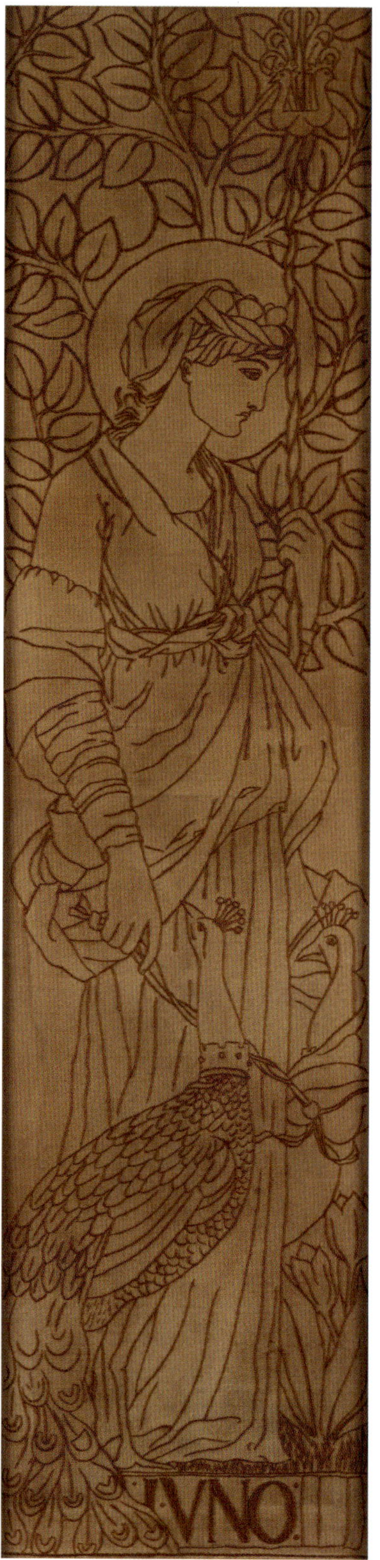

Opposite: fig.34 Selwyn Image (1849–1930), *Juno* panel, *c.*1879, embroidered by the Royal School of Art Needlework, late nineteenth century, monochrome silk on linen, 114 × 28 cm. Private collection.

The principal stitches found in art embroidery are long & short, satin, stem, split, darning, couching, laid work and French knot. May used all these stitches for her designs as well as chain, fly, herringbone, buttonhole, running, back, seeding and speckling stitch. A selection of these stitches and their uses are discussed below.

Darning

Morris & Co.'specially recommended' darning stitch to its customers because it could be worked easily in the hand, though as May observed, it was not a simple technique for a beginner to master without a few hours of personal instruction.[131] Darning stitch had been used by the firm since at least the mid-1870s. In a letter dated 20 July 1877, William Morris asked Catherine Holiday to embroider a large coverlet and a door hanging in 'darned work' using filoselle on loose Indian cotton.[132] The *Acanthus and peony* panel in **fig.35**, which is attributed to her, is worked mainly in darning stitch on a silk ground.

Surface darning stitches were a characteristic feature of the Islamic embroideries collected by William and May Morris. The technique was regularly used to work the repeating patterns of stylised flowers on Ottoman wall hangings or quilt facings. For instance, in the seventeenth-century hanging illustrated in **fig.36**, the motifs are filled by stitching in straight rows over five warp threads and under one, with each new row starting three threads higher or lower than the previous one until the whole of the design was covered in silk.[133]

By the time May took over the running of the embroidery department, darning stitch had become the Morris & Co. house style for domestic furnishings like the *Olive and rose* cushion cover in **fig.37**. The technique is explained in detail in *Decorative Needlework* and in May's lecture notes (**fig.38**) dating from the period spent teaching at the Birmingham Municipal School of Art (1899–1902) and the Central School of Arts and Crafts in London (1899–1905).[134] To stitch the background, the threads are laid in horizontal lines in an irregular brick pattern, the needle running in and out through the warp yarns of the material. Kits stitched on Manchester cloth were generally worked in horizontal rows, though vertical darning was used from time to time, as in the scrapbook covers discussed in Chapter 3. The background was left plain for the designs worked on silk.

Darning stitch was a quick and economic method utilised by several embroidery outlets to cover large surfaces such as curtains, portières and bedcovers, with the pattern worked in outline in stem stitch, as in **fig.39**. May described this method in her lecture notes as'good for big scroll work for wall hangings.'[135] At Morris & Co., a more intricate form of darning was used. This involved 'artistic knowledge' in drawing lines and shading colours to create the botanical motifs. The stitches radiate outwards from a common centre to

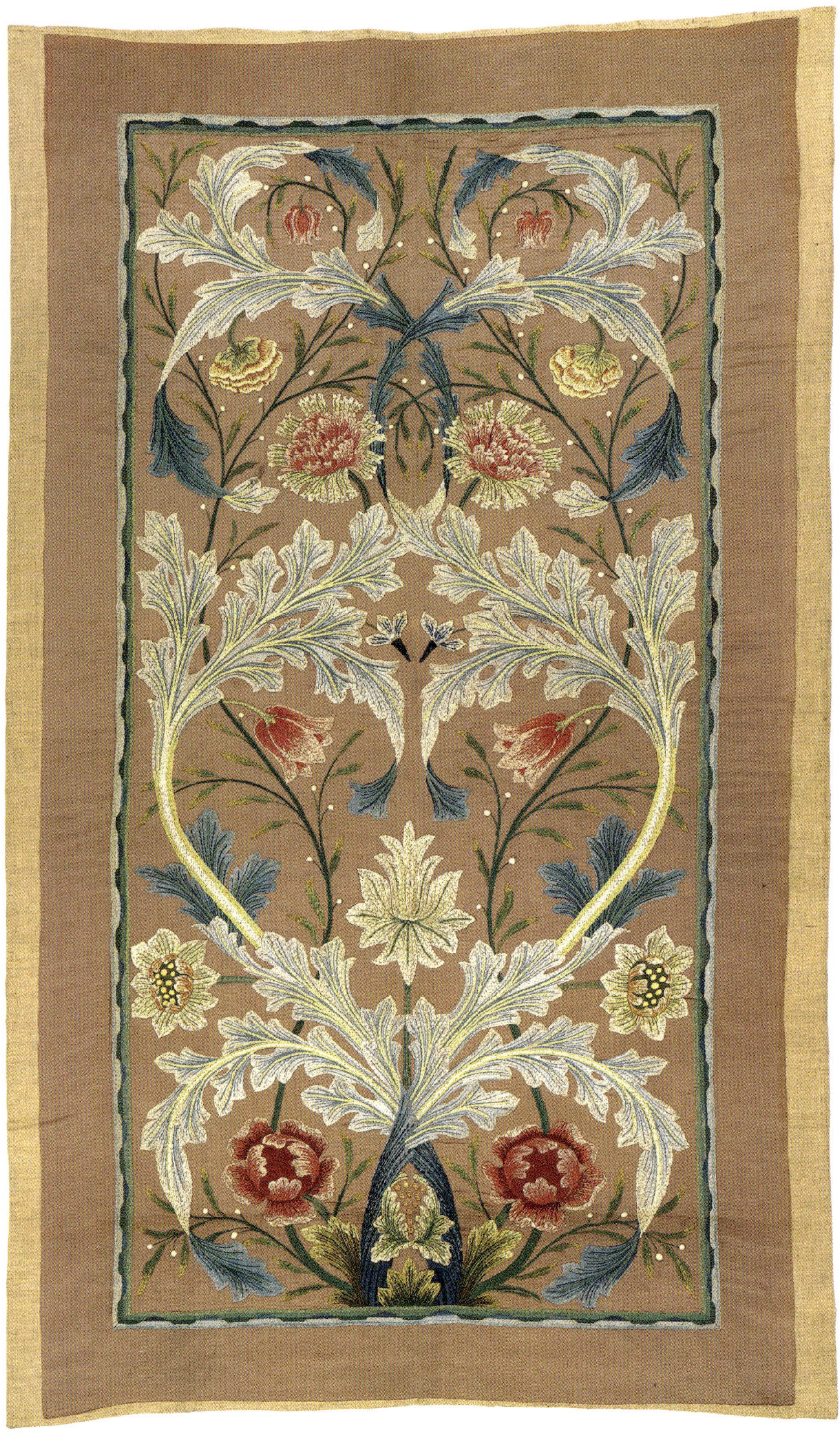

Fig.35 William Morris (1834–1896), *Acanthus and peony* panel, stitching attributed to Catherine Holiday, *c.*1875–80, polychrome silks on silk, 198.1 × 118.7 cm, Metropolitan Museum of Art, 1972.65.

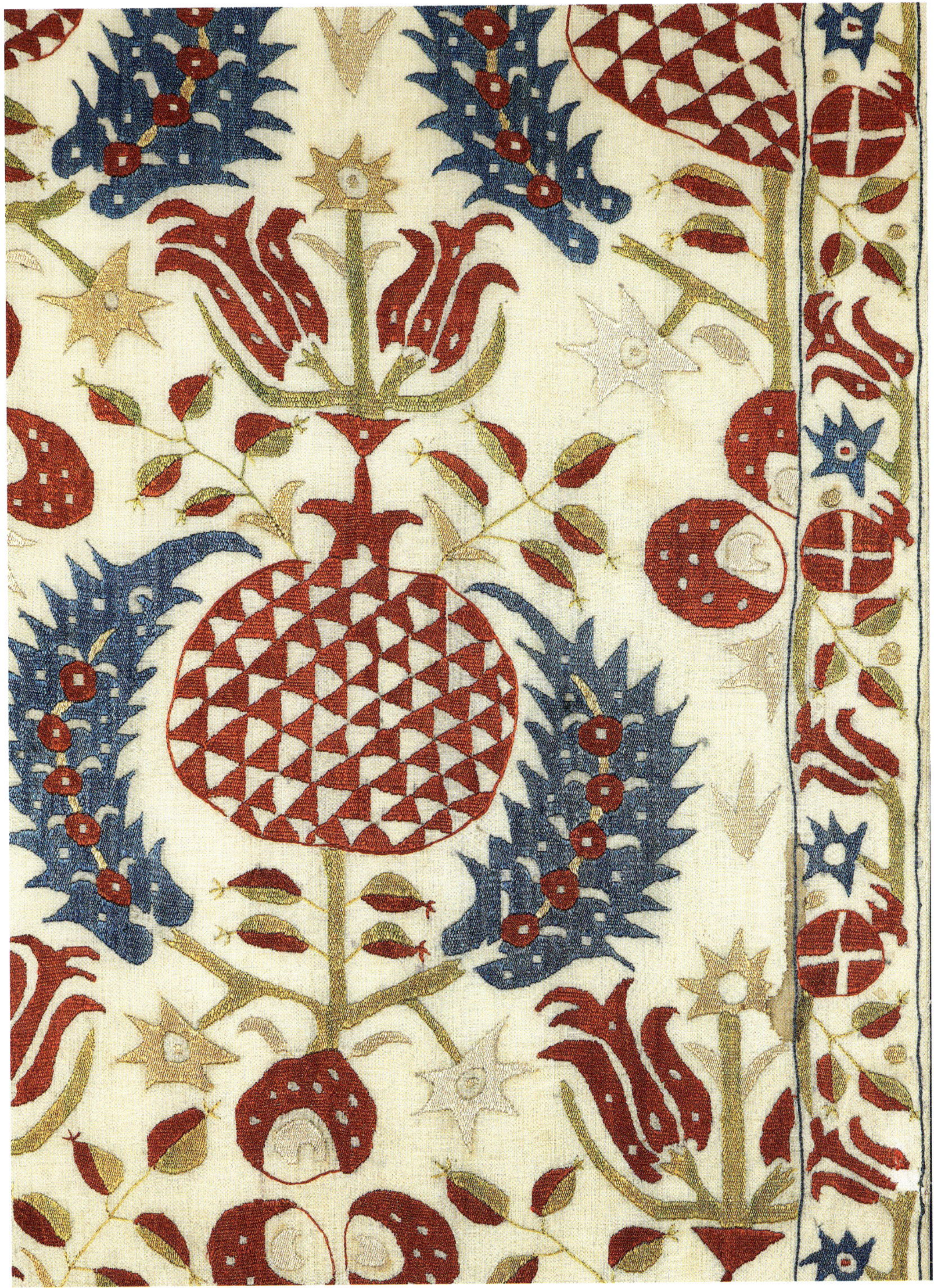

Fig.36 Detail from a wall hanging with tulips, pomegranates and serrated leaves, Ottoman Turkey, seventeenth century, polychrome silks on cotton, 235 × 130 cm. Ashmolean Museum (EA2007.104)

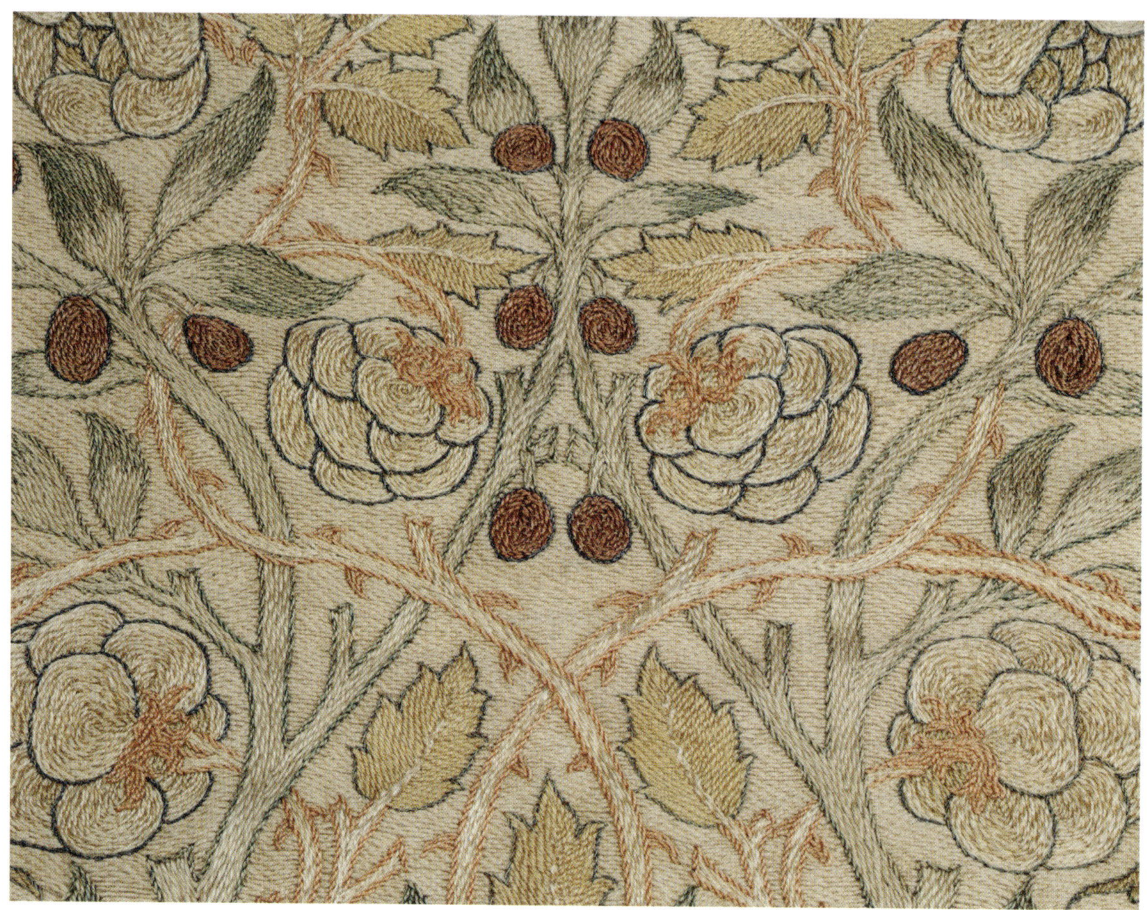

Fig.37 William Morris (1834–1896), Detail from *Olive and rose* cushion cover, *c.*1880, embroidered at Morris & Co. under May Morris's direction, 1885–96, polychrome silks on Manchester cloth, 48.5 × 49.5 cm. Private collection

Opposite: fig.38 May Morris (1862–1938), lecture notes, 1899–1905, ink on paper, 20 × 13 cm (page), William Morris Gallery, J561i.

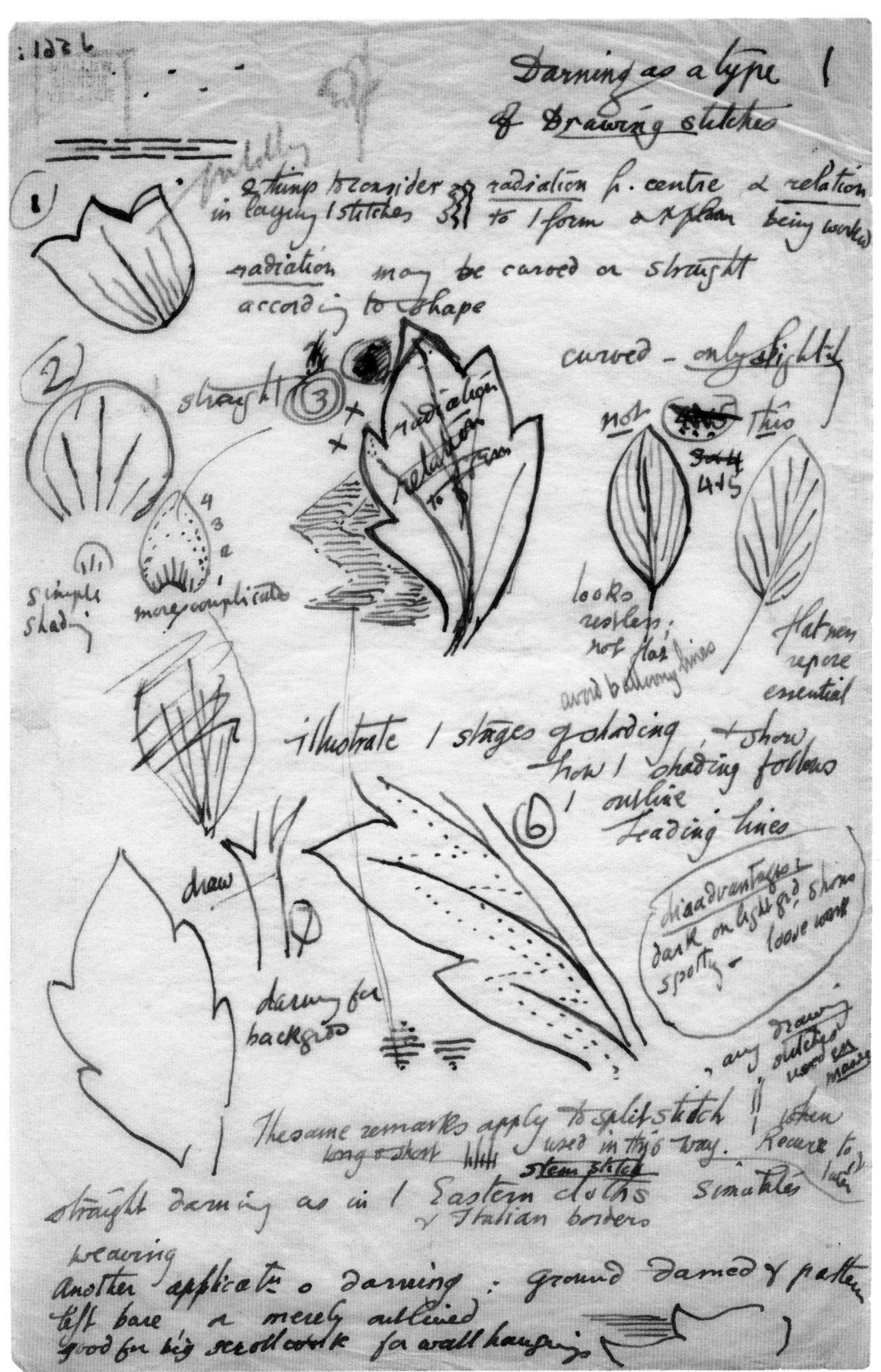
Darning as a type
of Drawing stitches
radiation may be curved or straight
according to shape
curved - only slightly
not this
straight
simple shading
more complicated
looks restless, not flat
flatness repose essential
illustrate stages of shading & show how shading follows outline
Leading lines
draw
darning for background
disadvantages: dark on light gd shows loose work spotty
The same remarks apply to split stitch when used in this way.
stem stitch
straight darning as in Eastern cloths & Italian borders
another application of darning: ground darned & pattern left bare or merely outlined
good for big scroll work for wall hangings

Fig.39 Detail from a wall hanging with flowers and peacocks, late nineteenth century, blue silk on linen, 160 × 102 cm. Private collection

replicate the natural growth of the flowers, stems and leaves (**figs 40–41**).[136] The botanical motifs are 'thrown slightly into relief' by outlining in light or dark silk as required.[137]

Long & Short

Long & short stitch, which May described as 'close & firm & laborious as darning is quick & loose & flowing', was regularly used by art embroiderers for shading flowers and leaves using different coloured threads to create subtle gradation (**fig.42**).[138] Nearly all of the technical guidebooks and stitch primers listed in **Table 2** advise dovetailing the stitches in between those worked in the preceding row so that the transition from one shade to another is 'quite

Right: fig.40 May Morris (1862–1938), *Decorative Needlework* (London, 1893), p.28, fig.9, 31.2 × 24.5 cm (page). Private collection

Below: fig.41 John Henry Dearle (1859–1932), *Anemone* screen panel, *c.*1885–90, stitched by May Morris, 1890s, polychrome silks on Manchester cloth, 132.5 × 53 cm. Private collection

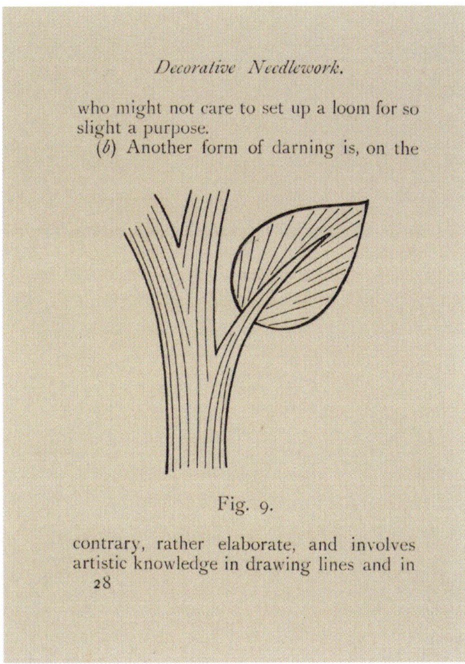

Decorative Needlework.

who might not care to set up a loom for so slight a purpose.

(*b*) Another form of darning is, on the

Fig. 9.

contrary, rather elaborate, and involves artistic knowledge in drawing lines and in

28

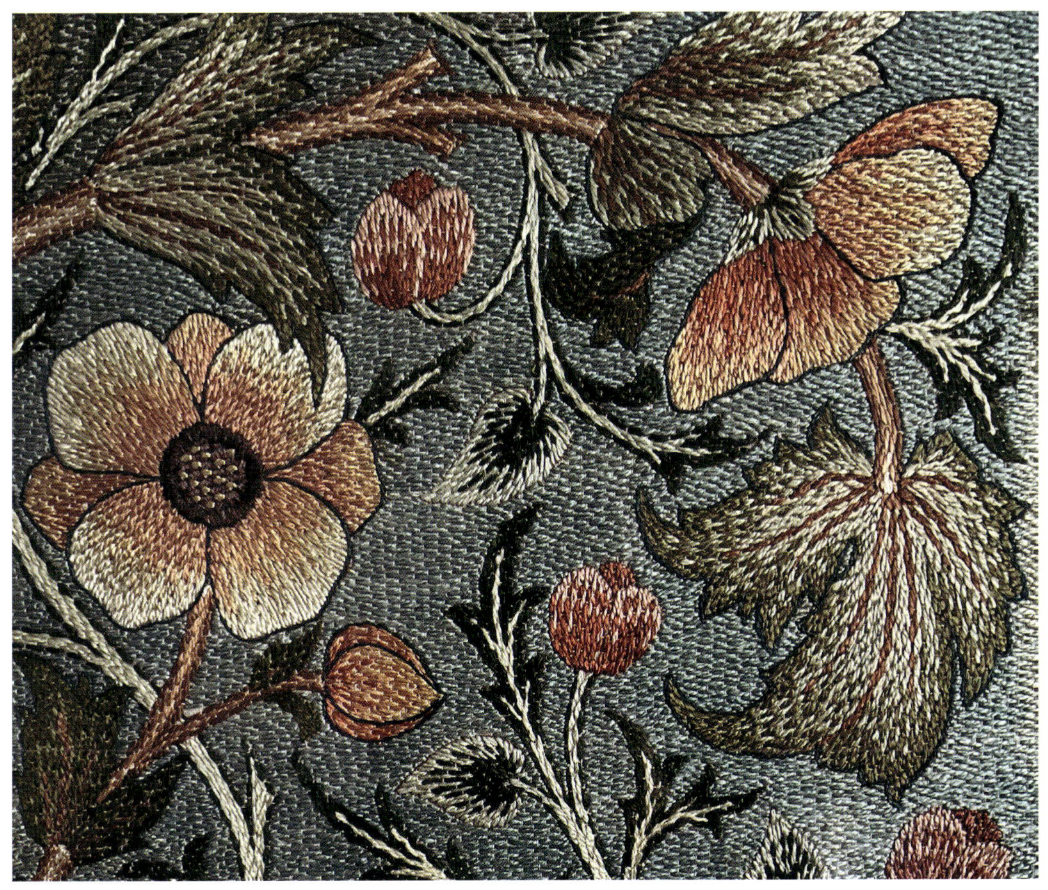

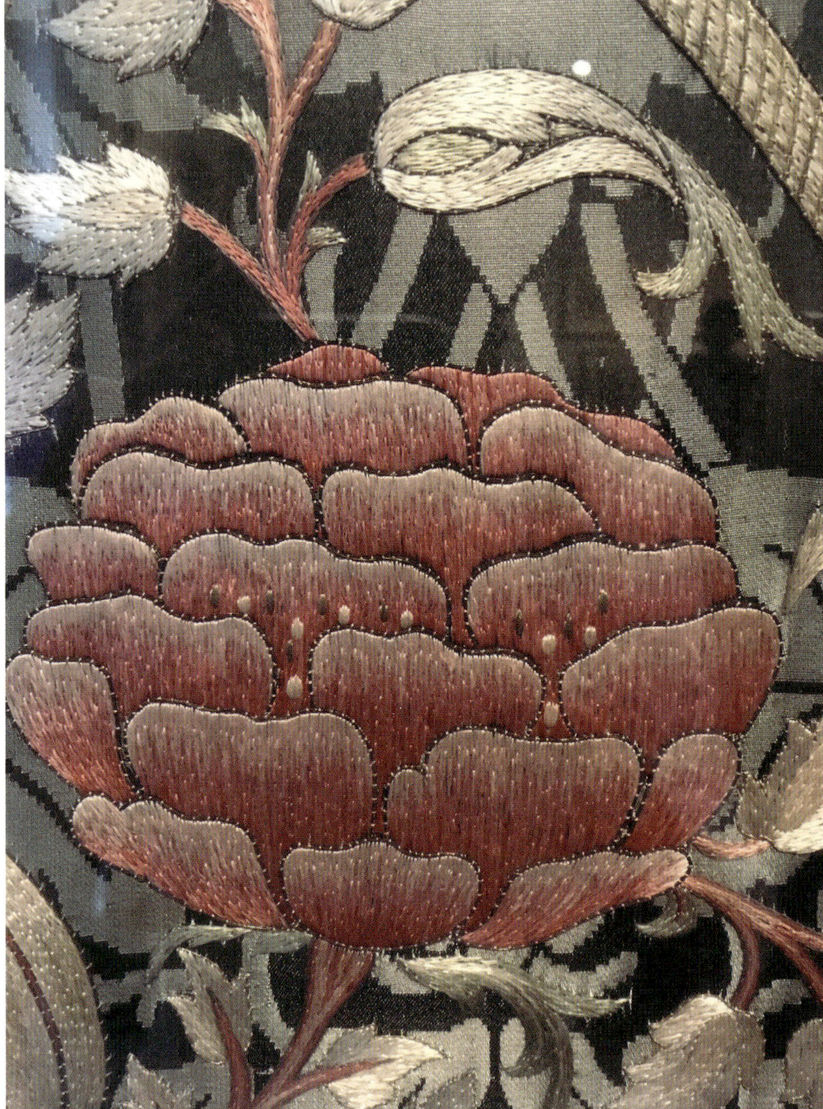

Fig.42 May Morris (1862–1938), Detail from the *Spring and Summer* panel, *c.*1894, polychrome silks on Morris & Co. *Oak* silk damask, 130.8 × 71.8 cm. Private collection.

unnoticeable'.[139] Day and Buckle and Mrs Townend also suggested splitting the stitches of the previous row, as today's embroiderers generally do: 'You will find it will be better, and cause a much nicer effect.'[140]

May proposed a third approach for working long & short, which she called 'feather-stitch', not mentioned by any other writer. While researching English crewel work of the seventeenth and early eighteenth centuries in the South Kensington Museum, she discovered that leaves were sometimes worked not from the top downwards but from the centre vein outwards: 'The stitches are built up from the centre line or stem, in close and compact rows, different gradations of colour being used where needed.'[141]

Chain

According to Higgin, chain stitch was 'but little used' in art embroidery during the last quarter of the nineteenth century, possibly because sewing machines could produce it mechanically on dress materials and domestic furnishings for little cost.[142] May's first published work on embroidery, printed in 1888 in *The Century Guild Hobby Horse*, was a rallying cry for the restoration of chain stitch. The stitch had been used 'with much skill and to great effect' in old work, but generally not by modern workers, she noted, 'excepting those of the east of Europe where embroidery is professional'.[143] Following in the footsteps of Daniel Rock, May cited the example of *opus Anglicanum*, noting that the faces and garments were worked in chain stitch, though some of her contemporaries had already begun to challenge this assumption.[144] In due course, she modified her view, noting in her 1894 article on figure work:

> It used to be the fashion to say that in this fine English work, the flesh was done in very minute chain-stitch. I am not quite of the same opinion. The work is so excessively fine that without unpicking, or even handling unduly, it is not easy to pronounce upon it; but I think... [it] is in split stitch... the stitches being so short that the appearance of chain-stitch is produced.[145]

May also referred to the use of chain stitch in late sixteenth-century Goa work that she had seen in the South Kensington Museum, stitched in yellow silk on a cotton ground,[146] and in the panel of Persian Resht embroidery which took pride of place in her own collection of Islamic textiles (**fig.14**). Appliquéd with different bits of coloured cloth decorated in chain stitch, the panel was 'a very flower-garden for colour and grace, and for skill and precision in the stitchery unsurpassed'.[147]

May encouraged modern embroiderers to use chain stitch for outline work and light veining in leaves and flowers. For more solid work, she recommended starting with the outline and working inwards until the whole space was filled up, a device prevalent in Indian textiles like this eighteenth-century example from Gujarat (**fig.43**).[148]

Chain stitch remained one of May's preferred techniques and features in several of her embroideries worked in silk or wool on a variety of cloths, including *Flowerpot*, designed by William Morris in *c.*1876 (V&A, T.68–1939), and a cloak in the form of an abba, inspired by her travels in Egypt in the winter of 1896–97 (**fig.44**).[149] Very few of May's designs contain suggestions for stitches, but among the items in the Ashmolean collection is a pattern inscribed in her hand: 'Sampler for chain stitch &c' (**figs 45 & 46**).[150]

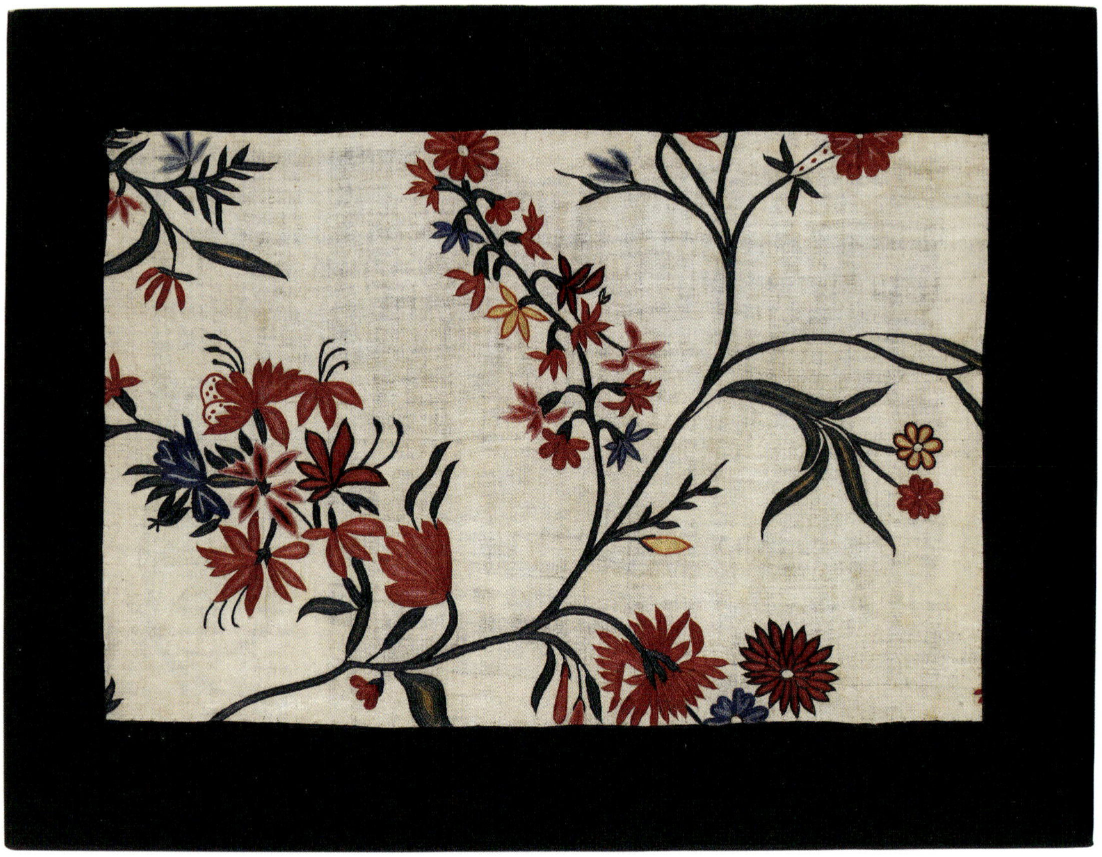

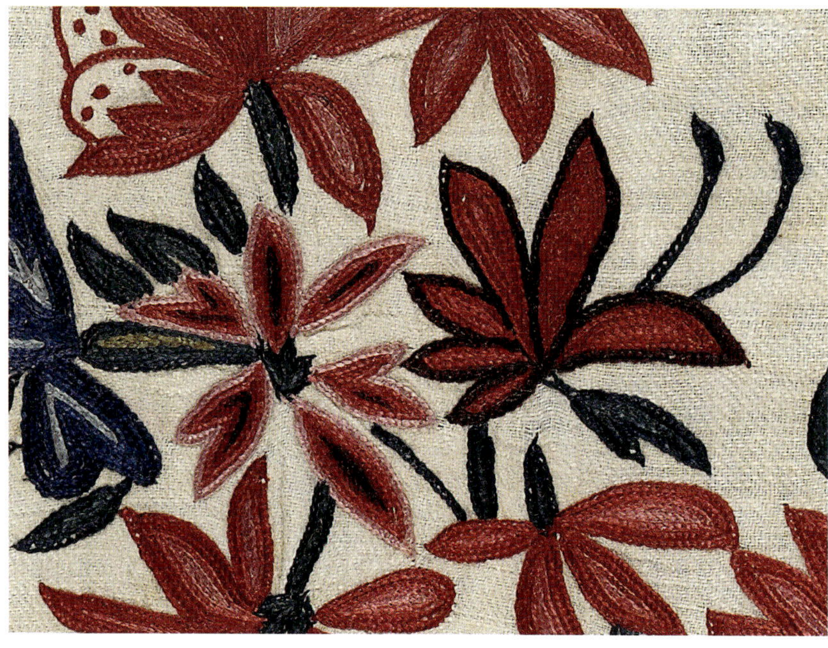

Fig.43 (with detail) Textile fragment with flowering branches or fronds, Gujarat, eighteenth century, polychrome silks on cotton, 20 × 32.5 cm. Ashmolean Museum (EA1993.383)

Fig.44 (with detail) May Morris (1862–1938), Cloak embroidered by May Morris and Maude Deacon, *c.*1897, polychrome silks on fine wool, 123 × 297 cm, William Morris Gallery, F204.

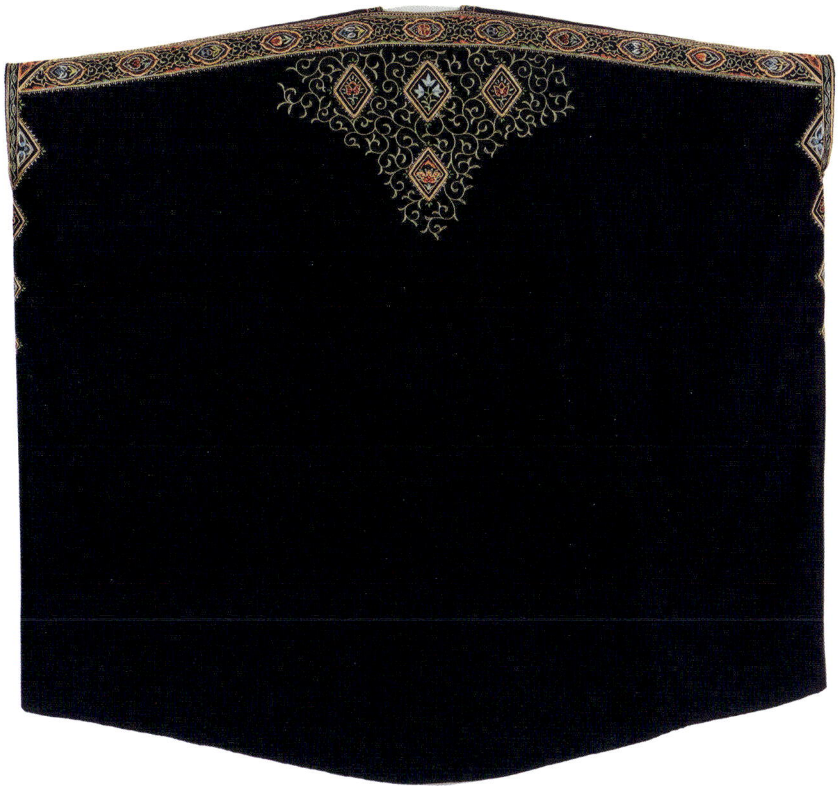

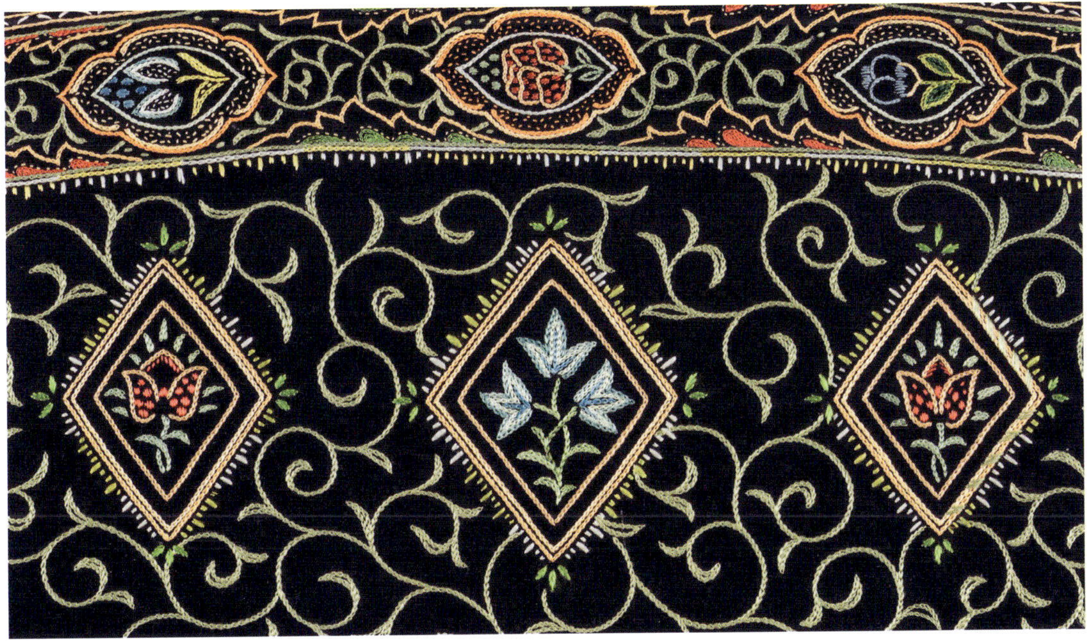

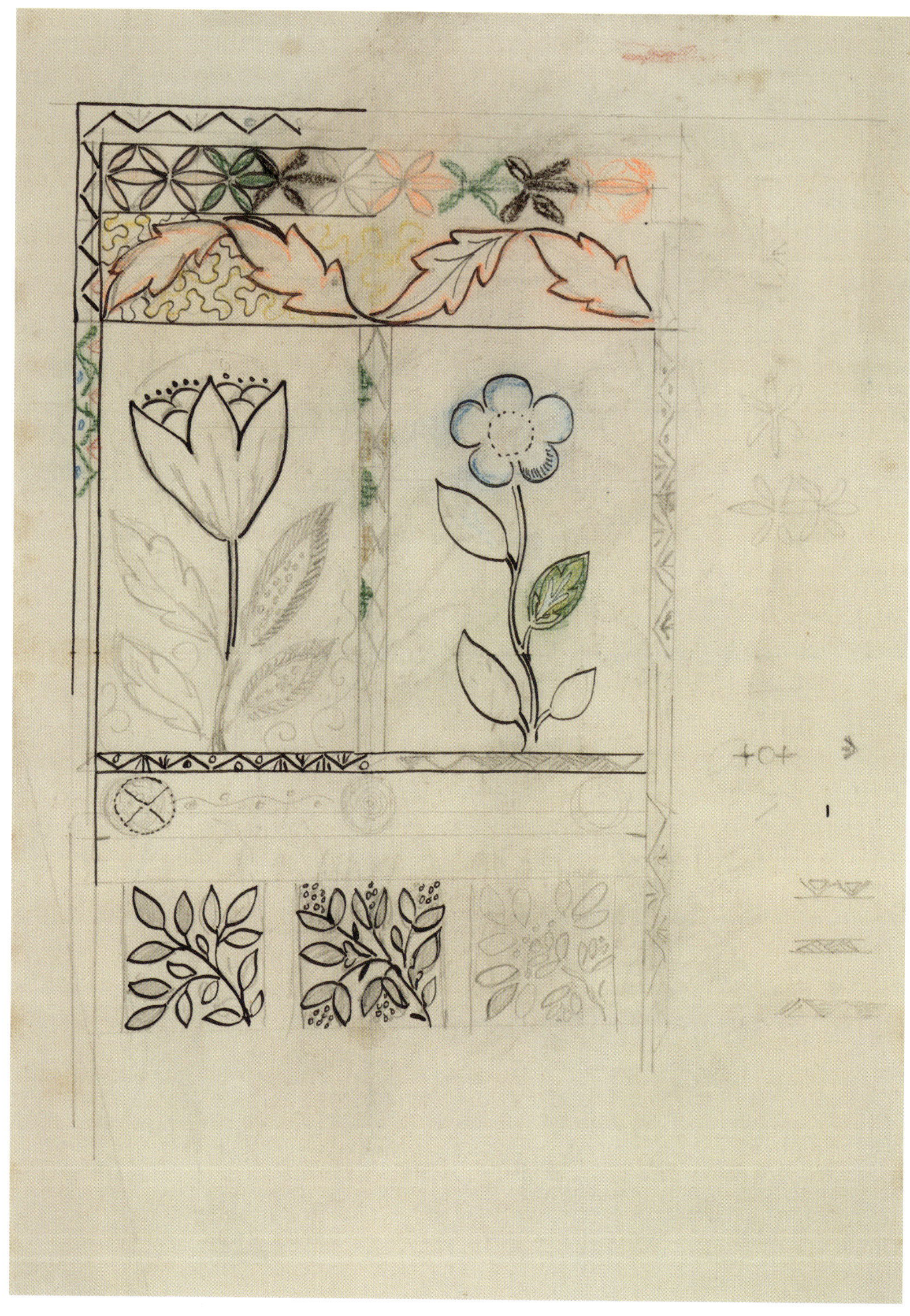

Fig.45 May Morris (1862–1938), 'Sampler for chain stitch &c', late nineteenth century, drawing on cream thick laid paper in graphite, pen and black ink, and polychrome chalks or pastels, 22.8 × 14.8 cm. Ashmolean Museum (WA1941.108.326.1)

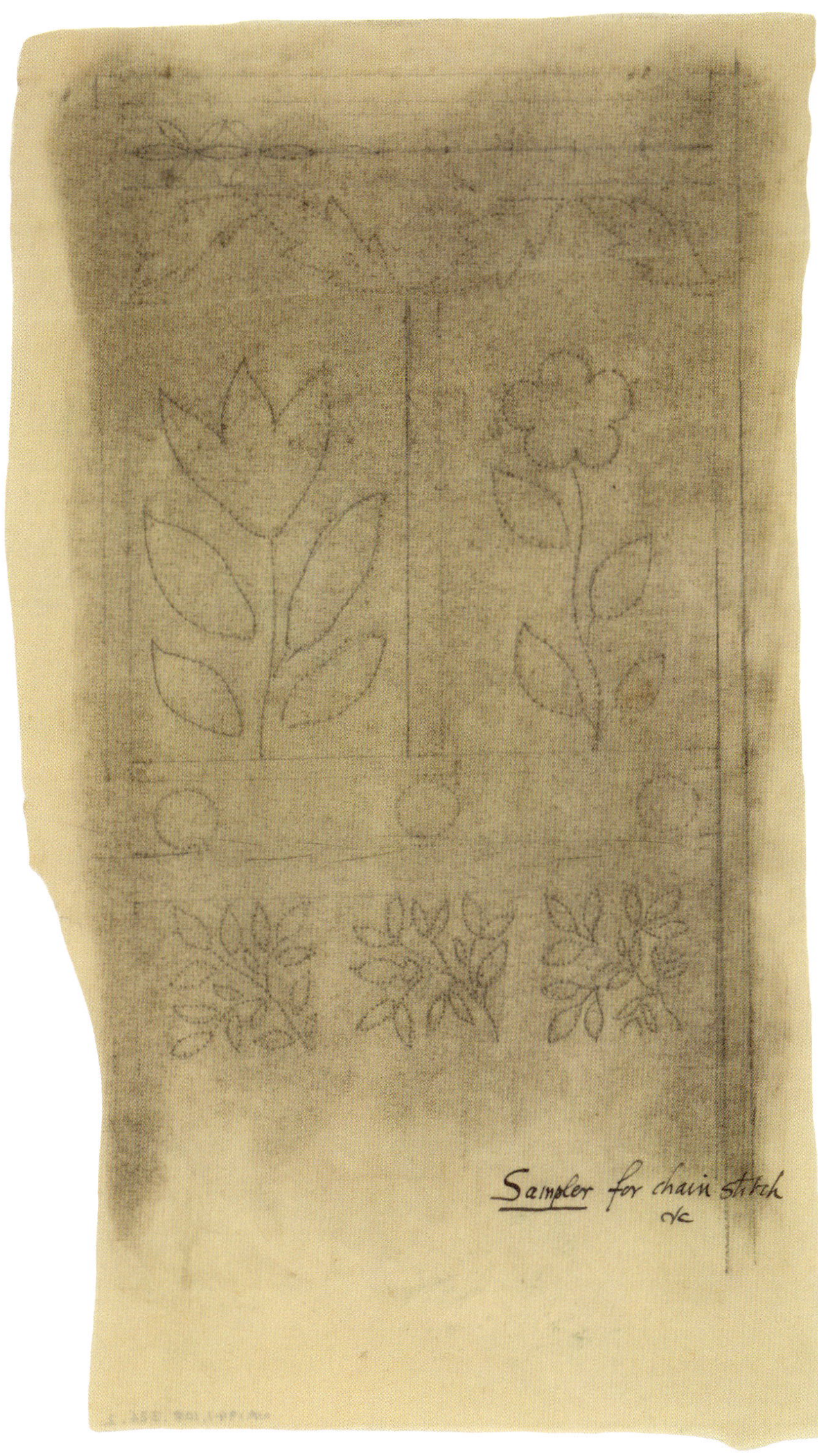

Fig.46 May Morris (1862–1938), 'Sampler for chain stitch &c', late nineteenth century, drawing on tracing paper in pen and black ink, pricked and pounced with charcoal, 23 × 14.9 cm. Ashmolean Museum (WA1941.108.326.2)

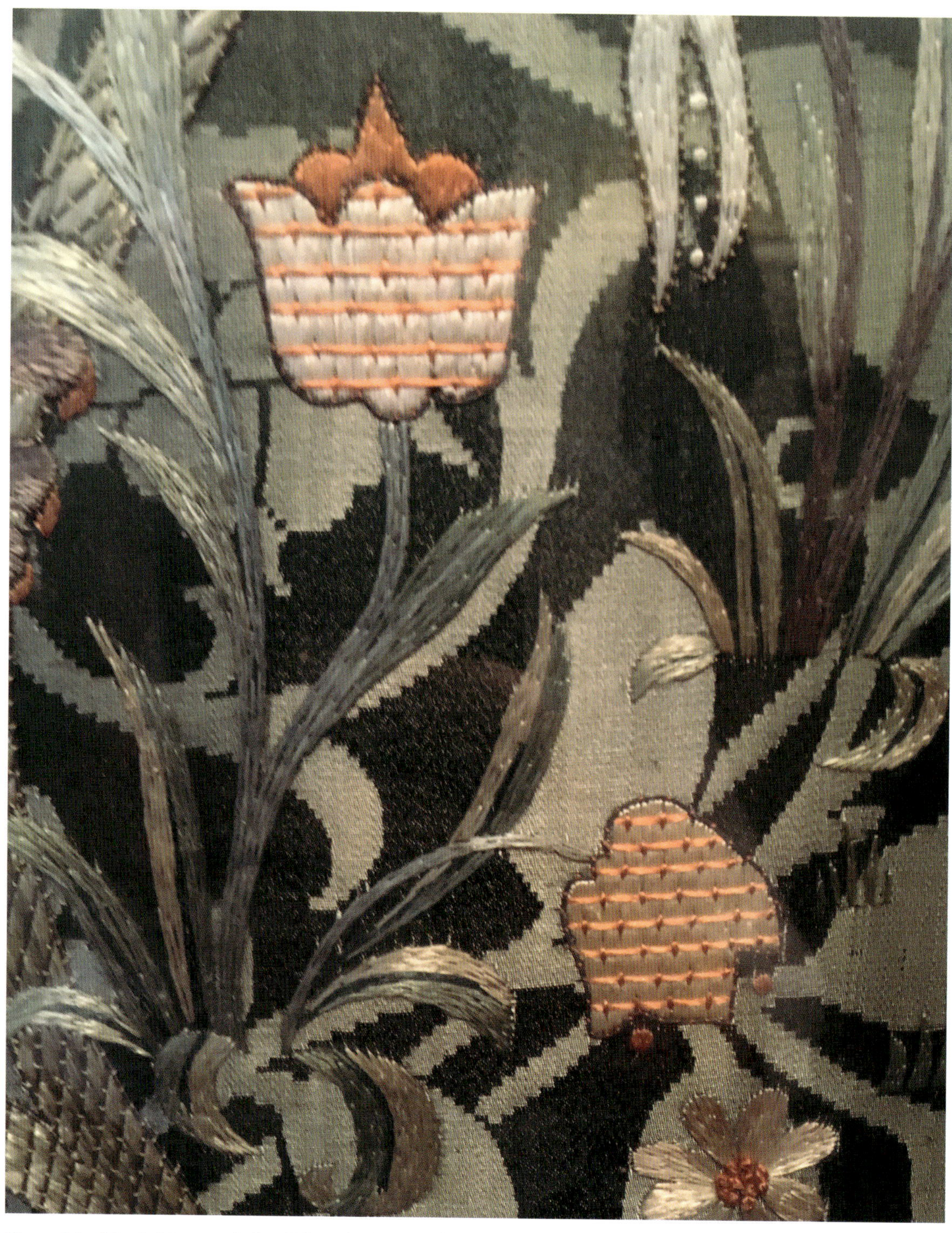

Fig.47 May Morris (1862–1938), Detail from the *Spring and Summer* panel, *c.*1894, polychrome silks on Morris & Co. *Oak* silk damask, 130.8 × 71.8 cm. Private collection.

Couching

May considered couching in silk and metal threads to be 'a particularly fascinating kind of embroidery, as it allows of much play of colour and invention and variety of stitching'.[151] Readers of *Decorative Needlework* were referred to old and modern Eastern embroidery and to Italian hangings of the seventeenth century in which the design was filled with satin stitch decorated with a diaper pattern of Bayeux stitch. May used this technique to execute the fritillaries in the *Spring and Summer* panel (**fig.47**). On the book bag that she designed for her father's medieval psalter, the pomegranate fruit is covered in a layer of brick-red floss silk couched with Japanese gold (**fig.32**).

Canvas Work

That May should have disliked modern canvas work should come as no surprise, given the negativity expressed towards Berlin wool work by the exponents of art embroidery. Unlike many of the other publications listed in **Table 2**, there are no instructions for tent or cross stitch in *Decorative Needlework*. However, May's bequest to the V&A included the *Vine* cushion cover or fire screen panel (1885–90), worked in cross, tent and condensed Scotch stitch (T.69–1939), reminiscent of the 'gay and amusing examples of *petit-point*' that she admired in bags and book covers dating from the seventeenth century.[152]

The historian and archivist Elfrida Manning (1901–1987), who visited May at Kelmscott in March 1925, reported in her diary: '*Petit point* she despises, but she works at it because of the great demand, making chair seats and table mats and designing them as she goes along.'[153] Canvas work was fashionable once again in the 1910s and 1920s. Stitched in thick wools on an open-weave canvas, it was less arduous and time-consuming than other types of embroidery. This may explain why May designed and stitched petit point table mats to raise funds for the building of the Morris Memorial Hall at Kelmscott. She displayed a set at the Arts and Crafts Exhibition in 1926 alongside a replica petit point chair seat.[154] May also produced small bags in cross and tent stitch as gifts for friends and for her own use, such as the one with the initial 'M' in **fig.48**.[155] In December 1931, she worked a bag in cross stitch for her former neighbour Dorothy Walker (1878–1963) to a design inspired by her father's poem 'Two red roses across the moon'.[156] She also taught cross stitch to her Australian cousin Una Fielding (1888–1969). '[I]t was great fun making patterns and springing them on one another,' recounted Fielding. 'She was always very kind to my efforts and helped me to realise the design I had in mind and never demolished my attempt to replace it by a better one of her own.'[157]

*

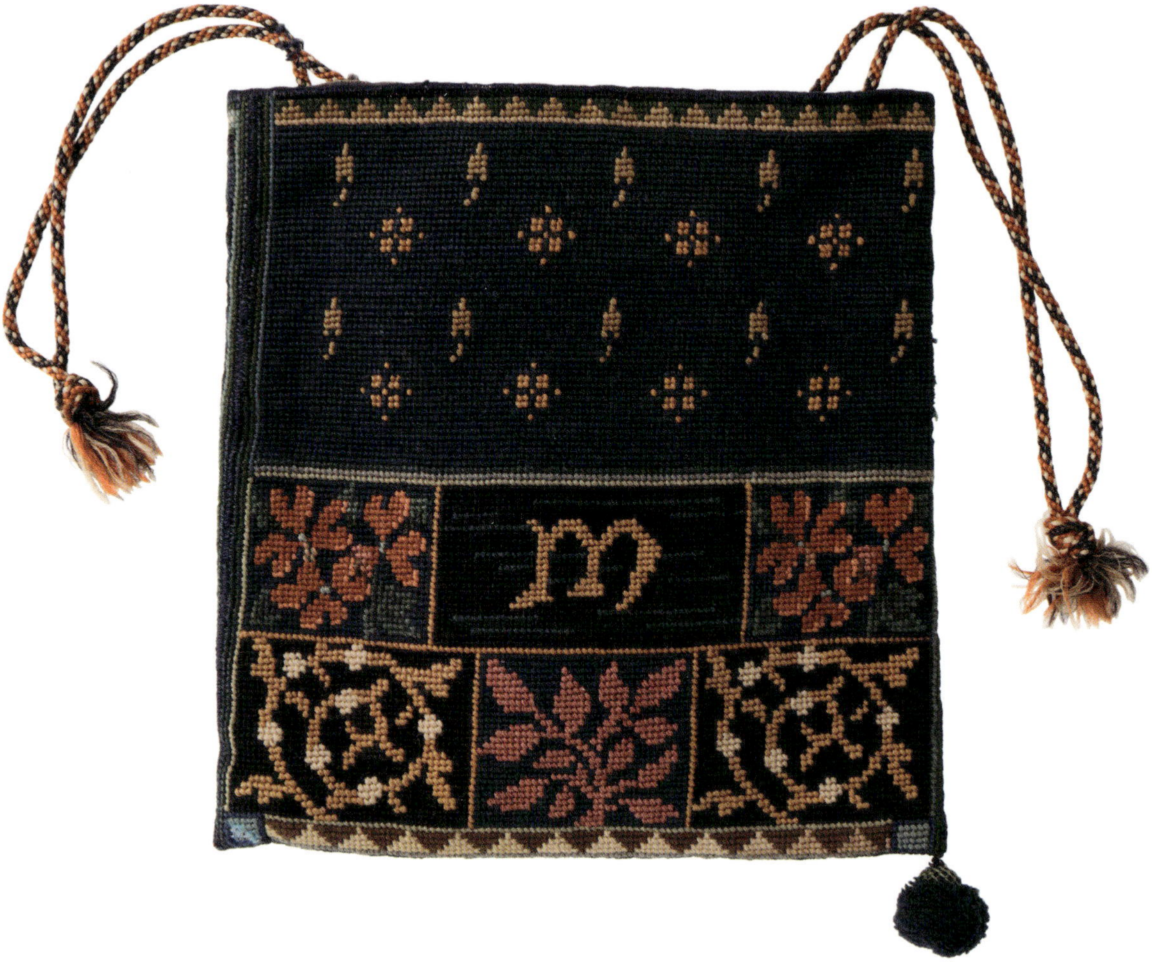

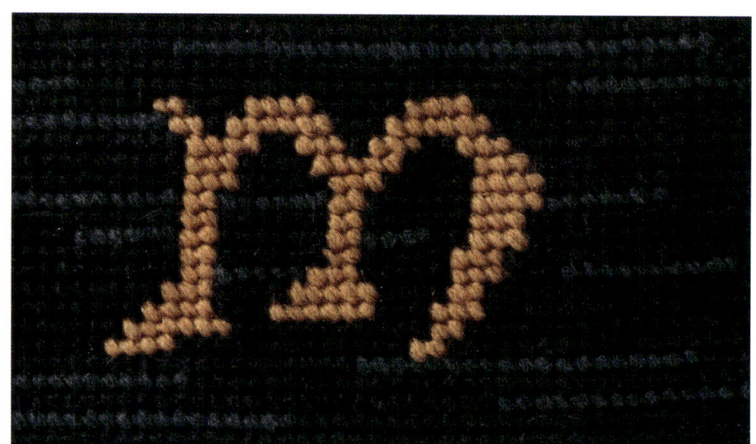

Fig.48 (with detail) May Morris (1862–1938), Embroidered bag, *c.*1932, wool on canvas, 25.7 × 25.4 cm, William Morris Gallery, F33.

The essential elements of art embroidery were to remain the touchstone for May's work throughout her life. Her views on the subject are summed up in the introduction to the catalogue of British Arts and Crafts displayed at the 1913 Ghent International Exhibition:

> A catalogue of stitches is dull reading even to an eager learner; and it is right that it should be dull, for in such work stitches matter wonderfully little, and sentiment matters so much. "Invention" does not lie in a profusion and ingenuity of stitching, but in the "finding" of a certain rhythm of line and mass, the certain loveliness of colour, the certain harmony of texture. As every painter will command his brush and place his touches rightly, so every skilled needlewoman will control her needle and place her stitches deftly, but she will not, in any serious work, make a forced exhibition of elaborate technique.[158]

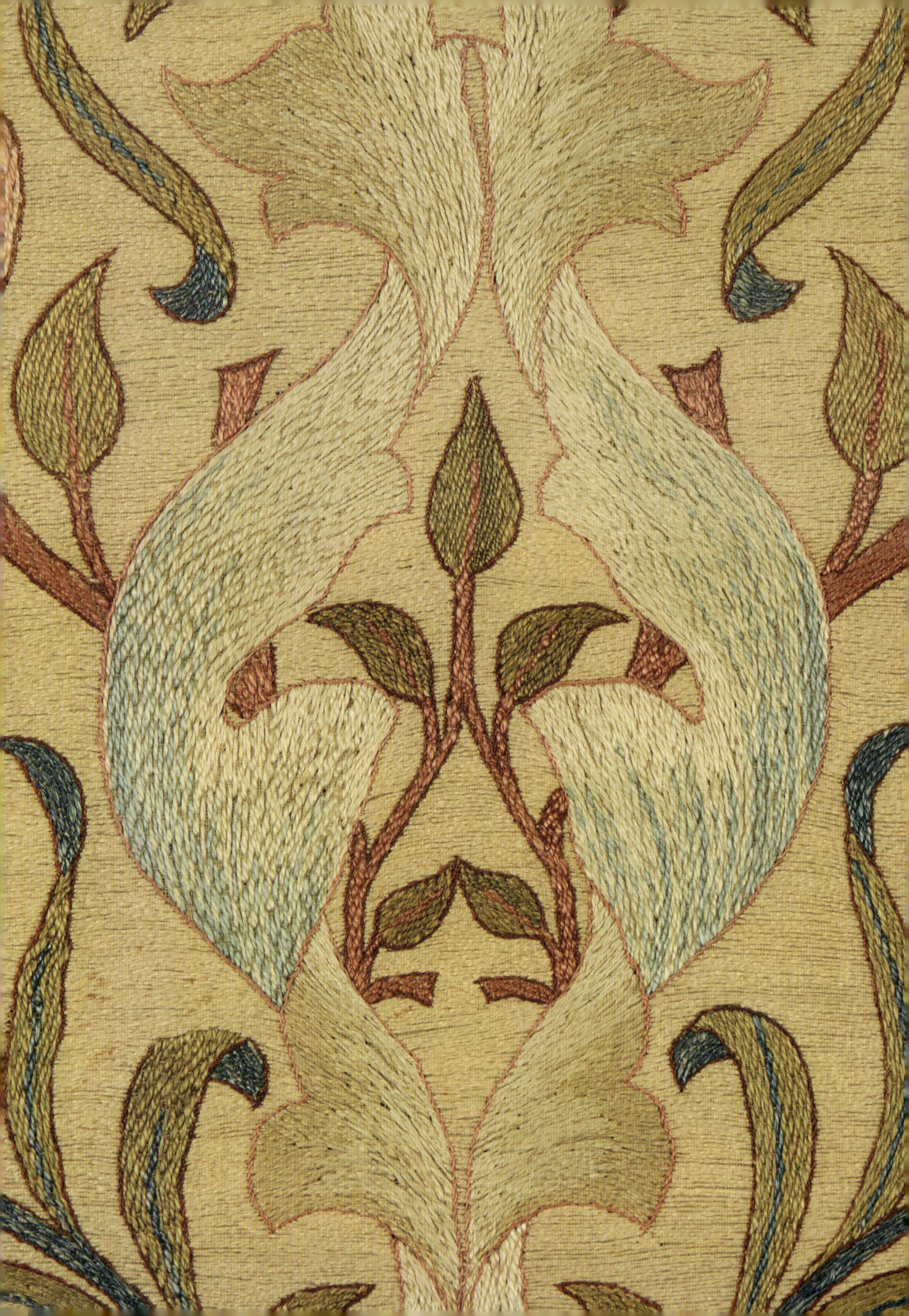

3 From Sketch to Finished Pattern

May Morris's extant needlework designs, which number several hundred, are divided between five repositories located in London and south-east England. The lion's share can be found in the Archive of Art and Design at the V&A and in the Western Art Print Room at the Ashmolean Museum, Oxford. The remainder are kept by The William Morris Society at Kelmscott House in Hammersmith, the William Morris Gallery in Walthamstow, and Kelmscott Manor in Oxfordshire.

The designs at the Ashmolean once formed part of the estate of Mary Lobb and were discovered at Kelmscott Manor several months after her death in March 1939. Purchased by the Museum in January 1941 for the sum of £12, the collection comprises more than 300 working designs together with botanical and landscape sketches and watercolours, and part of May's photographic archive of historic needlework.[1] The designs date from her years spent managing the embroidery department at Morris & Co. through to the First World War and beyond. Most of them are for domestic furnishings and include wall hangings, portières, screen panels, cushions, photograph frames, table covers and tea cosies. There are also designs for book covers, pin cushions, monograms, dress panels, workbags and sachets, as well as ecclesiastical embroidery. The V&A Archive of Art and Design and The William Morris Society possess duplicates of a few of the patterns.

Twenty-five of May's working designs have been selected for this volume and are discussed below. The designs themselves are set out in the second half of this book, with captions giving accession number, design dimensions (height × width in cm), and object type (drawing, tracing or pricking). Each two-page spread contains a photograph of May's original design together with an embroidery pattern for readers to transfer. To assist with scaling up or down, digitised versions of the latter can be accessed at www.ashmolean.org/may-morris-lynn-hulse-book-patterns. Technical samples are included at the end of the volume to demonstrate May's approach to stitch.

PREPARING THE DESIGNS

The featured designs reflect each stage of May's working process, from roughly sketched ideas based on studies taken directly from nature through to finished outline patterns. They are executed in pencil, pen and black or brown ink, black ink wash or charcoal, occasionally enhanced with coloured pastels or watercolours, on a variety of drawing surfaces. Pieces of thick laid or lightweight drawing paper, tracing paper, and even the odd sheet of cheap ruled writing paper were pressed into service.

Opposite: detail of fig.55

The next step was transferring the design to the cloth ready for stitching. In her manual *Art Needlework*, Masé recommended drawing directly on the material as this resulted in the work having a 'greater freedom of effect'.[2] Generally though, art embroiderers, regardless of their skill in draughtsmanship, used the technique of tracing and transferring, for which several methods existed in the late nineteenth century. One option was to pin tarlatan, a starched, loosely woven muslin, to the design and trace the outline with a pencil or brush. The tarlatan was then laid on the chosen material and the traced lines drawn over with a pen or brush dipped in Indian ink or Chinese white paint. In the 1870s, the London embroidery manufacturer Benjamin Francis (fl. 1870s) invented a tracing cloth in blue or white as a substitute for carbonised tracing paper. The tracing cloth was placed between the material and the paper pattern, and the design transferred using a hard pencil supplied for the purpose.[3] Around the same time, William Briggs & Co. developed the hot-iron transfer method. The design was printed on paper using a bituminous substance that adhered to the cloth when heat was applied to the back of the transfer.[4] Briggs transfer papers were widely available from embroidery outlets and through mail-order advertisements placed in the press. The needlework department at Liberty & Co. also produced its own transfer papers for domestic furnishings and garments and supplied printed catalogues of the latest patterns. **Fig.49** contains designs for a table cover and a sideboard cloth produced by Liberty in the early 1900s.

Church workrooms and embroidery societies generally used the traditional prick and pounce method in preference to the other systems outlined above, despite the fact it was more laborious. The RSAN experimented with all the methods that had been devised, including stamping with wood blocks and using hot-iron transfer papers, but concluded that designs 'can only be artistically and well traced on material by hand painting'.[5] Several of the volumes listed in **Table 2** offer guidance on the prick and pounce method, as did women's magazines like *The Queen*, which regularly published advice columns for amateur needlewomen.[6]

May utilised the prick and pounce method throughout her professional career. Kit designs were drawn onto glazed cotton which operated as a template for making multiple tracings. The traced outlines were then pricked at 1–2 mm intervals, probably using a fine darning needle topped with sealing wax, as suggested in *The Queen*.[7] **Fig.92** contains instructions in May's hand directing the worker to 'Tack lines round', 'Prick this side', and 'prick both roses like this'.[8] Drawings with their accompanying pricked tracings exist for some of the designs, as in **fig.68** and **fig.79**, revealing how sketched ideas were refined, ready to embroider.

Several of the designs were pounced with powdered charcoal or blue or white pipe clay, methodically rubbed over the pricks using a flannel stump. This left an outline of fine dots on the material that were joined up using

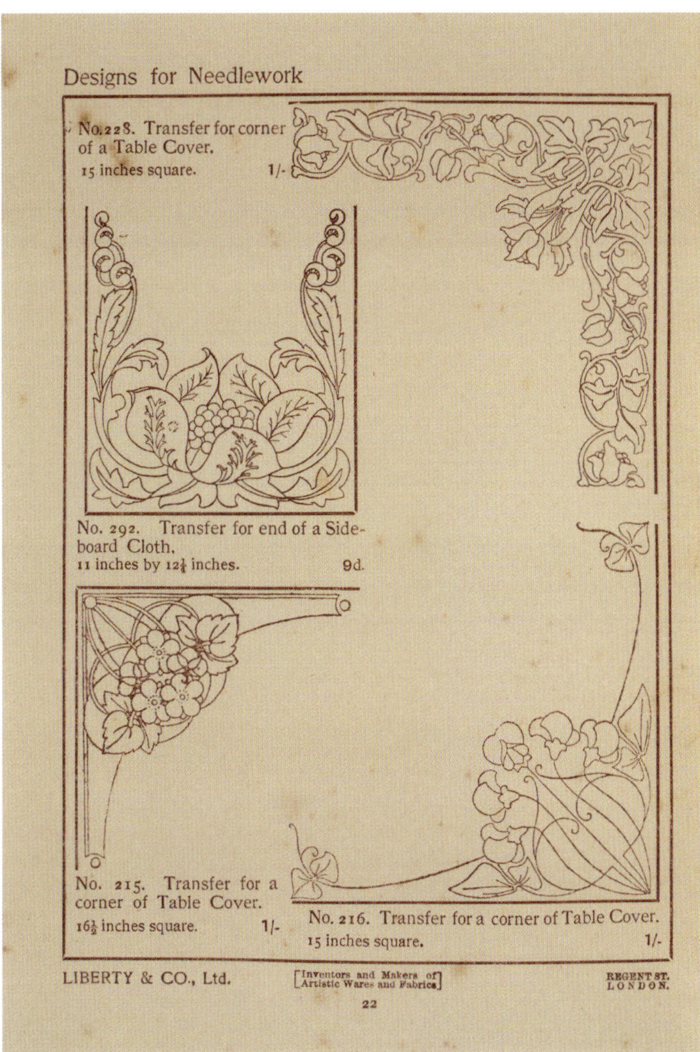

Fig.49 Liberty & Co. Embroidery catalogue, 1900s, 21 × 13.7 cm. Private collection

Indian ink. With careful handling, pricked tracings could be reused, as in the case of **fig.78**. This shows evidence of having been pounced with white pipe clay and charcoal, indicating that the design had been transferred first onto a dark cloth, then onto a lighter one. From time to time, May dispensed with the tracing stage of the process by pricking the drawings made on thick laid paper or ruled writing paper, and pouncing them straight onto the cloth.

When using designs with quartered pattern repeats (a typical feature of May's table covers), Masé advised folding the tracing paper in four with the drawn pattern on the upper side only, and pricking the holes through several layers at once to save time and ensure greater accuracy.[9] May preferred to add crosses to each corner of the quartered design, visible in **fig.86**, to assist with lining up the pricked tracing when turning the pattern repeat through 90 degrees in the process of transferring it to the cloth. On some of the designs there are random pinholes in each corner or centre top and bottom, indicating that pins were used to anchor the design securely to a tabletop when making a tracing or transferring the pricked outline to the material, as in **fig.81**.

THE DESIGNS

The designs that follow are representative of the work produced by May during her tenure as manageress of the embroidery department at Morris & Co. and in the decades that followed. Some of the patterns would have been stitched in the house style, others worked in a variety of stitches commonly found in decorative needlework, described in the firm's *Embroidery Work* catalogue (*c*.1912) as 'fancy stitch'.[10] The Embroidery Day Book provides contextual information for several of the patterns.[11]

Book Covers

The art of embroidered bindings, once fashionable in sixteenth- and seventeenth-century Britain, witnessed a resurgence in the late Victorian period.[12] Magazines and histories of bookbinding were soon encouraging needlewomen with 'a taste for the older kinds of embroidery' to turn their hand to book decoration. 'There are few more pleasing accupations [*sic*] for the skilful fingers of a lady,' noted one commentator, 'than that of embroidering a book-cover.'[13]

May designed at least fifteen embroidered bindings and loose covers, mainly as private commissions or gifts for family and friends. In 1890, for example, she worked a book cover in green silk decorated with scrolling vines leaves and grapes for a copy of the *Rubaiyat of Omar Khayyam*, 'a labour of love in itself, which I intend for my Mother's birthday';[14] the design is now in the Ashmolean collection (WA1941.108.27). May is known to have studied historic bindings in the British Museum and replicated some of the materials in her own work, stitching in silk and metal threads with seed pearls on a plain silk or silk damask ground.[15]

Three designs for book covers are included here. The coloured drawing in **fig.69**, of a pomegranate tree set within a ring of five flowerheads, was probably designed for a loose cover. The pattern bears some resemblance to the stylised pomegranate tree on the book bag for William Morris's medieval psalter (**fig.32**). The chequered grid on the lower half of the design is partially filled with heart-shaped motifs in a brick pattern arrangement. The monogram on the back matches that found in Dante Gabriel Rossetti's art works.[16] If May intended the book cover to be a gift for the artist (d.1882), the Ashmolean drawing would be one of her earliest recorded works. If not, it may have been designed some time later for her mother's copy of Rossetti's *Ballads and Sonnets* (1881).[17] The painted areas give some indication of how May envisaged working the design, in all probability using floss silk and Japanese gold. The banding on the pomegranate fruit may have been stitched in laid work in two shades of pink floss, anchored with a row of fly stitches (indicated in the painted decoration), and the blossom end stitched in long & short in mid grey-green floss. The drawing suggests that the trunk and the seeded area were both executed in laid and couched work, the diamond-shaped patterning of the latter filled with French knots and fly stitches. The leaves were probably worked in long & short, one side pale grey-green and the other mid grey-green, echoing the colour scheme in the trunk. The hatched line suggests that the whole of the pomegranate motif was edged in couched Japanese gold, just like the book bag referred to above.

Fig.70 is a finely executed drawing in pencil for a book binding, the title of which remains unknown. On the left-hand side of the leaf is a faintly written note in May's hand that reads 'Back of book'. There is also a rough sketch mirroring the fish scale border on the front. This patterning appears in the cartouche on May's earliest recorded book cover, designed in 1888 for a vellum copy of William Morris's 1873 masque *Love is Enough* (**fig.50**).[18] A variant

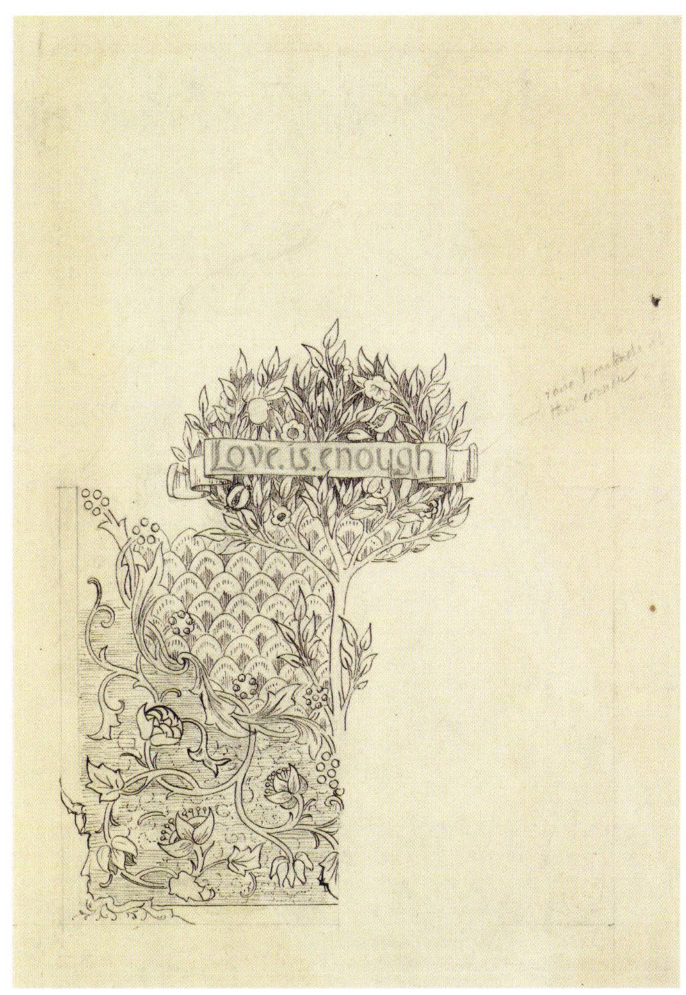

Fig.50 May Morris (1862–1938), design for the front of the book cover for *Love is Enough*, 1888, pen and black ink with graphite on off-white paper, 17.6 × 25.4 cm (sheet). Ashmolean Museum (WA1941.108.349)

on this fish scale motif also appears on the background of William Morris's book bag. The main body of the design comprises three registers set within a narrow chevron frame. The upper and lower registers are decorated with a fritillary motif. The acanthus leaves enclosing a central sunflower match May's pattern on a slipcover made for a copy of the 1919 edition of William Morris's *News from Nowhere*, once owned by George and Ada Culmer, who cared for her ailing sister.[19]

The rectangular frame in **fig.92** suggests this design may also have been intended for a loose cover or a book binding. The ogee-shaped motif, with tulips and roses and decorative curlicues, is typical of May's designs inspired by Islamic decoration, examples of which include a pair of portières specially designed for Mrs Munro Longyear.[20]

Scrapbook Covers

May also designed loose scrapbook or blotter covers in a variety of sizes that were sold commercially through Morris & Co. as part of its range of 'started' kits, of which *Rose and yew* (**fig.51**) is an example.[21] These were partly worked

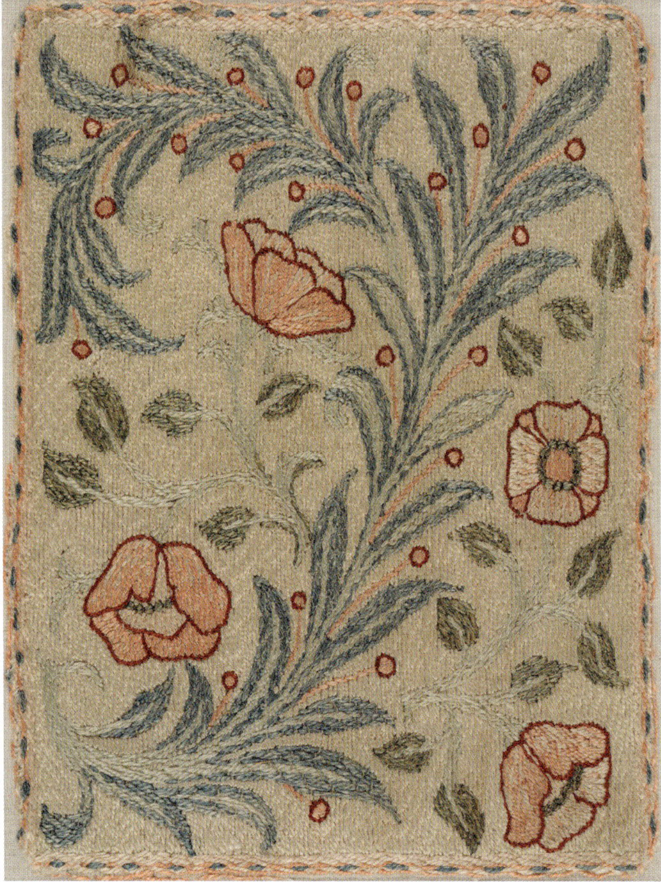

Fig.51 May Morris (1862–1938), *Rose and yew* scrapbook cover, 1890s, polychrome silks on Manchester cloth, 28.5 × 22 cm. Private collection

Fig.52 May Morris (1862–1938), *Tulip and acanthus* scrapbook cover, 1890s, polychrome silks on Manchester cloth, 30.8 × 19.5 cm. Private collection

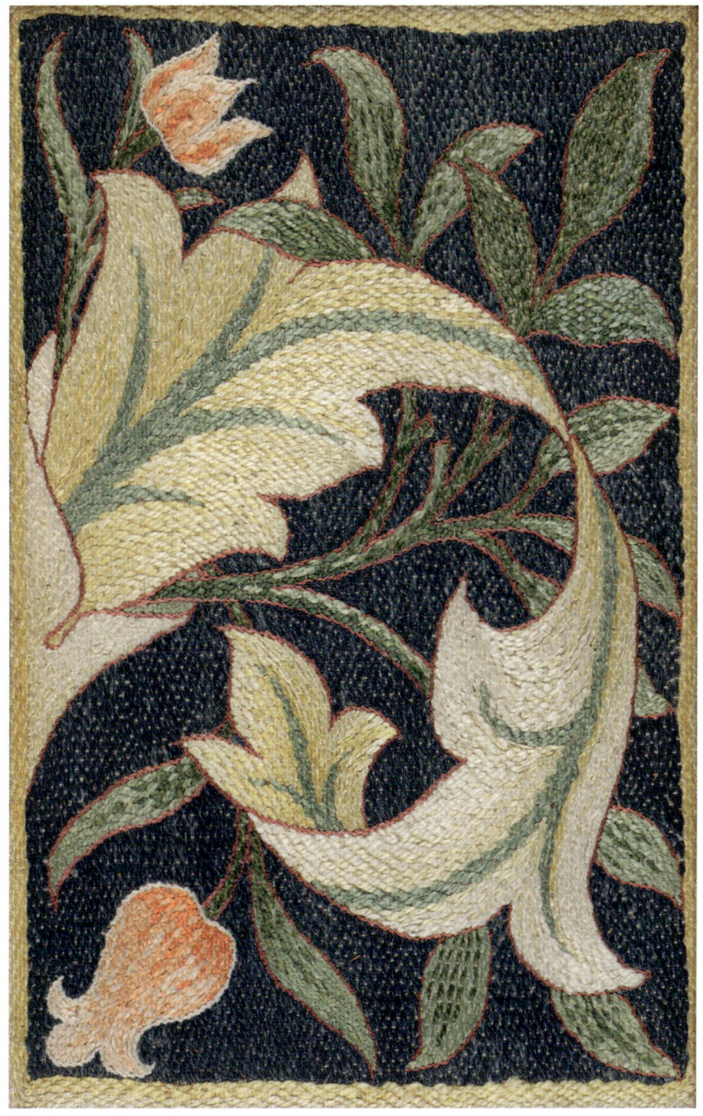

as a guide to the colouring and stitches to be used, and were supplied with sufficient threads for the customer to complete the design. Five orders made for stock, priced at 10s each and darned in silk thick twist on Manchester cotton, are listed in the Embroidery Day Book, along with an order for a *Carnation* blotter cover that was started in fine twist silk on a silk ground for the sum of 7s 6d.[22]

At least two of May's working designs in the Ashmolean collection can be identified as scrapbook or blotter covers and are included here. The *Tulip and acanthus* leaf pattern in **fig.88** may correspond with the *Tulip* kits made for the Oxford Street shop in November 1895. An embroidered version of the design is illustrated in **fig.52.**[23] The second scrapbook cover, **fig.82**, contains a berried sprig that resembles the one illustrated in **fig.51**, but in place of the trailing rose, May introduces a single stem of tulip, rose and harebell. All three designs feature the device of a dominant leafy scroll that follows the instruction described in *Decorative Needlework* on how to draw a curve: 'A beautiful curve has *variety* in every inch of it: that is to say, it changes its direction constantly.'[24]

Frieze

Fig.91 relates to one of the larger commissions undertaken by May during the period spent running the embroidery department. The tracing is inscribed 'Hudson frieze (middle)' and was designed in December 1893 for Gerda Hudson (1857–1932), wife of Robert William Hudson (1856–1937), who managed his father's soap-flake manufacturing business in Liverpool. The Hudsons were clients of Morris & Co. and friends of the family. In 1891, they built Bidston Court, a mock Tudor mansion house in Bidston Hill, Birkenhead, designed by the English architect Edward Ould (1852–1909). A letter addressed to May on 14 February 1893 provides a few details about the furnishings for the new house. It was Mrs Hudson's intention to decorate the drawing room with blue linen embroidery 'like that which Mrs Morris had worked for her'.[25] Over a period of twelve months she placed six orders with the firm for two flowerpot screen panels, one traced on linen and the other with a flower, leaf and rose pattern (5s and £1 16s respectively); one *Chippendale* screen panel, 'specially designed' by May, to be stitched in floss on silk by Mrs Hudson's companion Helena Wolfe (£3); a Persian design traced on linen (4s); a panel with small carnations in fine twist silk on blue linen, measuring 18 inches or 45.7 cm square (£2); and a tulip and rose cushion in fine silk twist on linen (15s).[26] On 21 December, she placed a seventh order, this time for a frieze measuring 4 feet 2¼ inches × 12 feet 7½ inches (127.6 × 384.8 cm). The design was worked by the embroidery department at Morris & Co. in fine twist silk on Mrs Hudson's own blue linen for the princely sum of £70.[27]

The pricked tracing in **fig.53** comprises one full pattern repeat of the central section of the frieze, decorated with ogee-shaped medallions filled with a single rose or an Ottoman-style tulip, perhaps mirroring the tulip and rose cushion which Mrs Hudson had purchased three months earlier. The medallions are interspersed with small circles containing a tulip motif; the background is powdered with small flowers. The design exemplifies 'the contrast of proportion' described by May in her article 'Design in Embroidery':

> If the leading forms, for instance, consist of large leaves and spreading flowers, the effect will be greatly enriched by the introduction of minuter [*sic*] work, a small leafage, clustering flowers, and so forth. It is customary sometimes to carry out this idea in such a way that the smaller parts of the design form a sort of under-pattern or

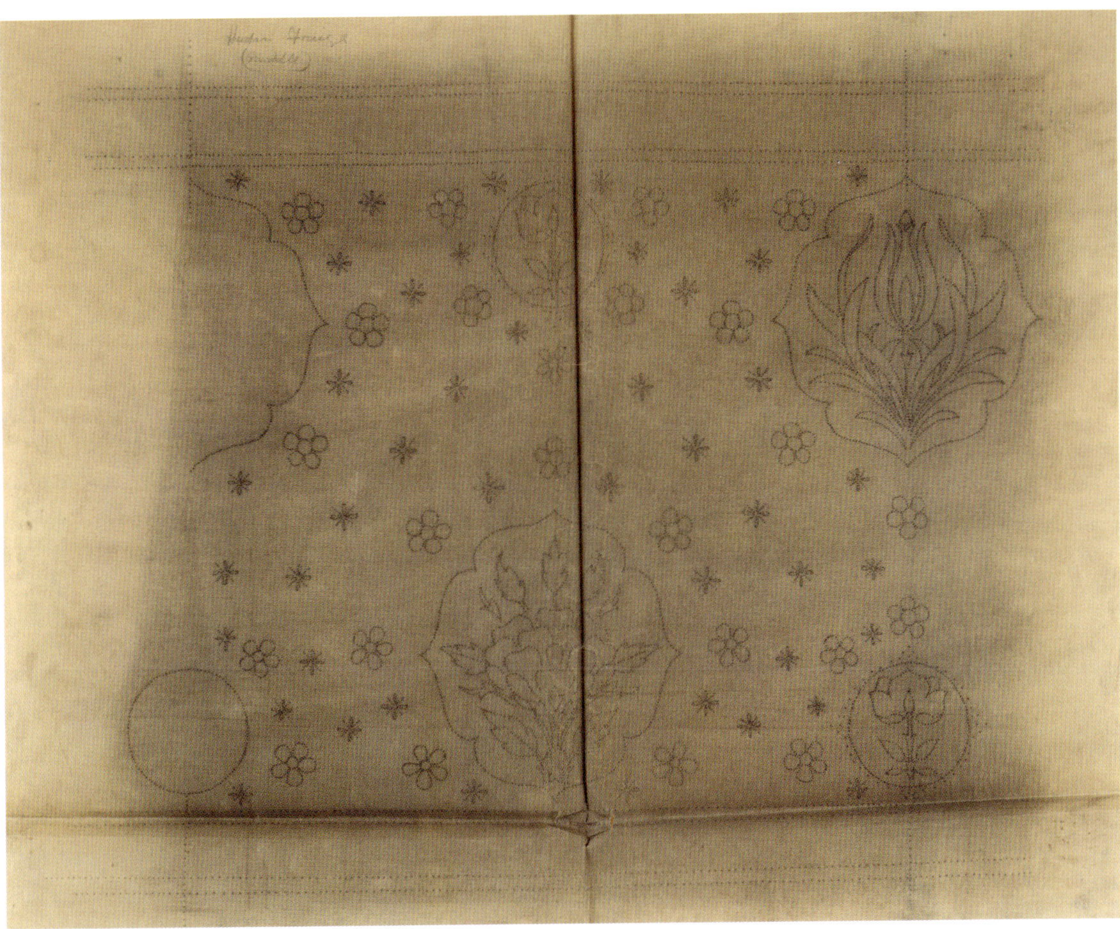

Fig.53 May Morris (1862–1938), Hudson frieze (middle), 1893, drawing on tracing paper in graphite, pricked and pounced with charcoal, 51.2 × 63 cm. Ashmolean Museum (WA1941.108.461)

> "mossing" on which the design itself is laid. This method has to be used cautiously, however, and should be so drawn and executed that the under-pattern is a mere mossing and background ornament very simply treated, and that it in no way professes to be as important in detail and finish as the design laid on it…[28]

One of the Ottoman-style tulip medallions is included in **fig.91**.

Cushion Covers, Fire Screens and Framed Panels

Cushion covers, fire screens and framed panels, worked in darning stitch in silk twist on Manchester cloth or twill silk, often to the same design, were sold by Morris & Co. as finished embroideries or in kit form, like *Tulip and pomegranate* (**fig.54**).[29] Once complete, customers could return panels to the firm to be stretched and mounted behind glass in a walnut or mahogany cheval screen that stood in front of an unused fireplace to decorate a room.

Several of the designs acquired by the Ashmolean were destined to become cushion covers, fire screens or framed panels. The four examples included

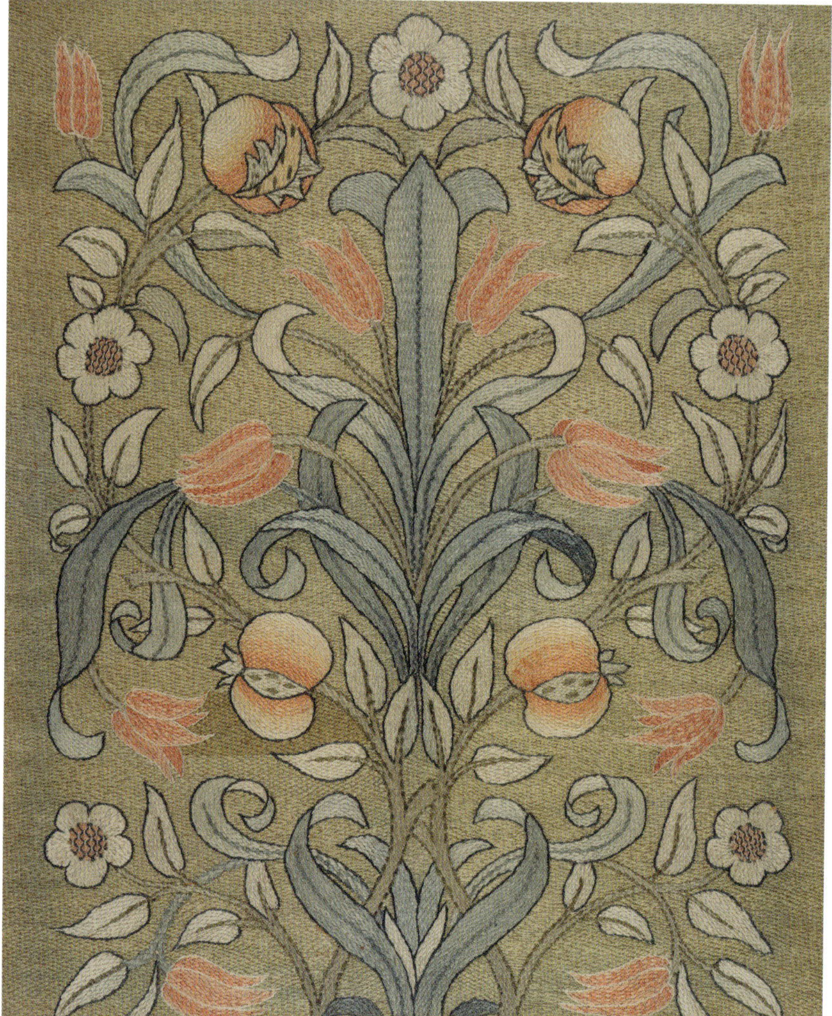

Fig.54 May Morris (1862–1938), *Tulip and pomegranate* fire screen panel or cushion cover, 1890s, polychrome silks on Manchester cloth, 58.6 × 49 cm. Private collection

here share the same format – they are all symmetrical along the vertical axis – and feature a variety of cottage garden plants and flowers such as tulip, lily, marigold, acanthus and pomegranate. **Figs. 87, 89** and **90** are similar in size, with the largest, **fig.93**, possibly being designed for a rectangular cheval screen. May created two versions of *Tulip and artichoke*, both of which are in the Ashmolean collection (**fig.89** and WA1941.108.456). Drawings of these patterns were donated to The William Morris Society in 1972, one in monochrome and the other in watercolour, inscribed 'adapted from Bell screen'.[30] The screen in question may have been designed for the Yorkshire industrialist Sir Isaac Lowthian Bell (1816–1904) and his wife Lady Margaret (1820–1886), who were important clients of Morris & Co. A framed panel of **fig.89**, worked in darning stitch with a stem stitch outline, was acquired in 2024 by the Society (**fig.55**).[31] The V&A Archive of Art and Design (AAD/1990/6) holds a second copy of the *Lily, tulip and marigold* pattern in **fig.90**.[32]

Fig.55 May Morris (1862–1938), *Tulip and artichoke* fire screen panel or cushion cover, c.1885, polychrome silks on Manchester cloth, 50 × 41 cm, The William Morris Society, WMS–T183.

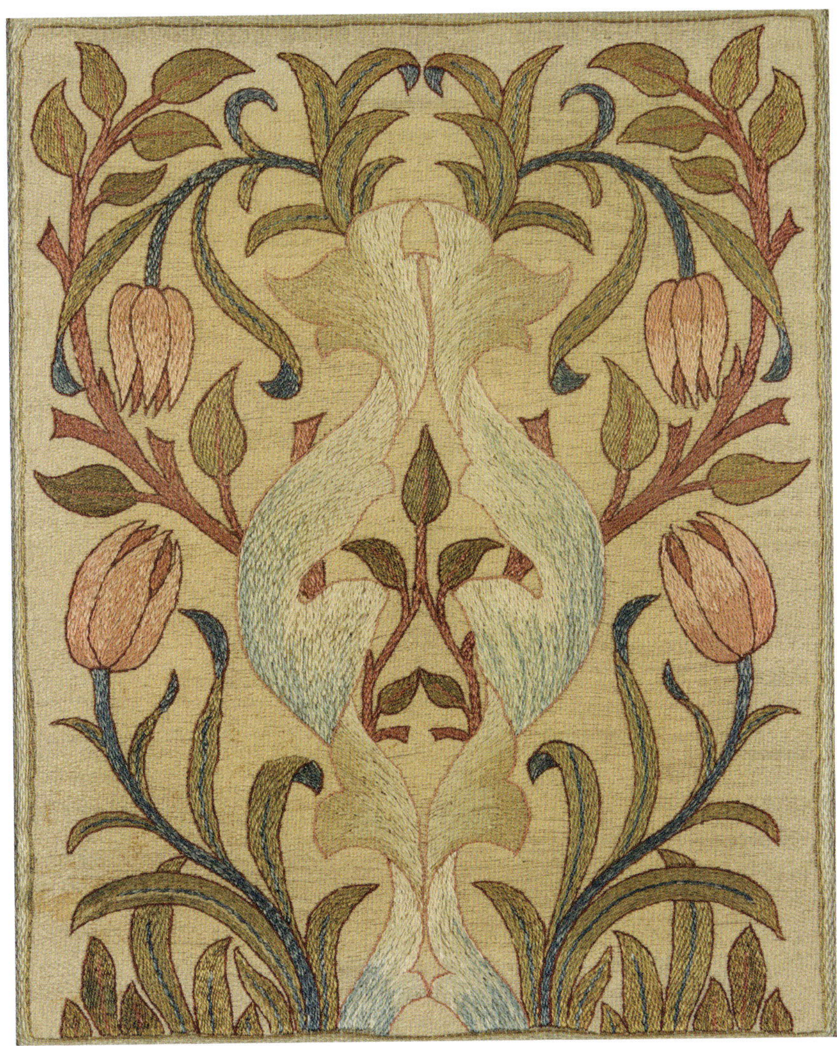

Pomegranate (**fig.78**) mirrors the composition of the other designs listed above, but with dimensions at a quarter of the size, it is unlikely to have been for a cushion cover or fire screen. It may have been designed as a picture panel, or alternatively as a sachet or mat. Over the winter of 1892/93, nine orders for mats were worked to the design *Lily*: four for stock and five for customers, priced between 5s 6d and 7s each, all on Manchester cloth.[33]

Cabinet Panels

Among the Ashmolean designs are an ink study (**fig.56**) and two pricked patterns for the *Autumn* and *Winter* roundels (**fig.77** and WA1941.108.3.1–2) from the *Seasons* panels (**fig.22**), thought to have been commissioned for a cabinet by Mrs Mawns in August 1894. The panels were stitched in floss silk on Morris & Co.'s green *Oak* silk damask at a cost of £150 and are the most expensive item listed in the Embroidery Day Book.[34] The roundels sit in the

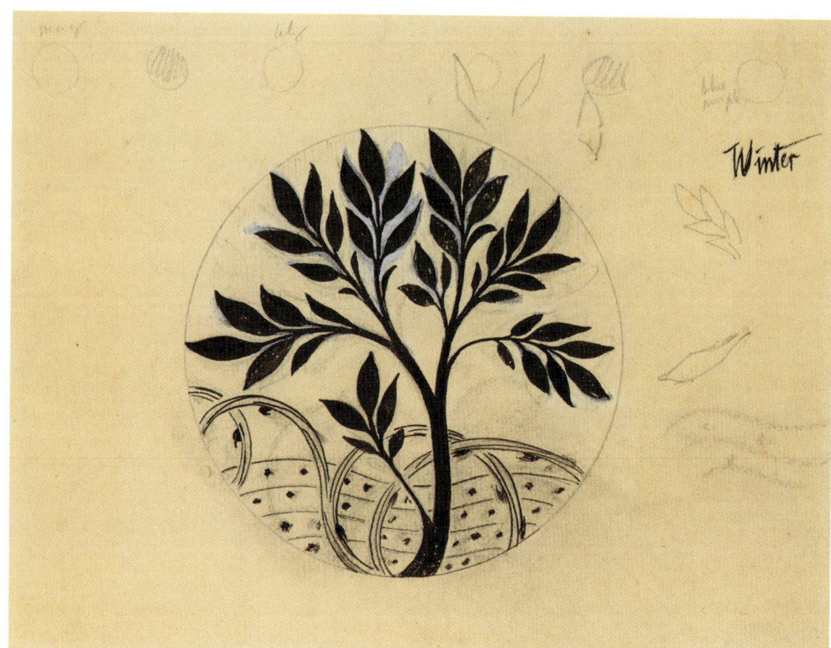

Fig.56 May Morris (1862–1938), Design for *Winter* roundel from the *Seasons* panels, *c.*1894, drawing on off-white paper in pen and black ink, with white body colour over graphite, sheet 24.6 × 32.8 cm. Ashmolean Museum (WA1941.108.3.2)

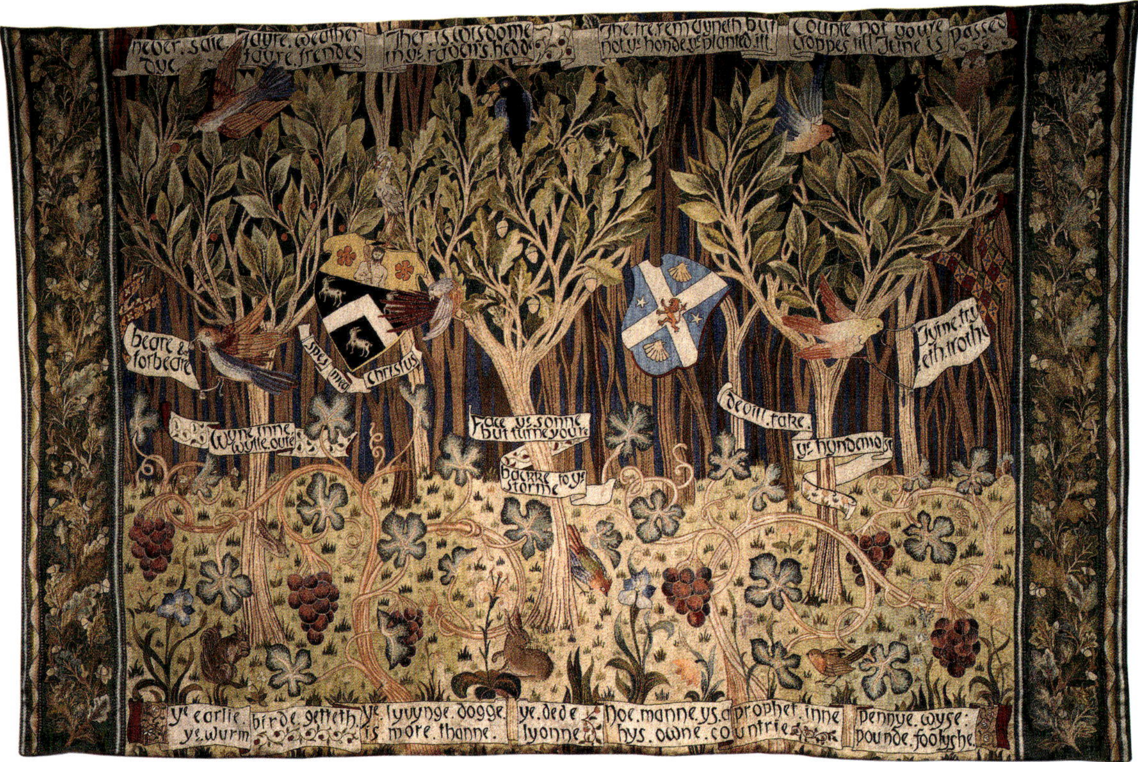

Fig.57 May Morris (1862–1938), Battye wall hanging, *c.*1890–1900, polychrome silks on canvas, 188 × 296 cm, William Morris Gallery, F101.

top register and are set within a lattice work frame decorated with highly conventionalised floral motifs. The *Autumn* roundel, which bears a striking resemblance to the grapevine in the Battye wall hanging, *c*.1890–1900 (**fig.57**), is worked in long & short, satin and stem stitch, with French knots. Both the stem and the grapes are outlined in black, which gives the roundel a stained glass feel. This technique was also used in Eastern embroidery for separating banks of colour. In addition, the grapes are foregrounded by filling up the spaces in between in black, just like the flowers, fruits and leaves in the pomegranate trees depicted on the Kelmscott bed hangings. May had seen this method used to good effect on the appliquéd trees that formed part of her father's decorative scheme for the dining room at Red House, like the pomegranate tree in **fig.26**, and replicated it in her own work.

Photograph Frame

The Morris & Co. *Embroidery Work* catalogue contains eight designs for photograph frames available in two sizes: 10¼ × 8½ in, or 26 × 21.6 cm, and 17 × 15 in, or 43 × 38 cm (**fig.58**). The frames are decorated in a variety

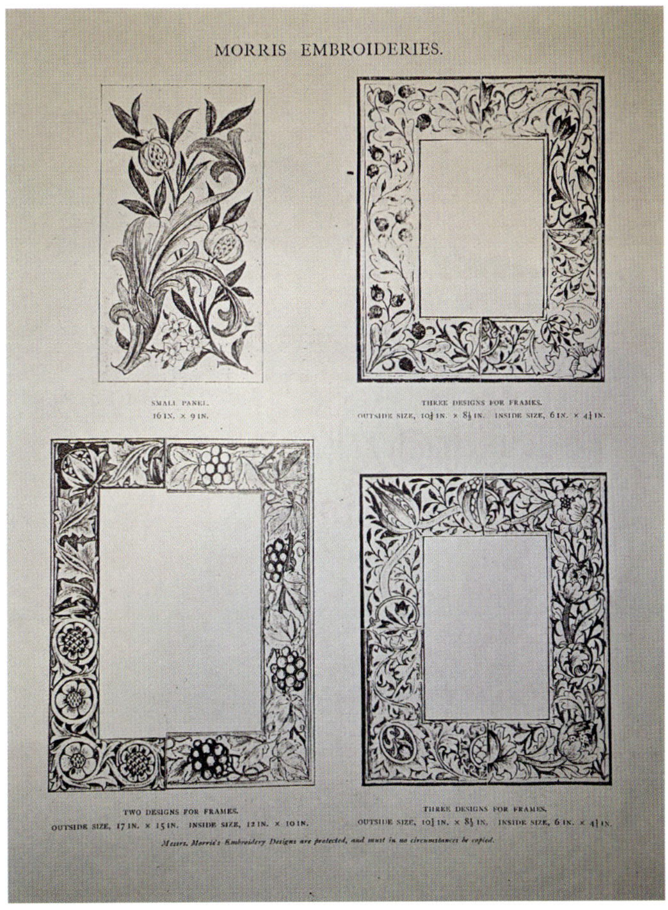

Fig.58 Morris & Co. *Embroidery Work* catalogue (London, *c*.1912), photograph frames, 27.7 × 22.7 cm.

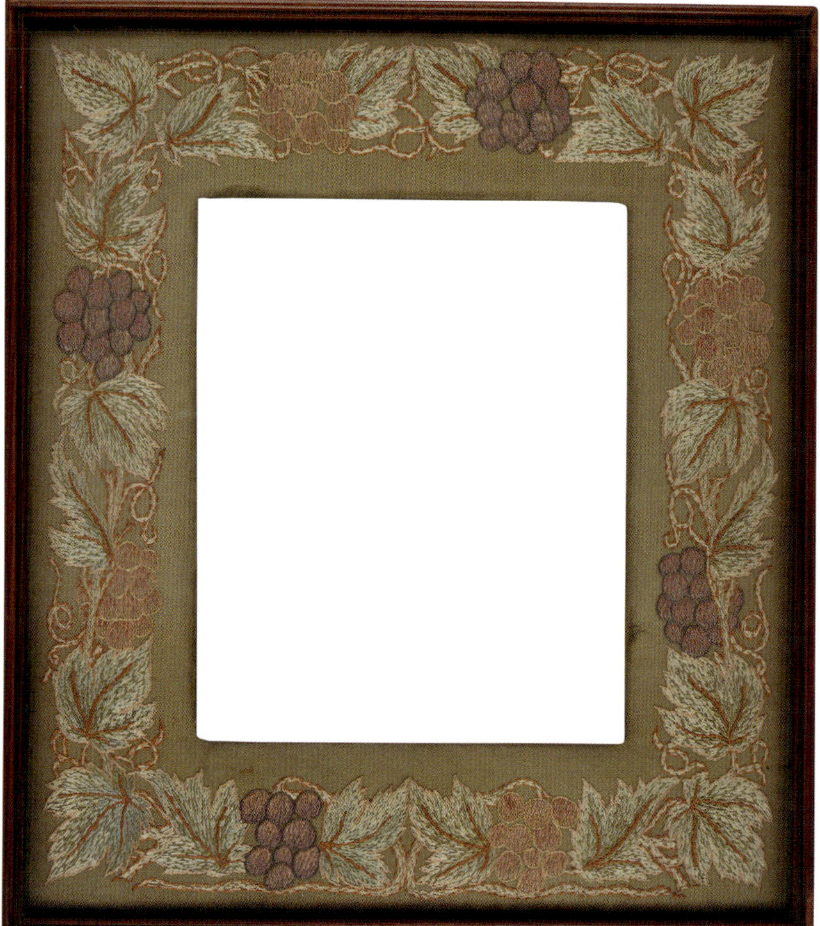

Fig.59 May Morris (1862–1938), *Grapevine* photograph frame, 1890s, stitched by Mrs Joanna Hawker, *c.*1900, polychrome silks on silk, 45 × 40 cm. Private collection

of styles, ranging from highly conventionalised floral motifs reminiscent of medieval plasterwork to ornamental borders like those found on Middle Eastern carpets. The Ashmolean collection contains a handful of designs suitable for photograph frames, including *Rose and grapevine* (**fig.85**), which closely resembles the grapevine border illustrated in the catalogue, bottom left. A worked version of the latter, made by Mrs Joanna Hawker (1866–1963), daughter of the firm's Australia-based client Mrs Joanna Barr Smith (1835–1919), is illustrated in **fig.59**.[35]

Table Cover and Runner

Fig.86 is one of several borders for a table cover in the Ashmolean collection. The design consists of a quartered pattern repeat with a scrolling grapevine entwined around stems of dianthus, lily and tulip. More than one copy of the pattern must have been pricked at the same time as there is no evidence of any outline drawing on this version. A second, pricked and pounced copy, inscribed 'Vine and pinks table cover 65', is in the V&A Archive of Art and

Design. May adapted the pattern for a linen tray cover worked in chain stitch and French knots in shades of blue, green, pink and cream silk (**fig.60**), which she bequeathed to the V&A, T.120–1939.

The grapevine motif in **fig.76** was probably designed for a table centre, or runner. The arrangement of the vine tendrils, which resemble a Celtic knot, is reminiscent of the central motif in the *Vine leaf* table cover (**fig.13**).

Fig.60 May Morris (1862–1938), *Vine and pinks* tray cover, 1890s, polychrome silks on linen, 86.4 × 52.1 cm, V&A, T.120–1939.

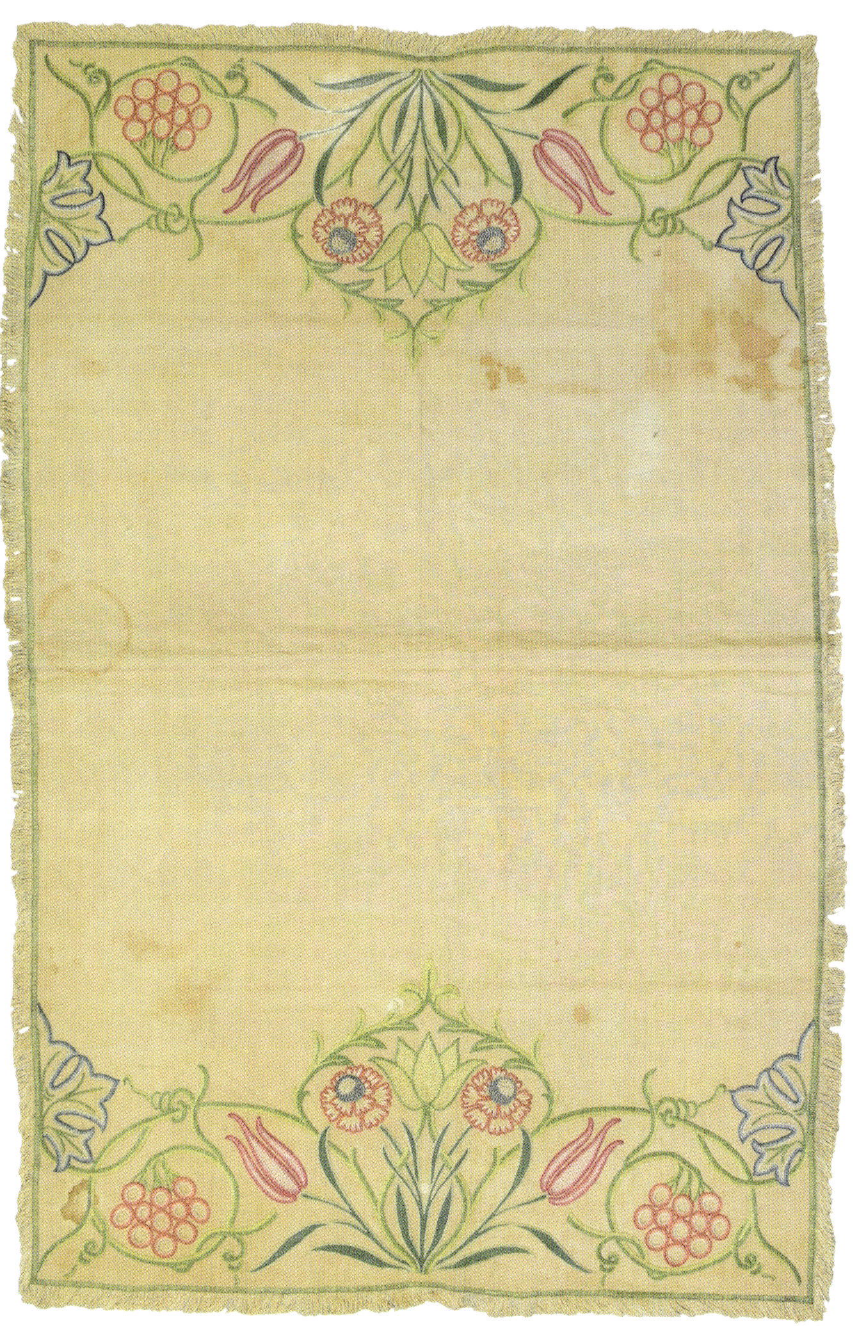

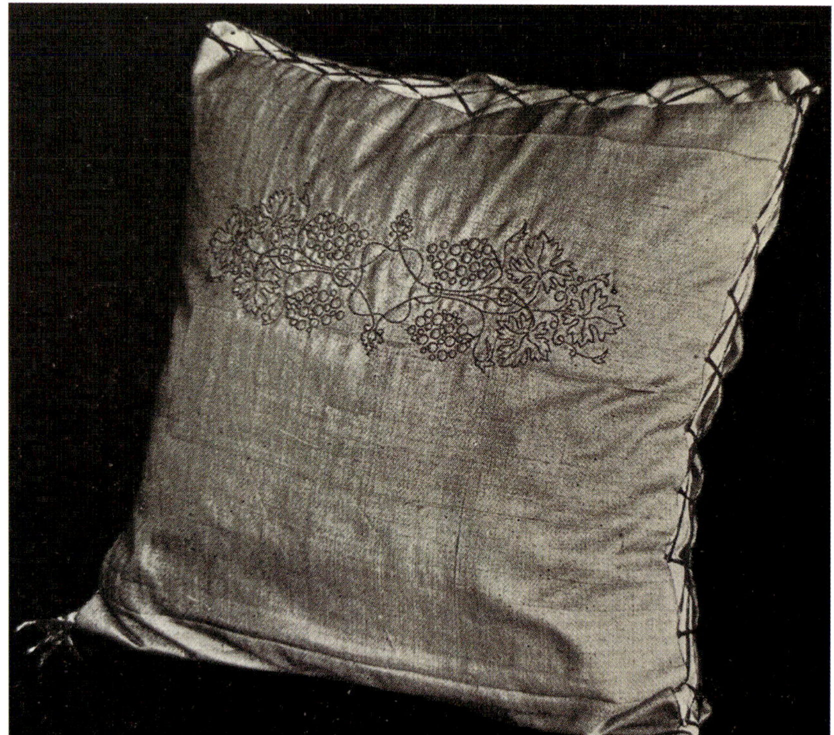

Fig.61 May Morris (1862–1938), Cushion, *c.*1907, monochrome silk on tussar silk, 31.9 × 23.7 cm (page), illustrated in *The Art Journal* (1907), p.323. Private collection

The Embroidery Day Book contains orders for seven 'started' kits for table centres, six to the design *Van Ingen*, for which this may be the working pattern, stitched in fine silk twist mainly on a fine silk.[36] A version of the design, stitched in outline in brown silk on a tussar silk ground and made up into a cushion cover, was illustrated in *The Art Journal* in 1907 (**fig.61**).[37]

Sofa Back

The viola pictured in **fig.72** is one of eight botanical motifs designed for a sofa back (*c.*1920s); the others are dianthus, fritillary, crocus, apple blossom, wood sorrel, hops and harebell (WA1941.108.73–74, 79, 88, 90, 92, and 93).[38] The patterns for viola and dianthus closely resemble motifs in *The heavens declare* panel and the *June* frieze; apple blossom is a reworking of the tree in the *Spring* roundel from the *Seasons* panels. Each sofa back motif was sketched on a single sheet of cheap ruled paper, pricked and pounced with charcoal.

Washable cloths made from a variety of needlework techniques such as crochet or tatting first appeared in the early nineteenth century to prevent seating from being soiled by macassar hair oil. By the 1870s, art embroiderers began to produce chair and sofa backs decorated in wool or silk. A notable example is the sofa back cover designed by William Morris, which the RSAN sent to the Philadelphia Centennial Exhibition in 1876, worked in outline on handwoven linen in two shades of gold-coloured silk.[39]

The sofa back was probably designed for May Elliott Hobbs (1877–1956), whose in-laws had rented Kelmscott Manor to the Morrises in 1871. Prior to her marriage, Hobbs had trained as a pianist in Weimar and Munich with a pupil of Liszt. She went on to perform across Europe before settling in Kelmscott in 1906, where she developed a close friendship with May. Both women shared an interest in folk dance and were passionate about rural issues and the role of women in society. In 1916, they founded the Kelmscott branch of the Women's Institute, which helped to develop community life and rural arts and handicrafts in the village. At the Kelmscott sale in 1939, Hobbs acquired one of May's personal treasures, *The Homestead and the Forest* quilt, reacquired by the Manor in 2016.[40]

The embroidered sofa back has remained in private hands, passing down through the Hobbs family line to the current owner. The rustic flowers are worked in long & short and stem stitch in shades of blue, coral, lime green and cream silk on handwoven linen (**fig.62**). There is no record of Hobbs

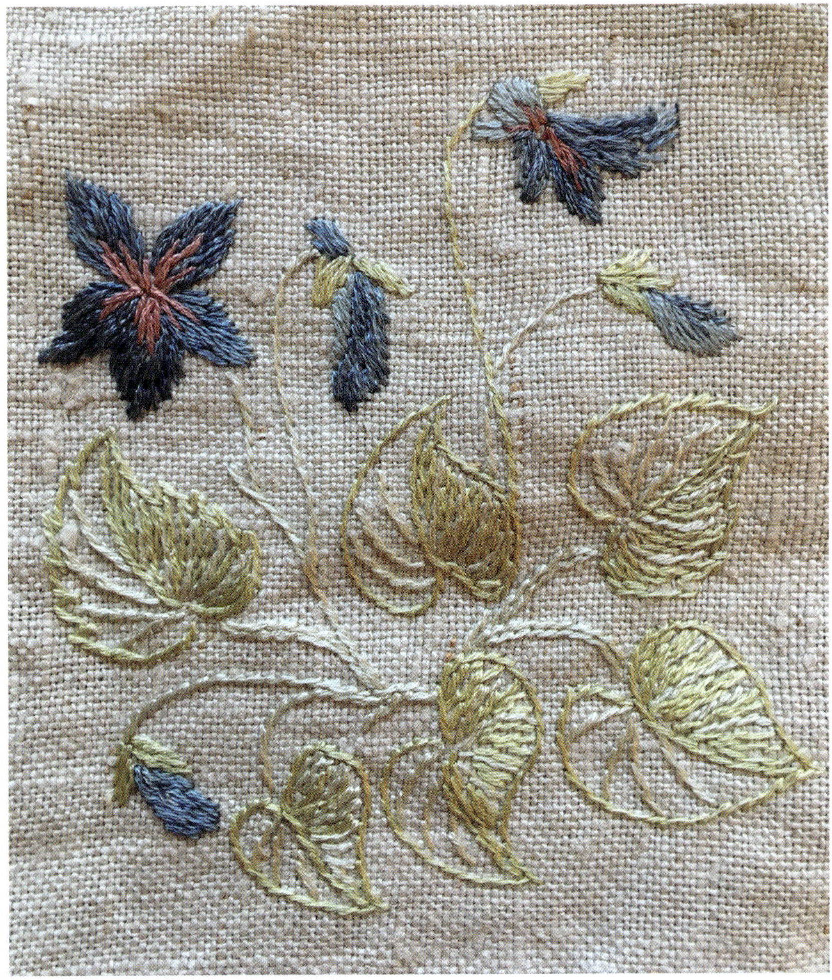

Fig.62 May Morris (1862–1938), *Viola* from a sofa back cover, *c*.1920, possibly stitched by members of the Kelmscott Women's Institute, polychrome silks on linen, 19 × 19 cm. Private collection.

being the maker, but the fact that each motif was stitched on a single linen square before being joined together to form the front panel of the sofa back suggests that it could have been a collaborative project.[41] This sofa cover may have been worked by members of the Kelmscott WI.

Miscellaneous Designs

Several individual botanical motifs have found their way into the Ashmolean collection. A few are connected to the *June* frieze and the Kelmscott bed cover. Others cannot be linked to a specific utility. Two of these are included here: strawberry (**fig.71**) and rose (**fig.81**). Pricked on thick laid paper and pounced with blue pipe clay, **fig.81** is redolent of the appliquéd slips found in late sixteenth- and seventeenth-century English needlework, like the panel in **fig.63**. Single flowers in profile or in full bloom, with one or two buds on a cut stem, were an inherent feature of contemporary herbals and botanical woodblock prints produced specially for embroidery. May adopted this historic device for the Kelmscott bed cover, albeit working the rows of flowers, each set within or between knotwork compartments, directly onto the linen cloth. The floral motifs in both the Kelmscott bed cover and the smaller version made in the 1910s for May's London neighbour Mary Grace Walker (1849–1920), wife of the photographer and printer Sir Emery Walker (1851–1933), contain a rose, but the pattern differs from the one included here.[42]

Fig.63 Panel of slips for appliqué work, first half of the seventeenth century, polychrome silks on linen, 57.8 × 33 cm, Metropolitan Museum of Art, 28.53.

May also used knotwork patterns to embellish the border of a garment (see below) or soft furnishing like the coverlet (1910–30) made for the artist

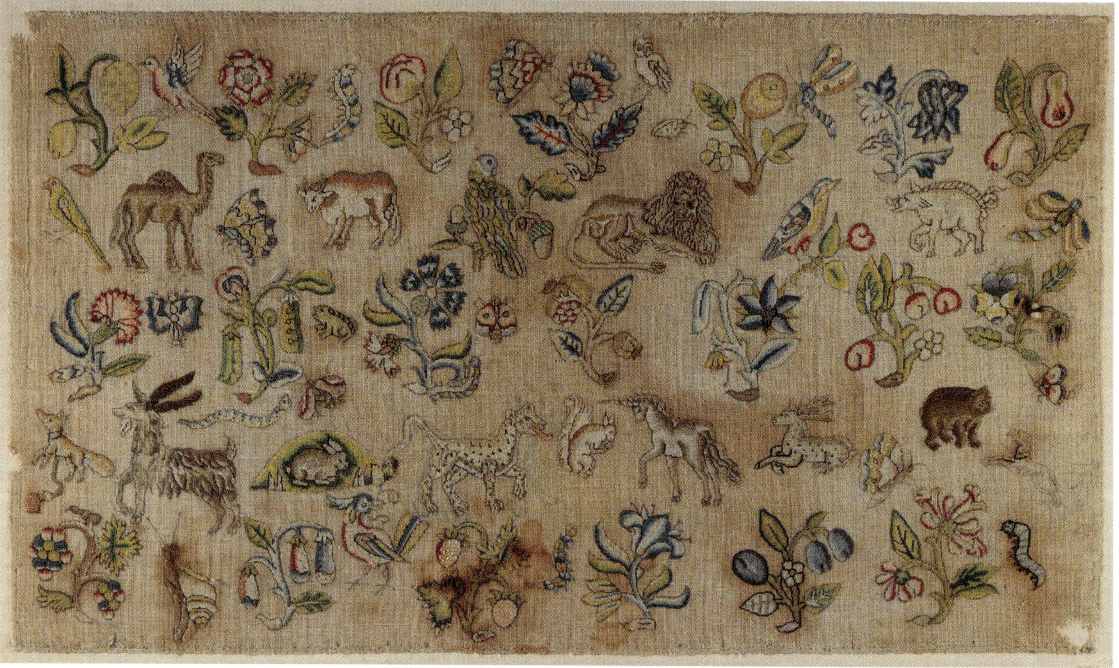

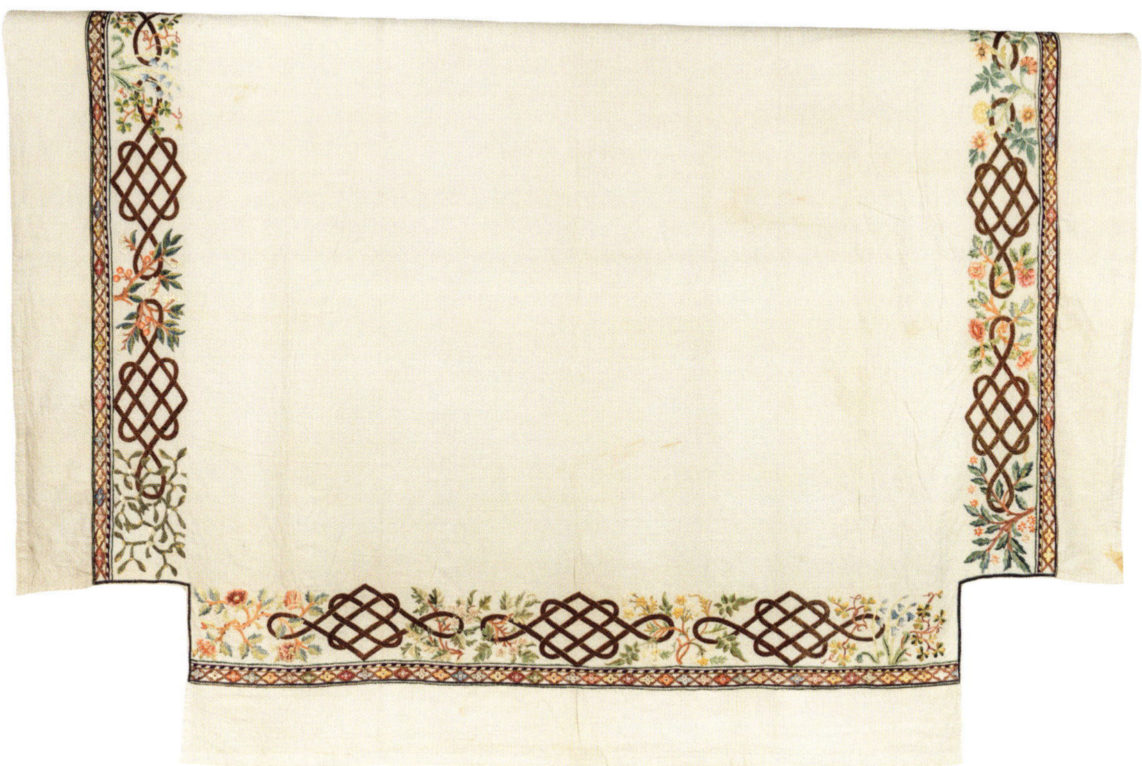

Fig.64 May Morris (1862–1938), Coverlet, 1910–30, polychrome silks on linen, 232.4 × 226.1 cm, William Morris Gallery, F203.

Mary Annie Sloane (1867–1961), in which Celtic knots alternate with sprays of hedgerow flowers, berries and mistletoe, worked in silk on a linen ground (**fig.64**). A truncated version of the same knot motif, decorated with highly conventionalised flowers, is included as **fig.83**.

Garments and Accessories

Morris & Co. occasionally undertook commissions for 'worked' yokes or dress panels on customers' own material.[43] In April 1894, Theodosia Middlemore supplied the silk for a dress panel to be designed and started in floss silk at a cost of £3 12s.[44] May promoted the loosely fitted, simple designs of the Artistic dress movement, inspired by the style of clothing worn in the Middle Ages. In 1892, she published an article exploring the use of embroidered ornamentation on medieval sleeves, and enjoined readers to pick up some ideas from the fashions of the past in creating their own attire.[45] Among the items sold at Kelmscott in 1939 was a pair of sleeves that May had decorated with a *rinceau* pattern in imitation of the embroidery found on late sixteenth- and early seventeenth-century costume (**fig.65**).[46]

The Ashmolean collection contains a handful of designs for clothing, two of which are included. **Fig.74** is a pencil, ink and charcoal sketch for the right sleeve of a garment with a peony and scrolling acanthus leaf design. The shape is roughly mapped out in the drawing with the directions 'right sleeve' and

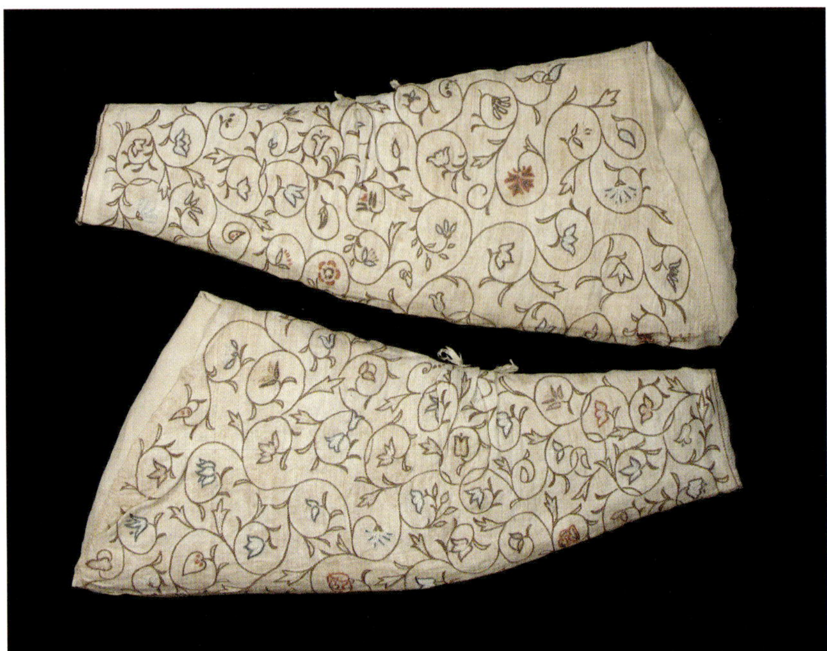

Fig.65 May Morris (1862–1938), Pair of sleeves in seventeenth-century style, *c*.1890, polychrome silks on linen, 62 × 29 cm.

'front edge' in May's hand. The repeated knotwork border with tulips and roses in **fig.73** may have been designed for the bottom of a dress not unlike the one May created in *c*.1905 for Mary Annie Sloane.[47]

Orders for workbags and offertory bags are listed in the Embroidery Day Book, but there is no mention of day or evening purses being executed by the firm. May is known to have created bags for her own use such as the one illustrated in **fig.48**. A handful of patterns for similar items exist in the Ashmolean collection, including a tracing for a blue silk bag designed by her father and worked by her mother, WA1941.108.459. Set within a reused metal frame engraved 'EW', the bag was among the treasured possessions that May bequeathed to the V&A, T.70–1939 (**figs 66 & 67**).[48]

Fig.75 may have been designed for a chatelaine bag that hung from the waist, like the medieval girdle bag, or *aumônière*, which May so much admired.[49] Chatelaine bags were a popular fashion accessory in Britain during the second half of the Victorian period. By joining the handles together in a clip that slid over a belt or sash, they were a convenient way of freeing the hands. Bags for outdoor wear were produced in leather, while those for home use were often made of embroidered velvet or wool work.[50]

In her article on designing for embroidery, May emphasised the importance of 'suitability of purpose'. In contrast to a large wall hanging or portière that required 'generous curves and forms' or a bold pattern repeat worked in large stitches, a little bag or girdle pouch called for 'minute work, rich and varied and complete in the small space, a design giving scope to the craftsman's skill in laying curious stitches, and heaping gold into precious masses'.[51]

Fig.66 William Morris (1834–1896), Design for a bag, *c.*1878, drawing on tracing paper in graphite, scored, 17.2 × 18.2 cm. Ashmolean Museum (WA1941.108.459)

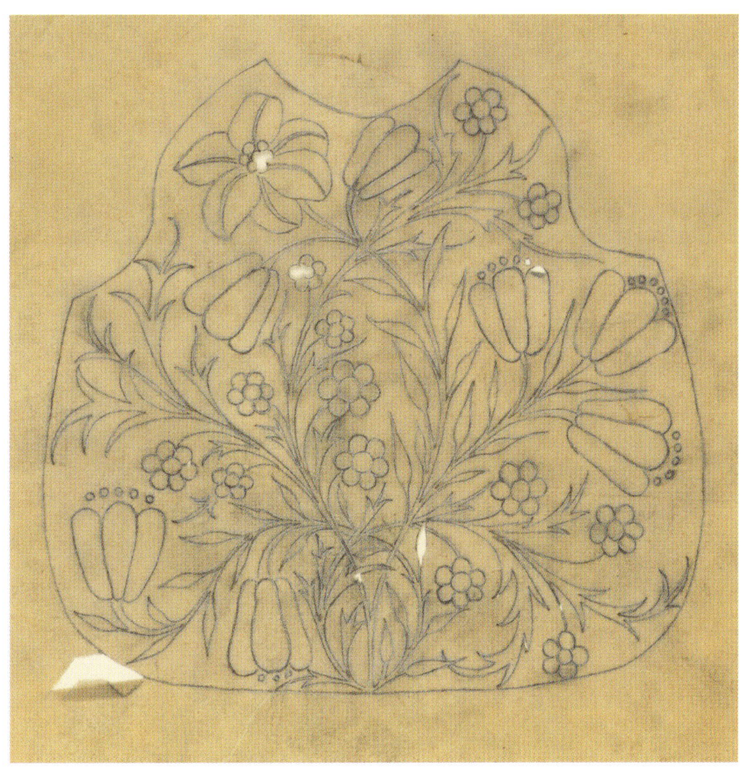

Fig.67 William Morris (1834–1896), Bag stitched by Jane Morris, *c.*1878, polychrome silks on silk, 24 × 24.5 cm (dimensions of board), V&A, T.70–1939.

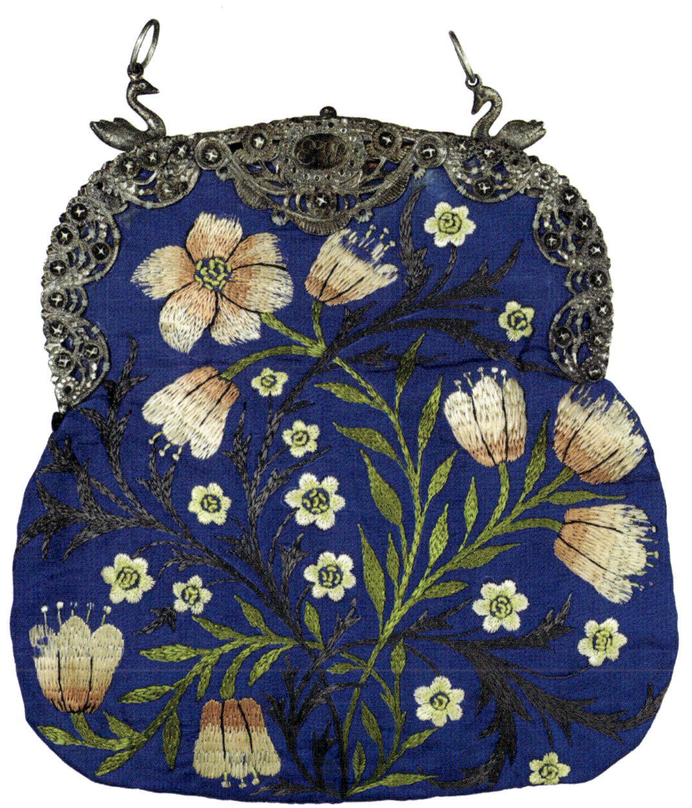

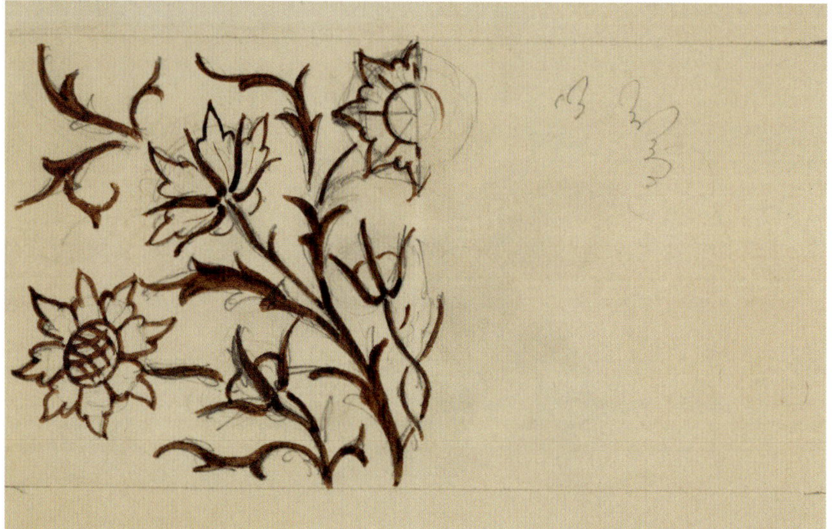

Fig.68 May Morris (1862–1938), Design for a workbag, 1890s, drawing on cream laid paper in pen and dark brown ink and wash over graphite, 11.4 × 17.9 cm (sheet). Ashmolean Museum (WA1941.108.267)

The pricked outline of the bag in **fig.75** bears some resemblance to a medieval round-top trapezoidal *aumônière*, but with a semicircular flap folded over the opening. The pattern of trailing flowers mirrored on the front panels is repeated on the flap.

Workbags and Sachet

May occasionally designed bands for workbags that were used by customers to store their embroidery threads and tools. On 25 May 1892, Mrs Barr Smith, who was a keen embroiderer, placed an order for a workbag in silk with decorative bands stitched on Manchester cloth for the sum of £2 7s 6d.[52] The Embroidery Day Book also lists a *King cup* border for a 'started' kit, stitched in thick silk twist.[53] Two of the oblong patterns (**figs. 79** and **84**) included in this volume were probably designed as borders for a workbag. **Fig.68** contains a roughly executed sketch of half the design with the flower heads mapped out in circles and ellipses, shown in bud, in full bloom, and from the back; the final version of the pattern is in **fig.79**. The clumps of poppies and fritillaries featured in **fig.84** are commonly found in May's embroideries dating from the late nineteenth and early twentieth centuries such as the Kelmscott bed hangings, *The heavens declare* panel, and the *June* frieze.

The floral wreath in **fig.80** can be identified as *Periwinkle*, illustrated in the *Embroidery Work* catalogue. The measurement of the Ashmolean pricking matches that printed in the brochure (3½ in, or 8.5 cm, in diameter). *Periwinkle* may have been designed for a small handkerchief sachet. Three examples are listed in the Embroidery Day Book: two 'started' kits in fine silk twist on a silk ground, priced £1 6s and £1 8s, and a cheaper version stitched in filoselle on Manchester cloth, at 7s 6d.[54]

Original Designs and Embroidery Patterns

Twenty-five of May's working designs are set out in the following pages. Each two-page spread contains a photograph of May's original design, together with an embroidery pattern for readers to transfer. To assist with scaling up or down, digitised versions of the latter can be accessed at www.ashmolean.org/may-morris-lynn-hulse-book-patterns. The captions to the original designs give accession number, design dimensions (height × width in cm), and object type (drawing, tracing or pricking).

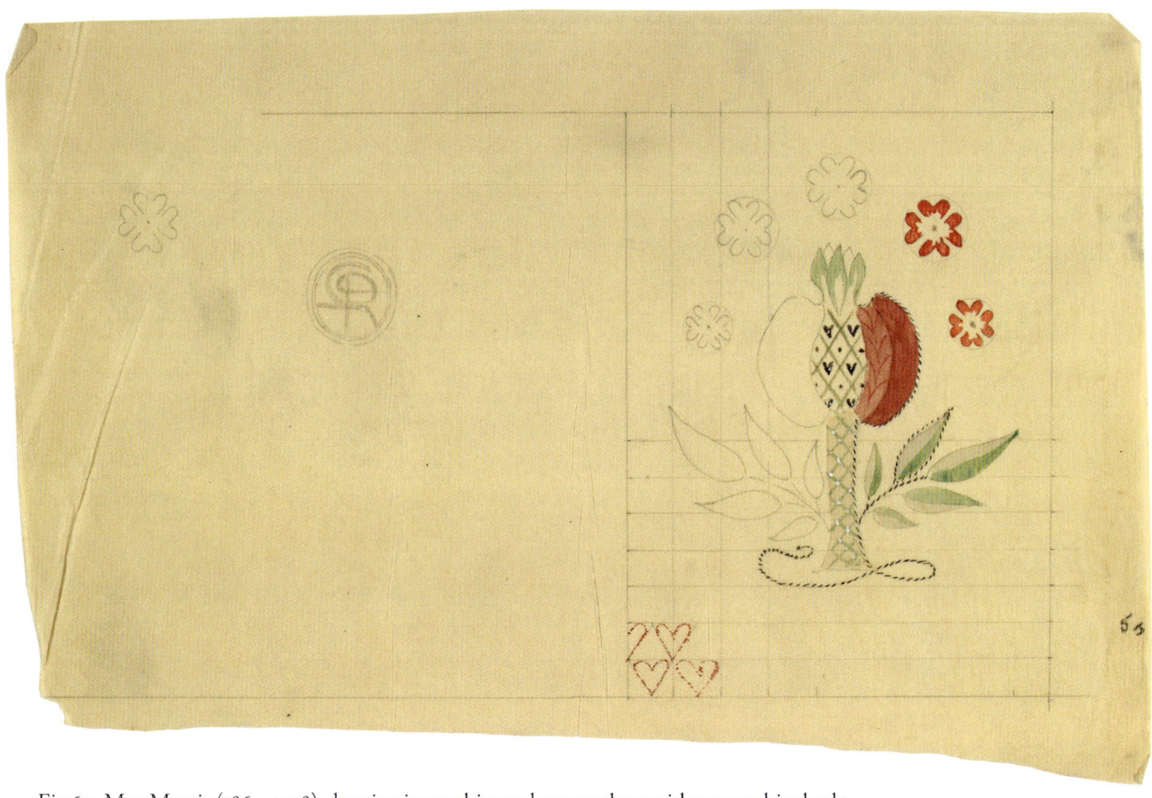

Fig.69 May Morris (1862–1938), drawing in graphite and watercolour with some white body colour on light cream paper, 15.2 × 11.3 cm. Ashmolean Museum (WA1941.108.36)

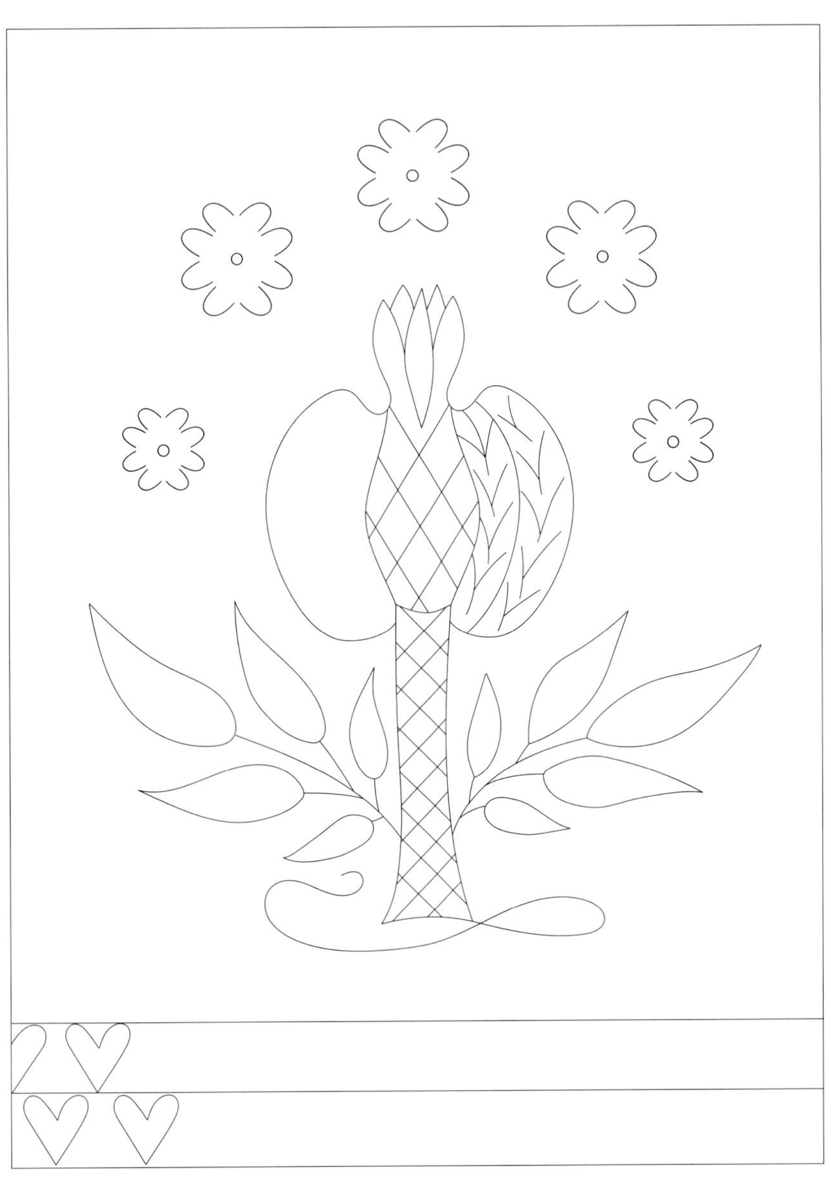

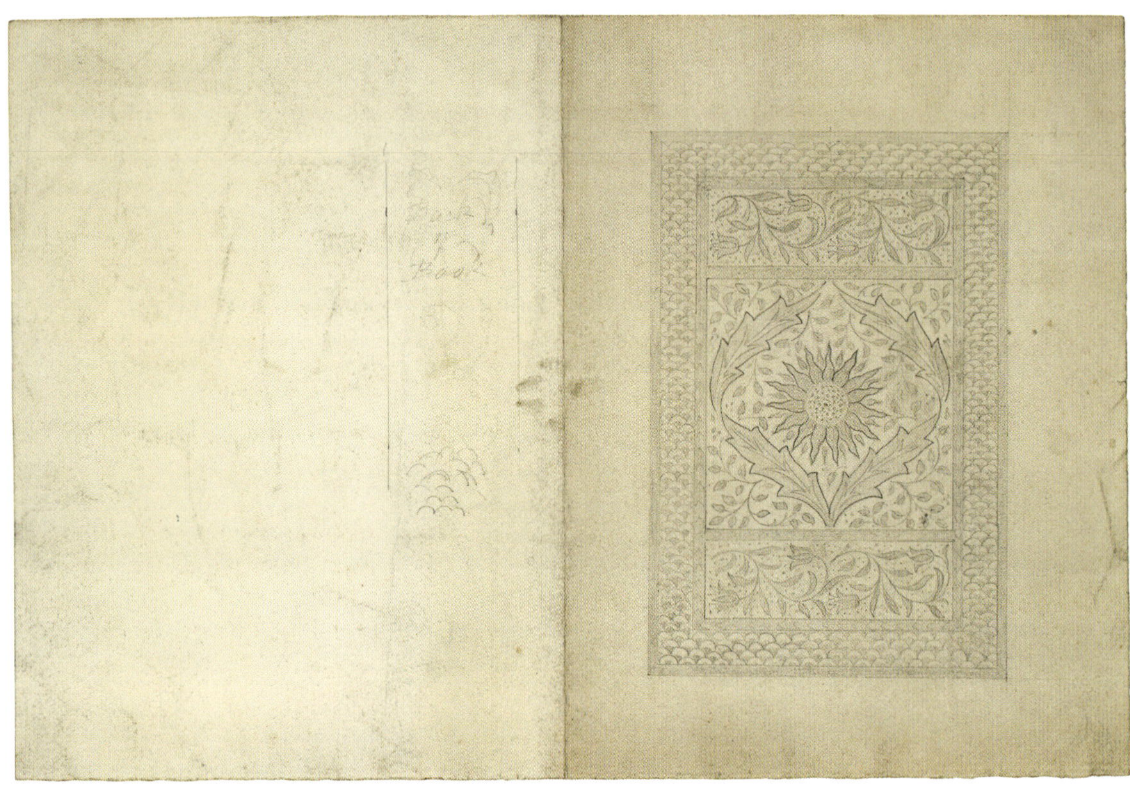

Fig.70 May Morris (1862–1938), drawing in graphite on white thick laid paper, 18.5 × 12.5 cm. Ashmolean Museum (WA1941.108.37)

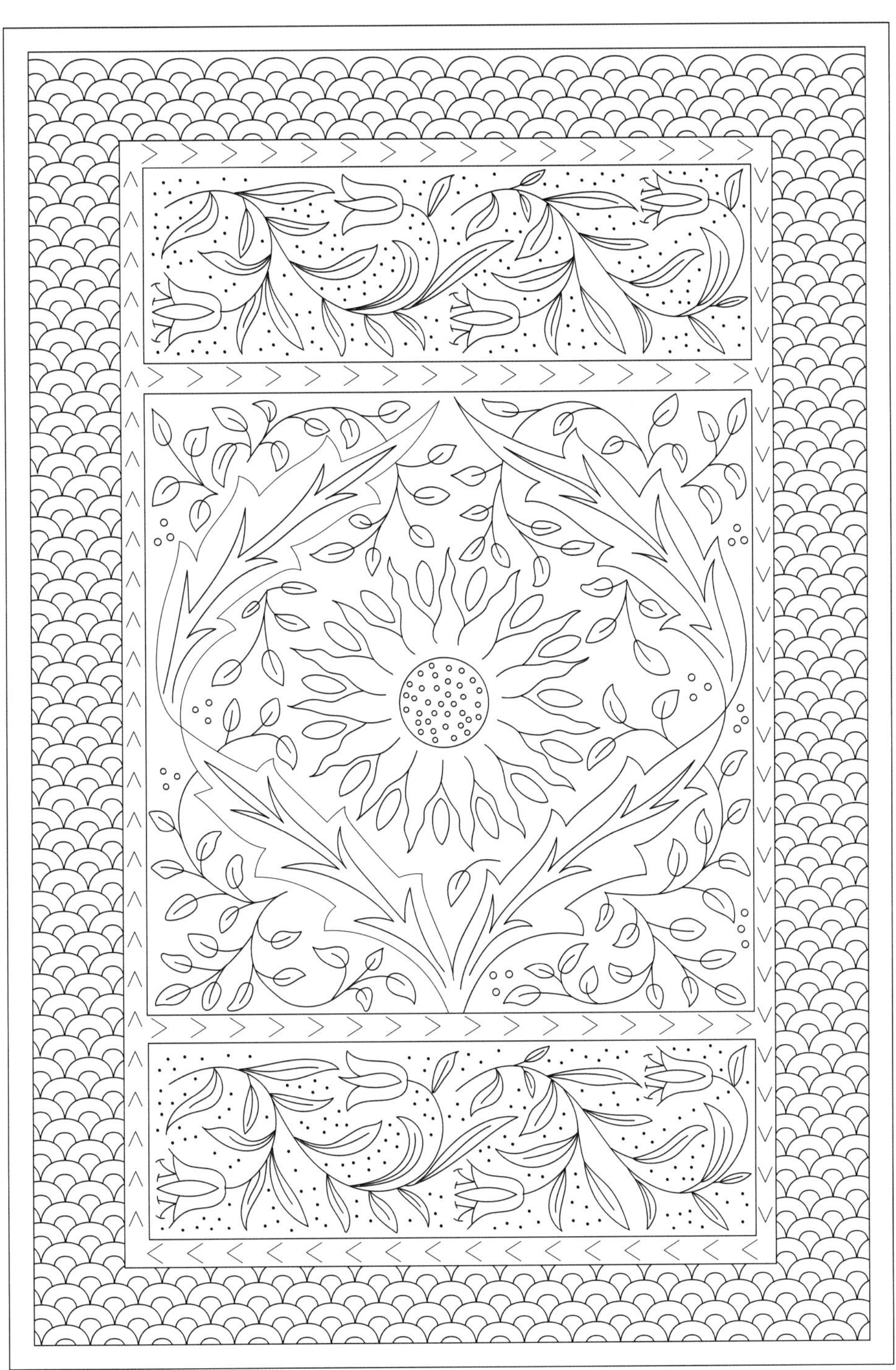

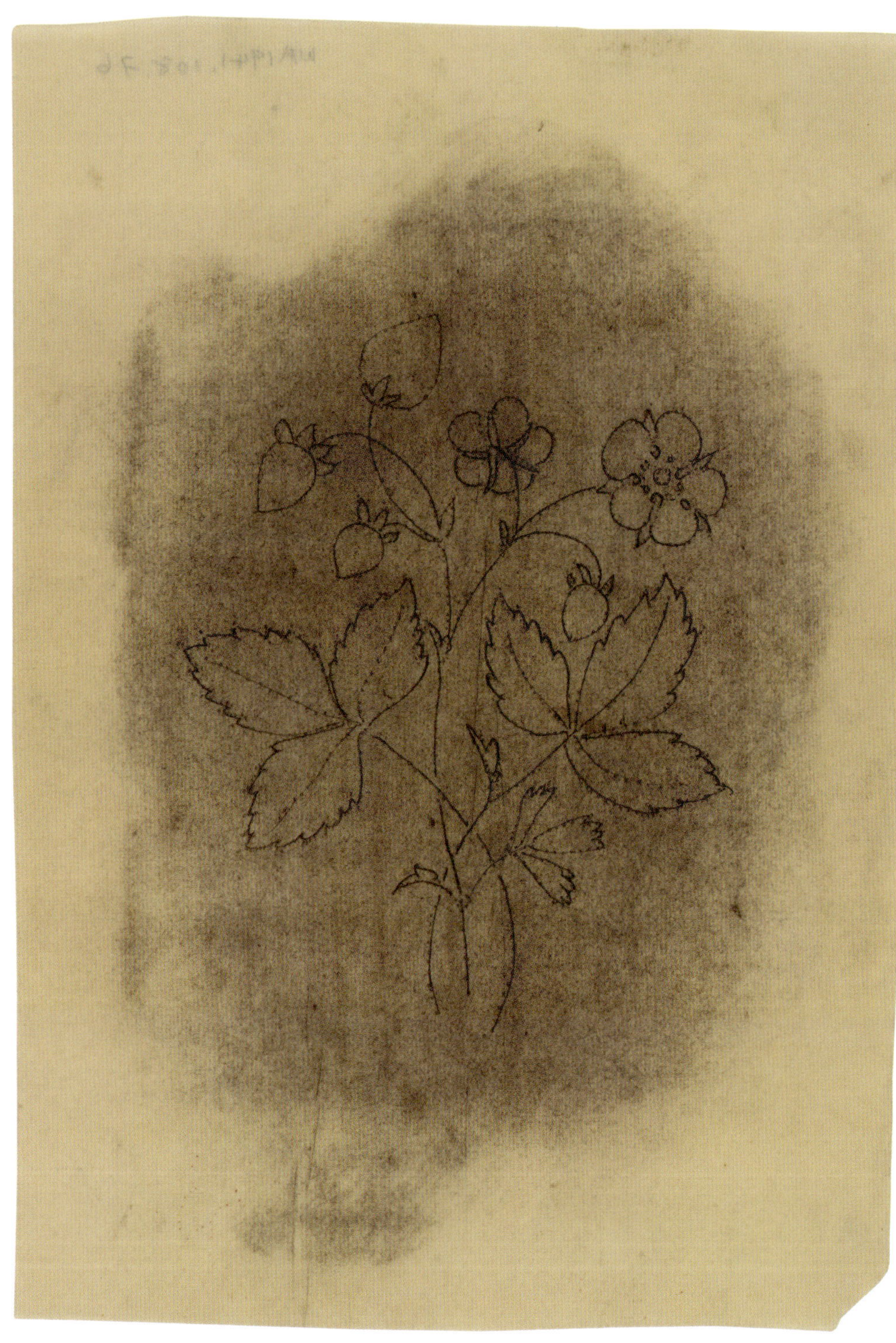

Fig.71 May Morris (1862–1938), drawing in graphite and pen and black ink on tracing paper; pricked and pounced with charcoal, 13.3 × 10.2 cm. Ashmolean Museum (WA1941.108.76)

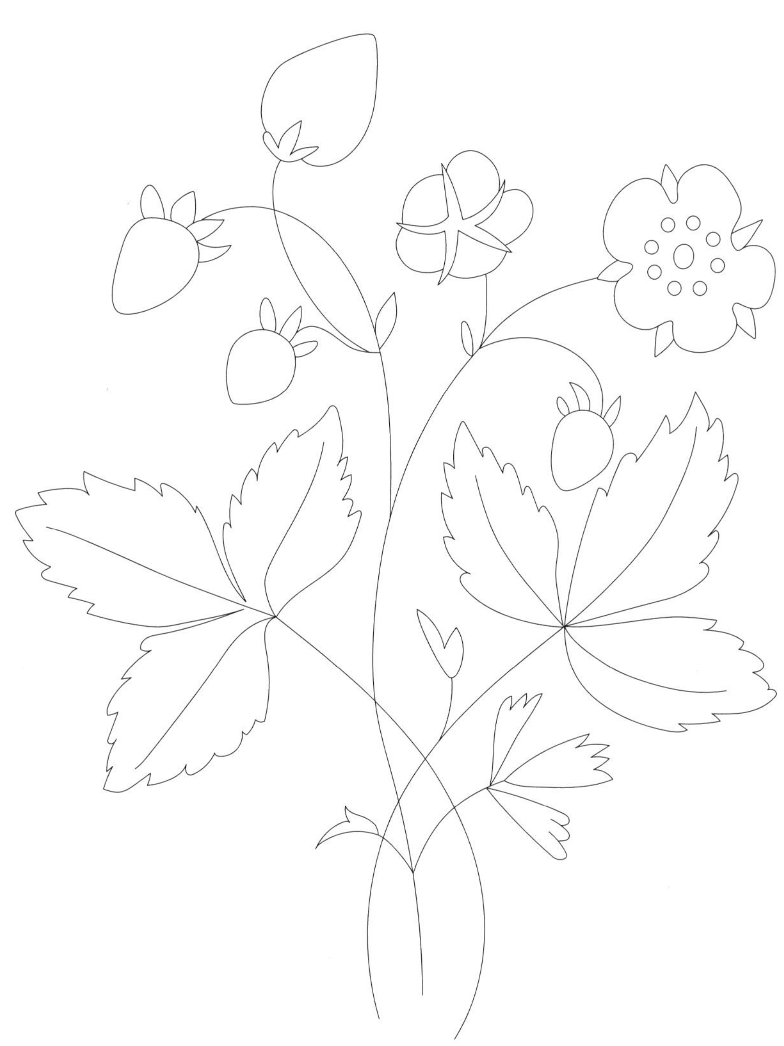

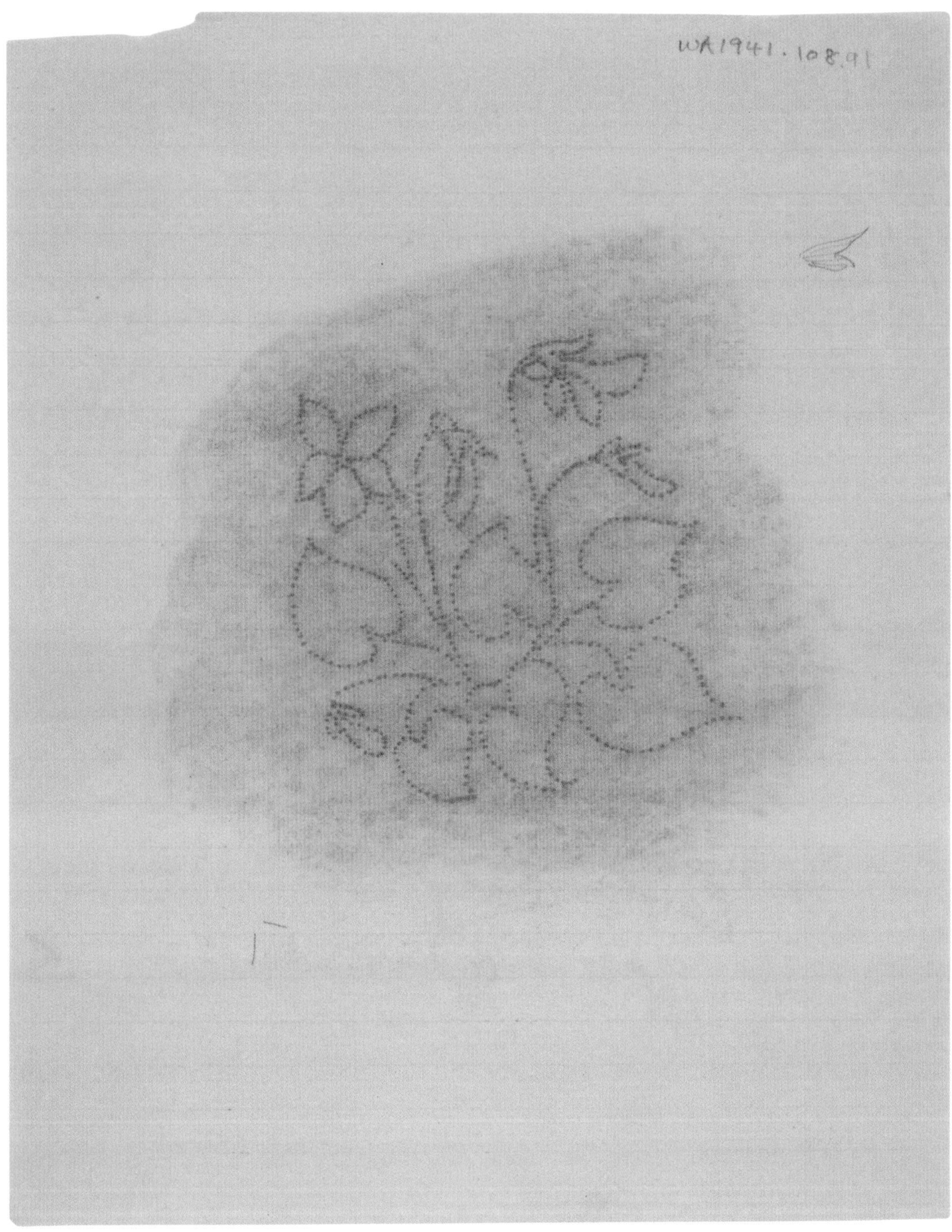

Fig.72 May Morris (1862–1938), drawing in graphite on cheap ruled paper; pricked and pounced with charcoal, 9.7 × 9.6 cm. Ashmolean Museum (WA1941.108.91)

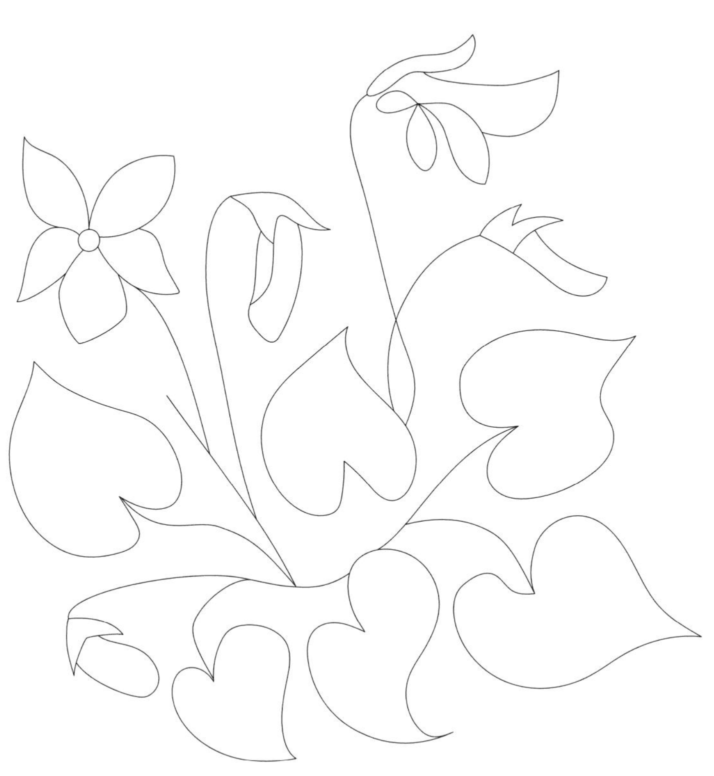

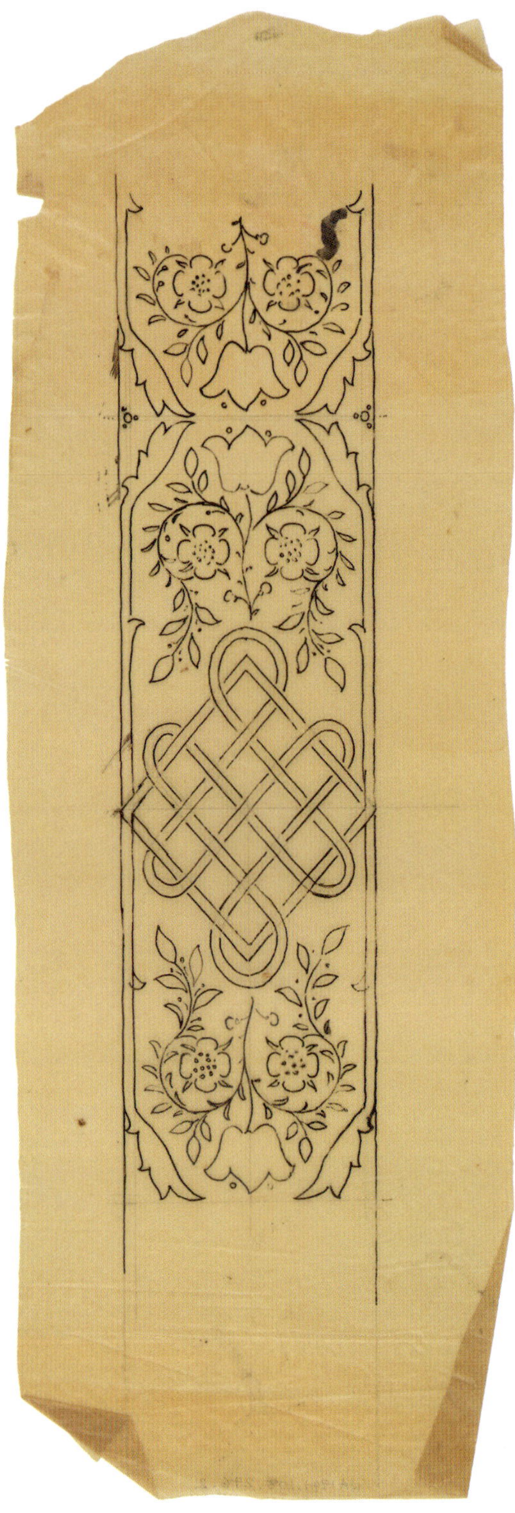

Fig.73 May Morris (1862–1938), drawing in pen and black ink, with some graphite, on tracing paper, 29.8 × 7.1 cm. Ashmolean Museum (WA1941.108.276.2)

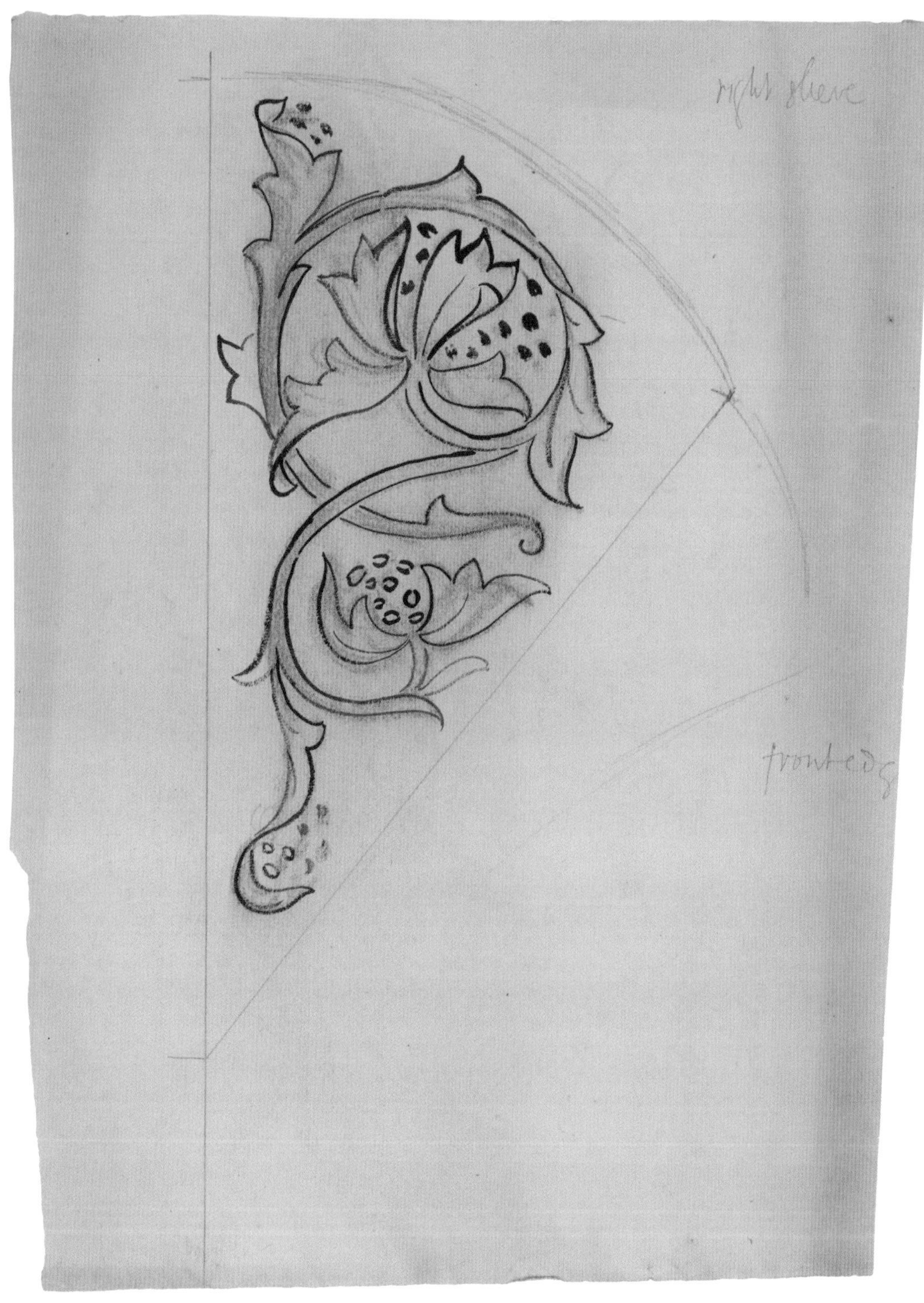

Fig.74 May Morris (1862–1938), drawing in graphite and charcoal, with brush and black ink, on cream thick laid paper, 33 × 21 cm. Ashmolean Museum (WA1941.108.297.1)

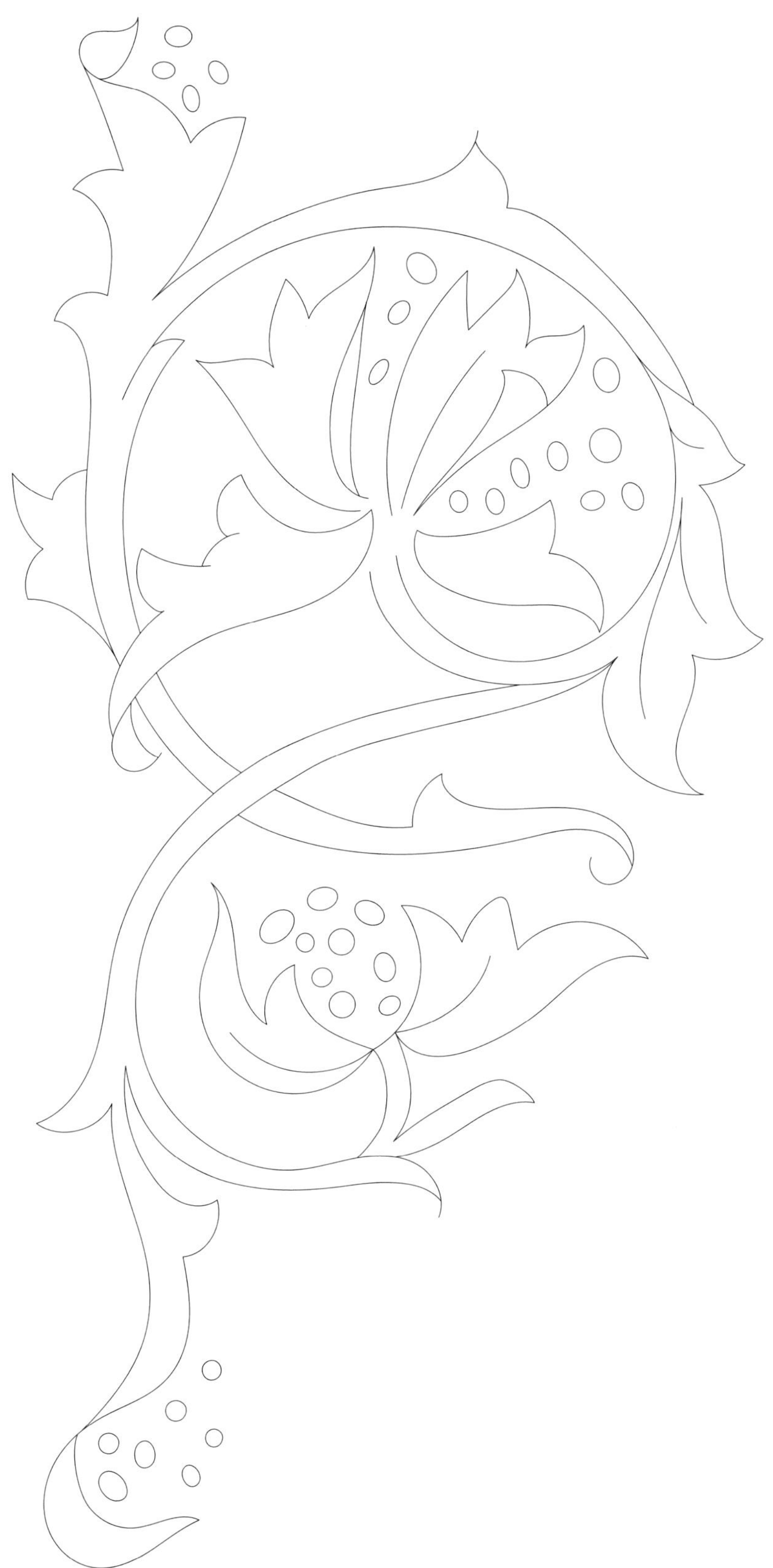

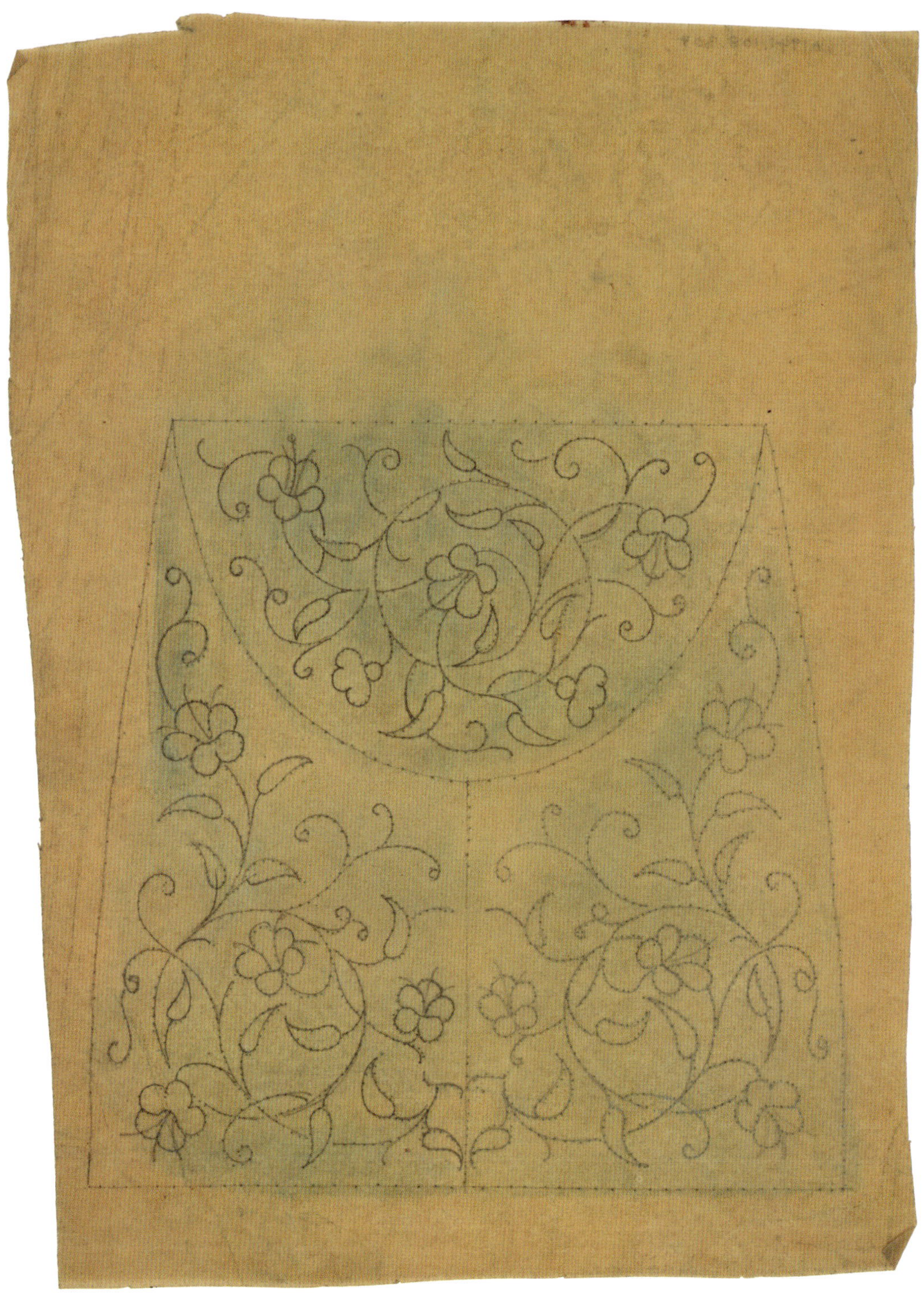

Fig.75 May Morris (1862–1938), drawing in graphite on tracing paper; pricked and pounced with blue clay powder, 19.2 × 15.3–19.5 cm. Ashmolean Museum (WA1941.108.307)

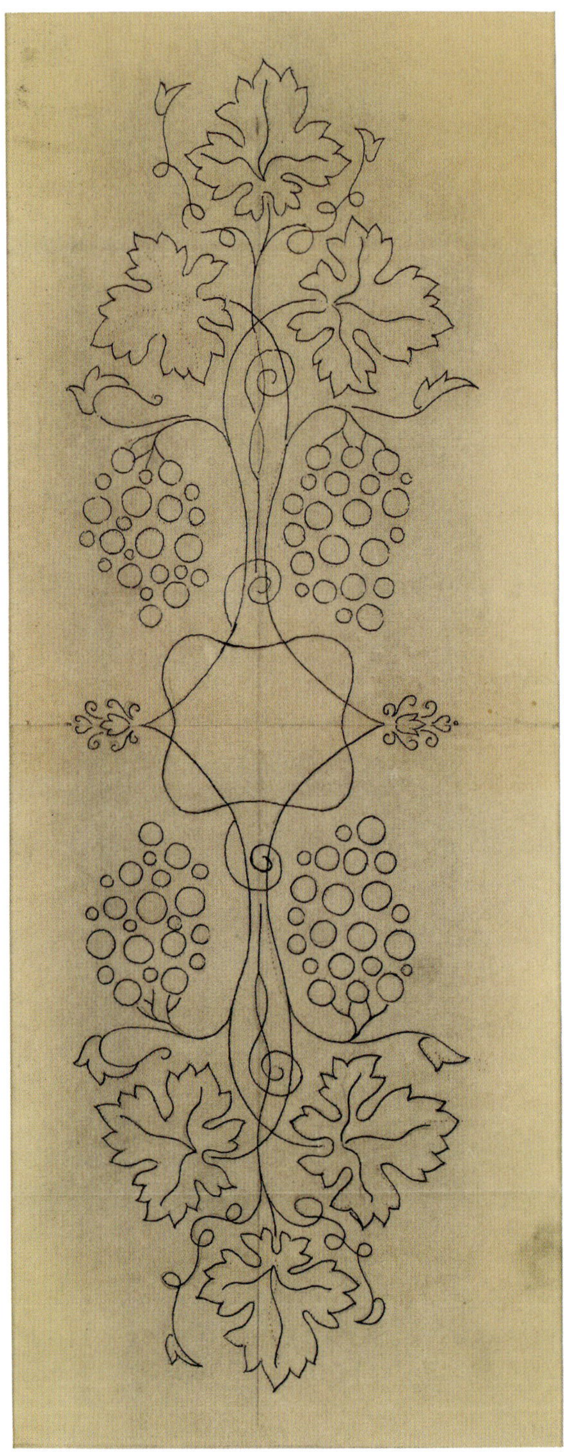

Fig.76 May Morris (1862–1938), drawing in pen and black ink on tracing paper; pricked and pounced with charcoal, 36 × 10.4 cm. Ashmolean Museum (WA1941.108.342)

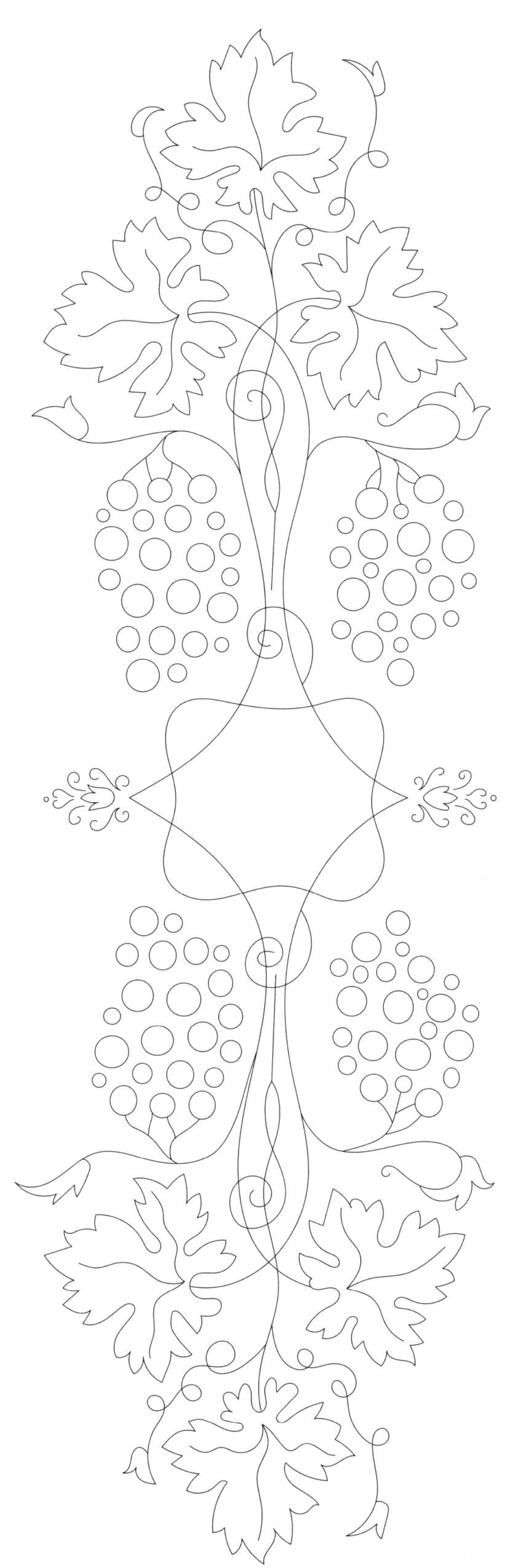

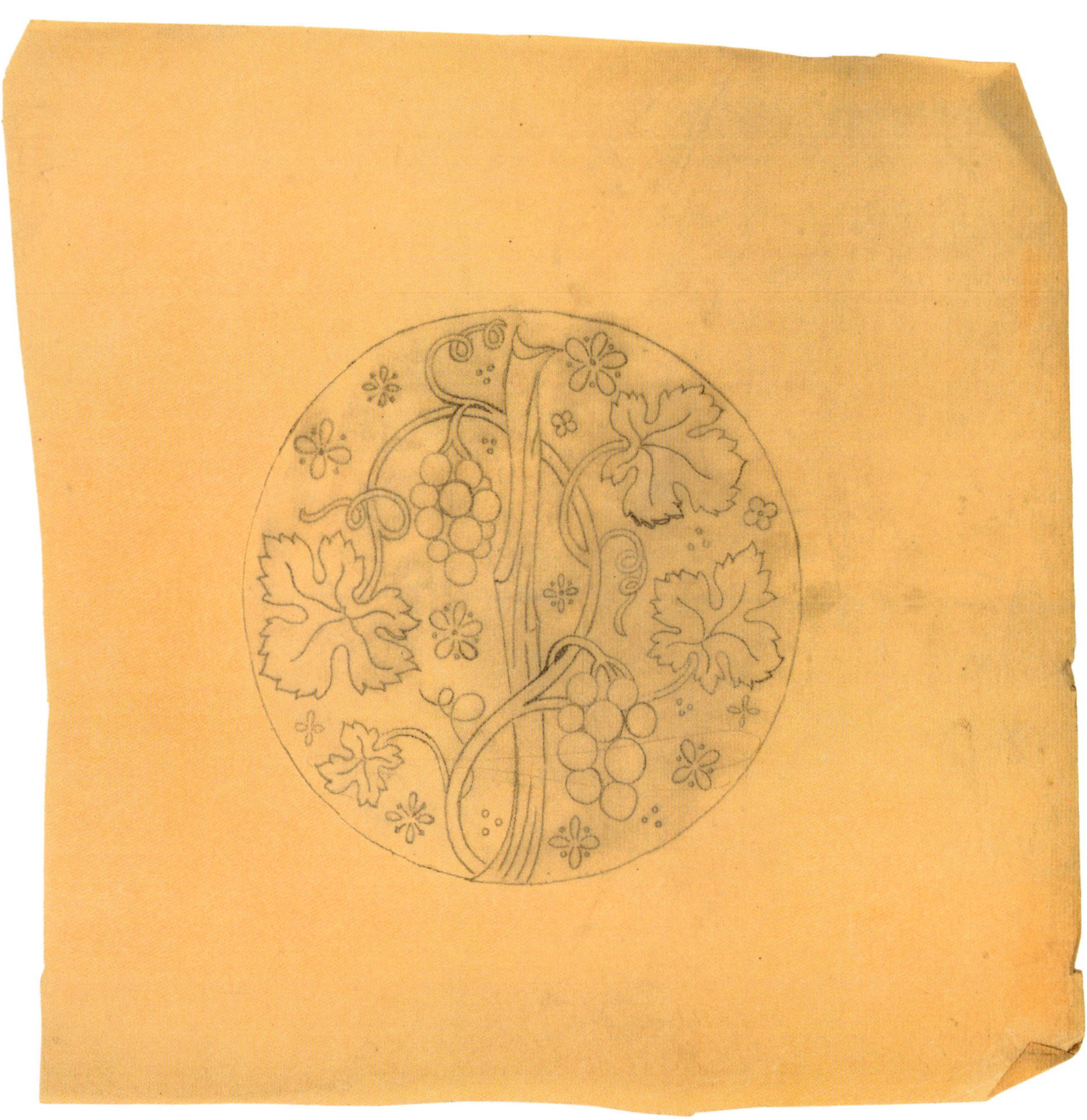

Fig.77 May Morris (1862–1938), drawing in graphite on tracing paper; pricked with some evidence of pouncing with charcoal, 17.2 cm in diameter. Ashmolean Museum (WA1941.108.350)

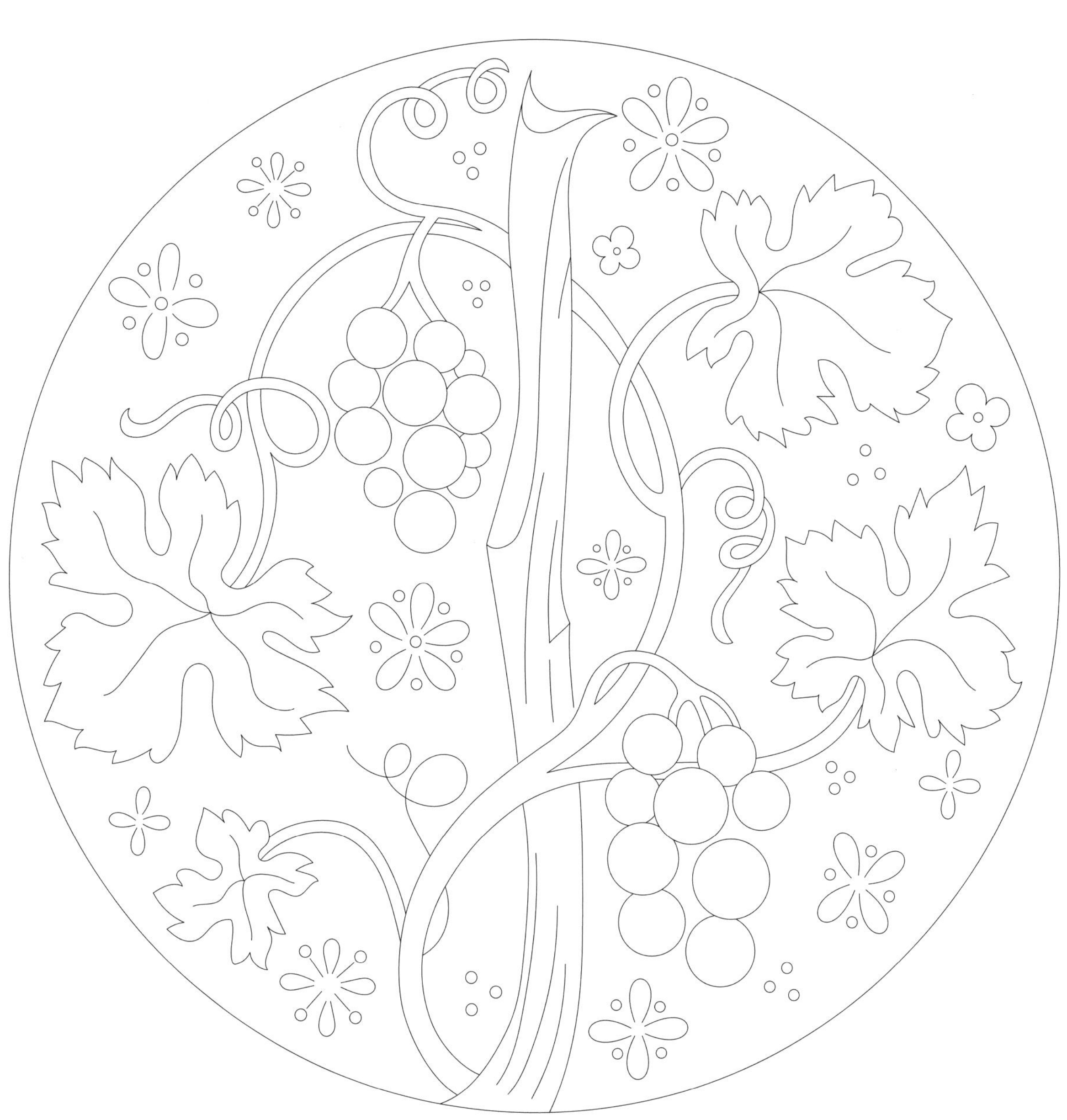

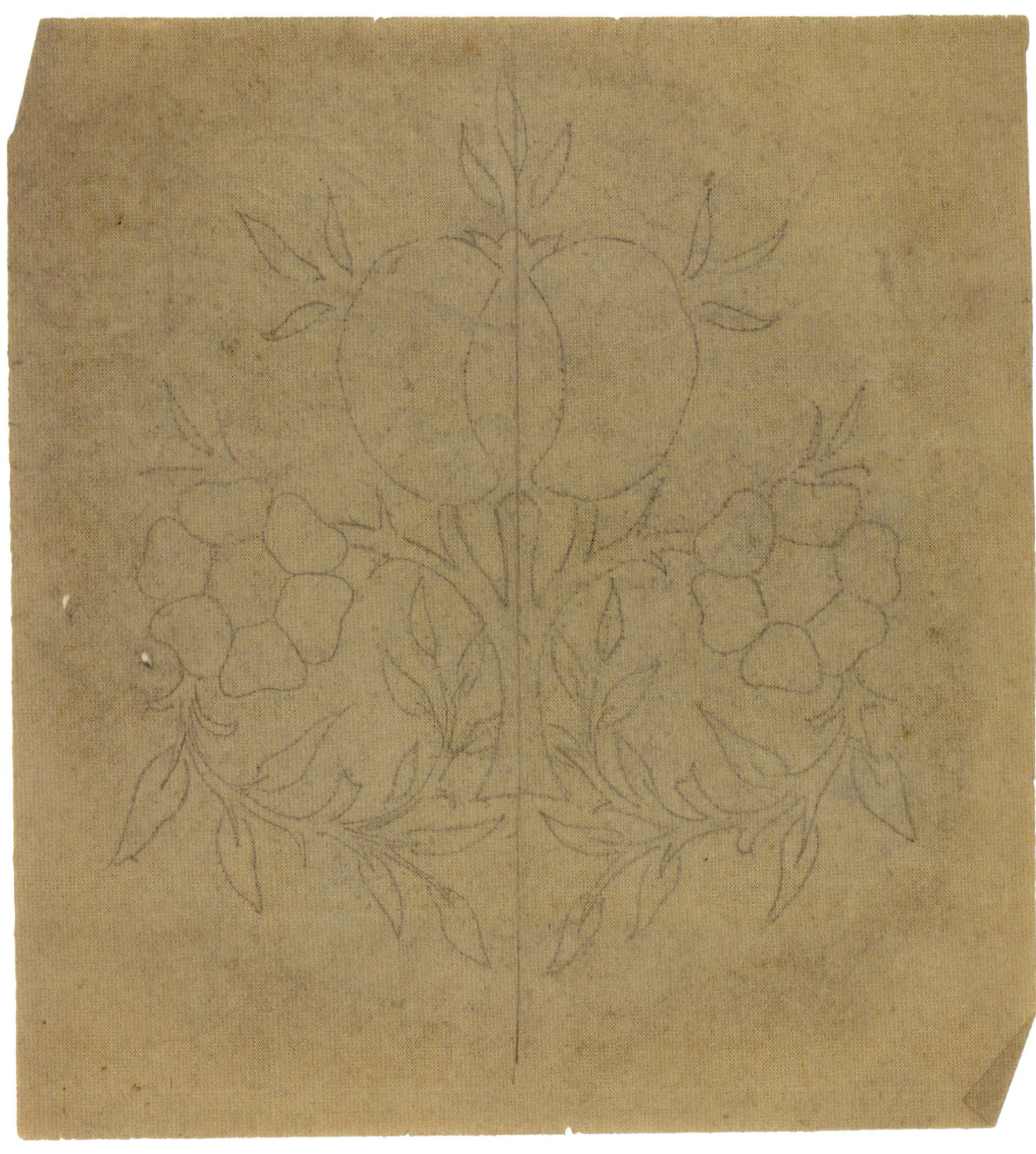

Fig.78 May Morris (1862–1938), drawing in graphite on tracing paper; pricked and pounced with charcoal and white clay powder, 15.7 × 14 cm. Ashmolean Museum (WA1941.108.391)

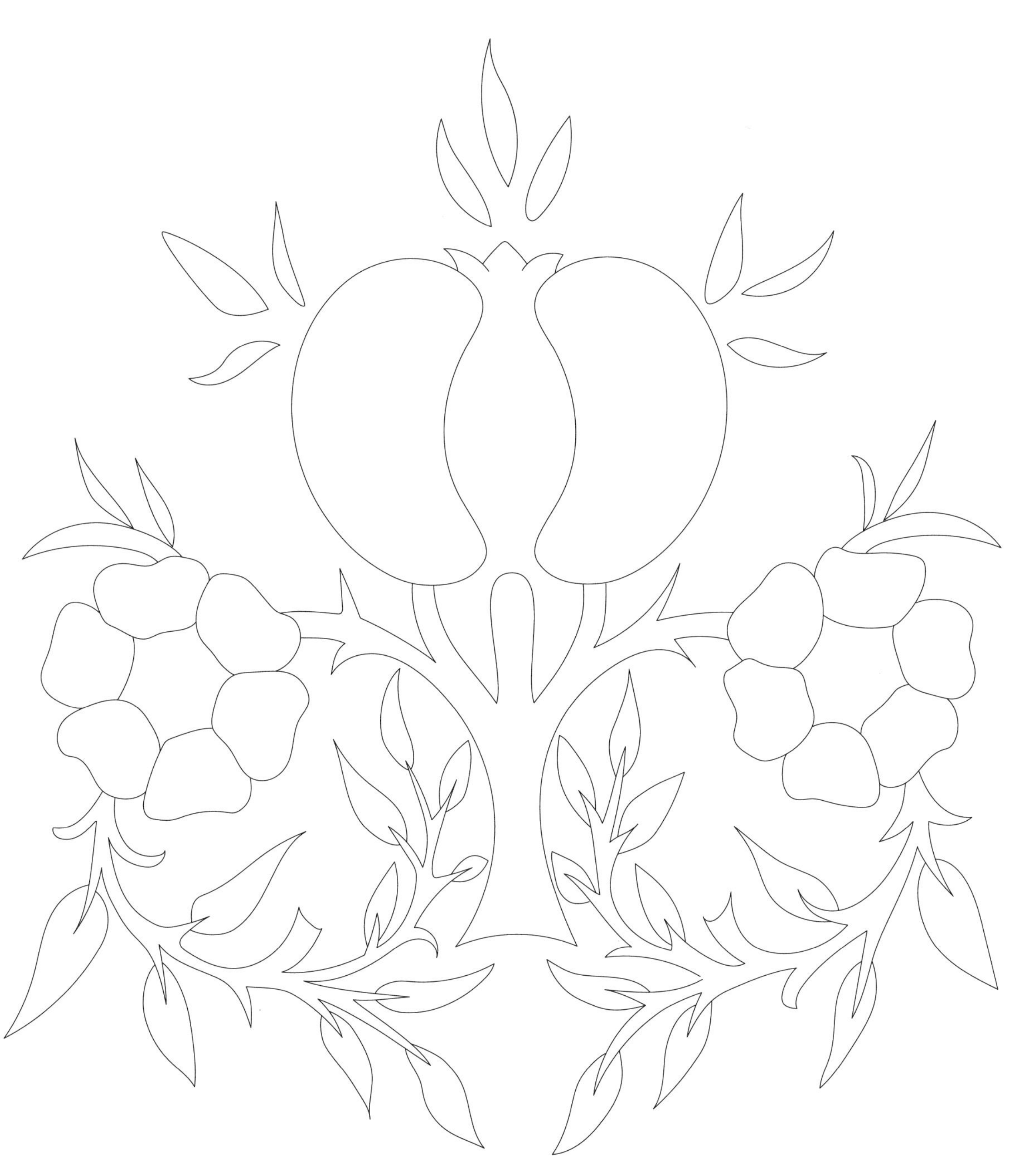

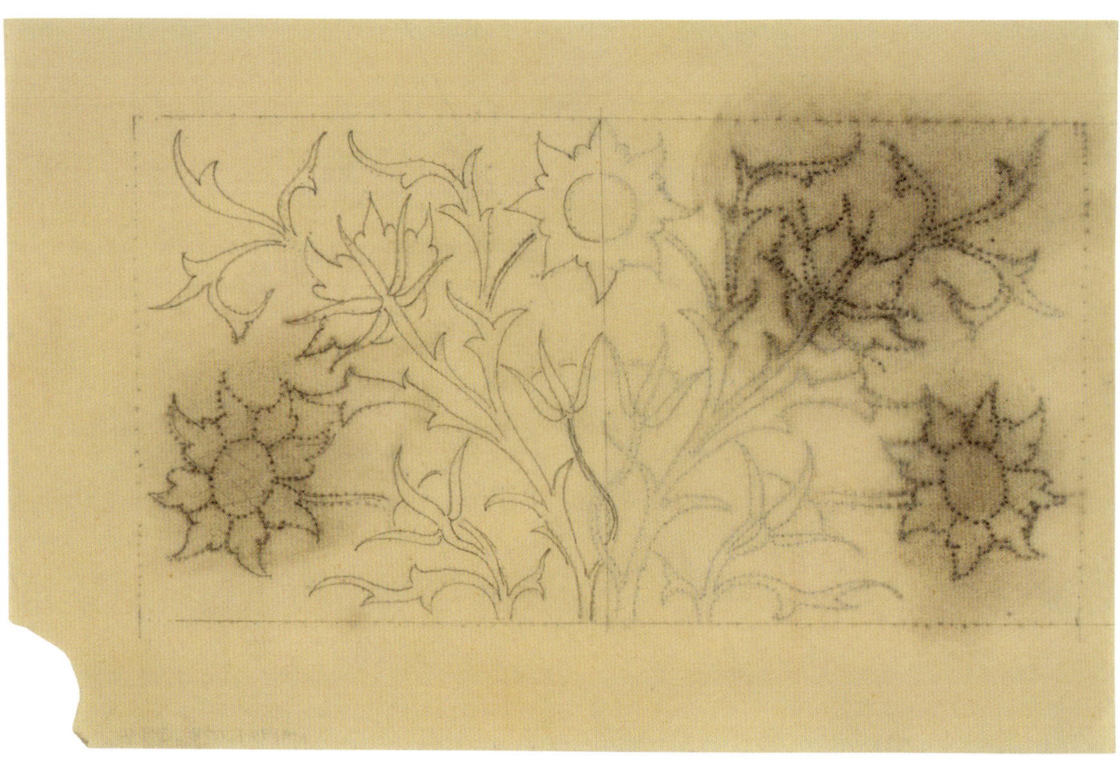

Fig.79 May Morris (1862–1938), drawing in graphite on tracing paper; pricked and pounced in some areas with charcoal, 9.3 × 18 cm. Ashmolean Museum (WA1941.108.394)

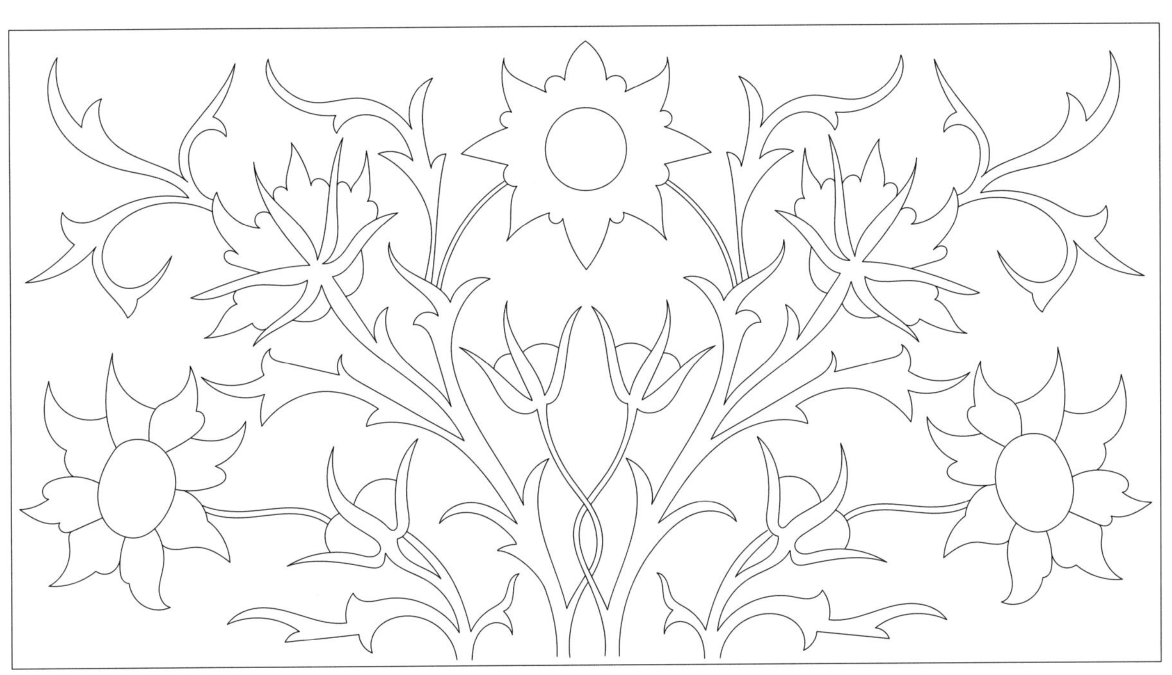

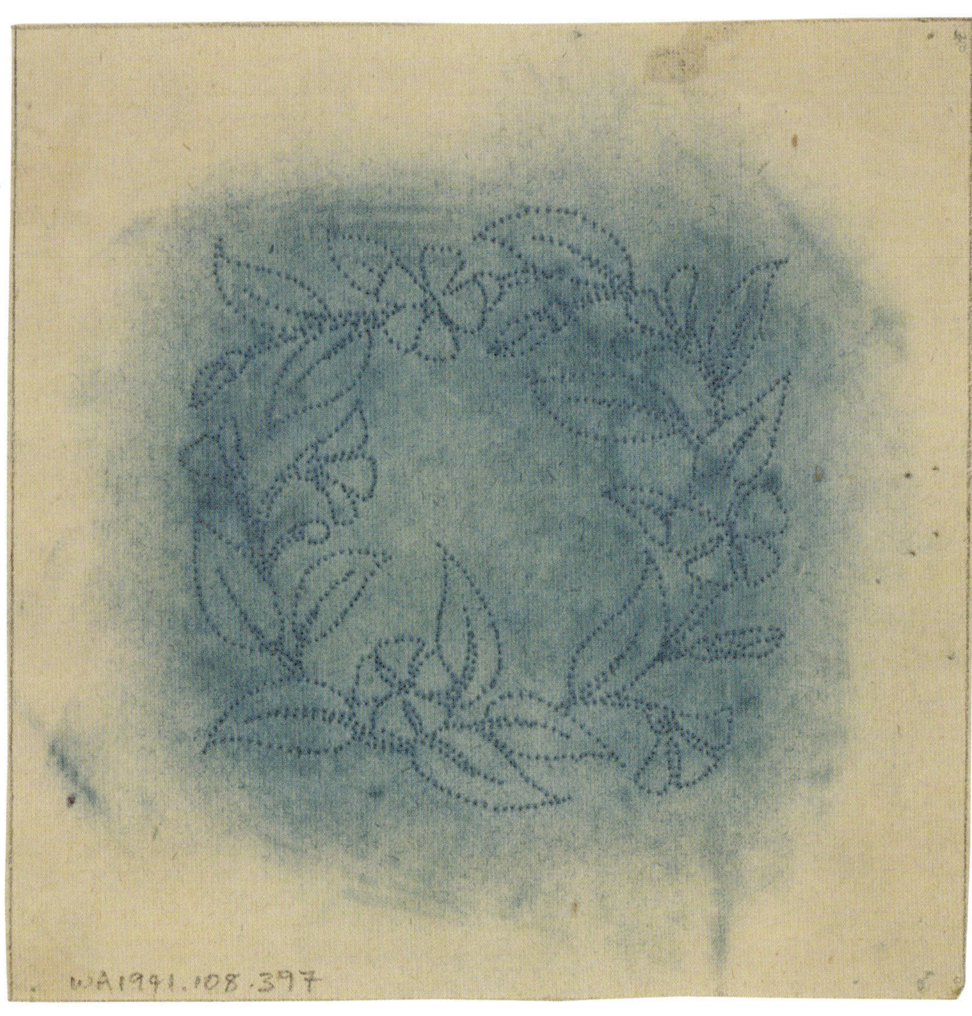

Fig.80 May Morris (1862–1938), drawing in graphite on fine cream paper; pricked and pounced with blue clay powder, 8.5 × 8.5 cm. Ashmolean Museum (WA1941.108.397)

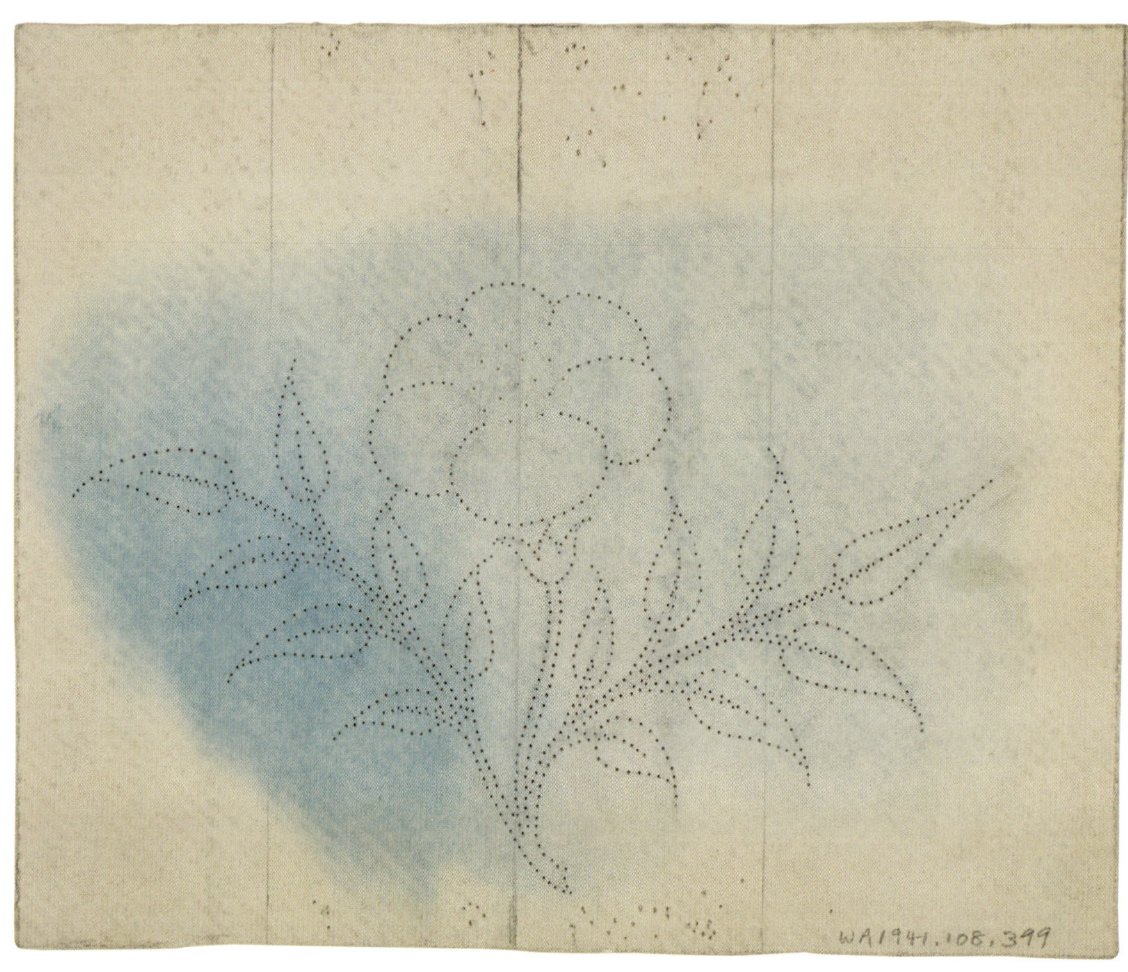

Fig.81 May Morris (1862–1938), drawing in graphite on cream thick laid paper; pricked and pounced with blue clay powder, 12.2 × 19 cm. Ashmolean Museum (WA1941.108.399)

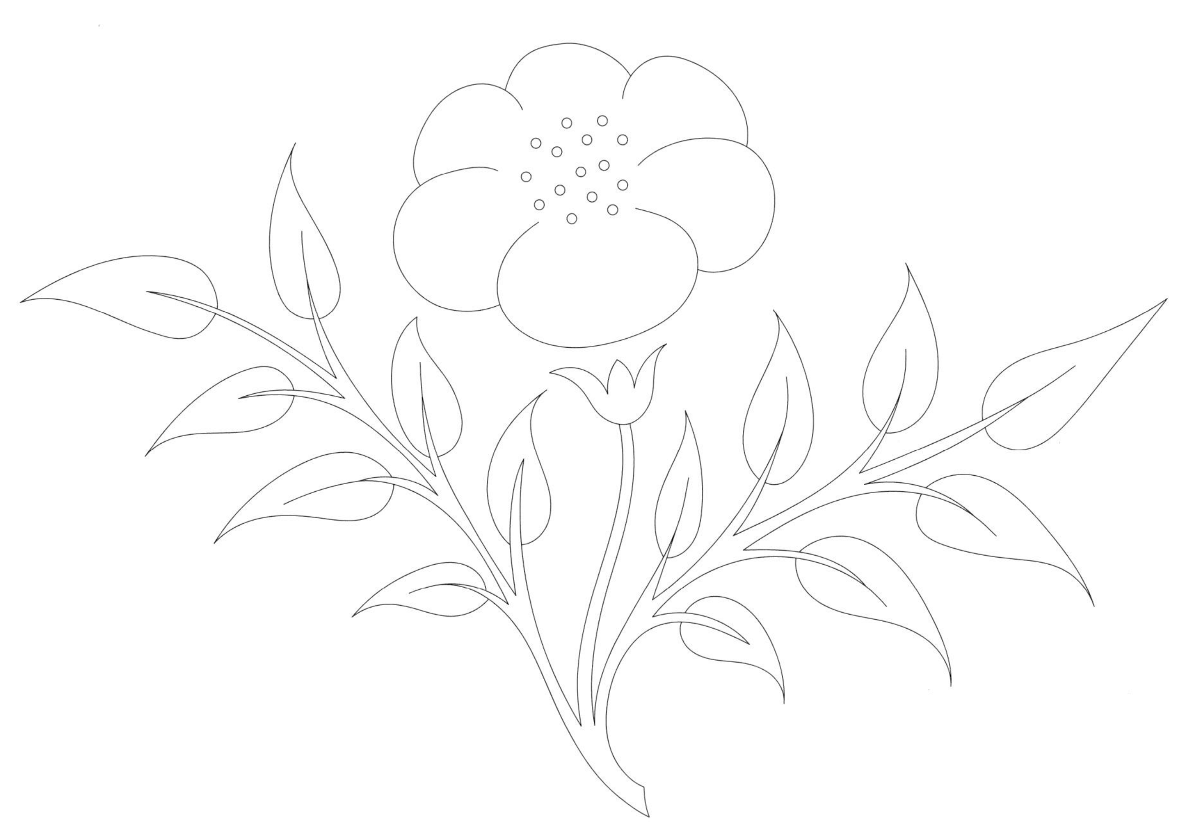

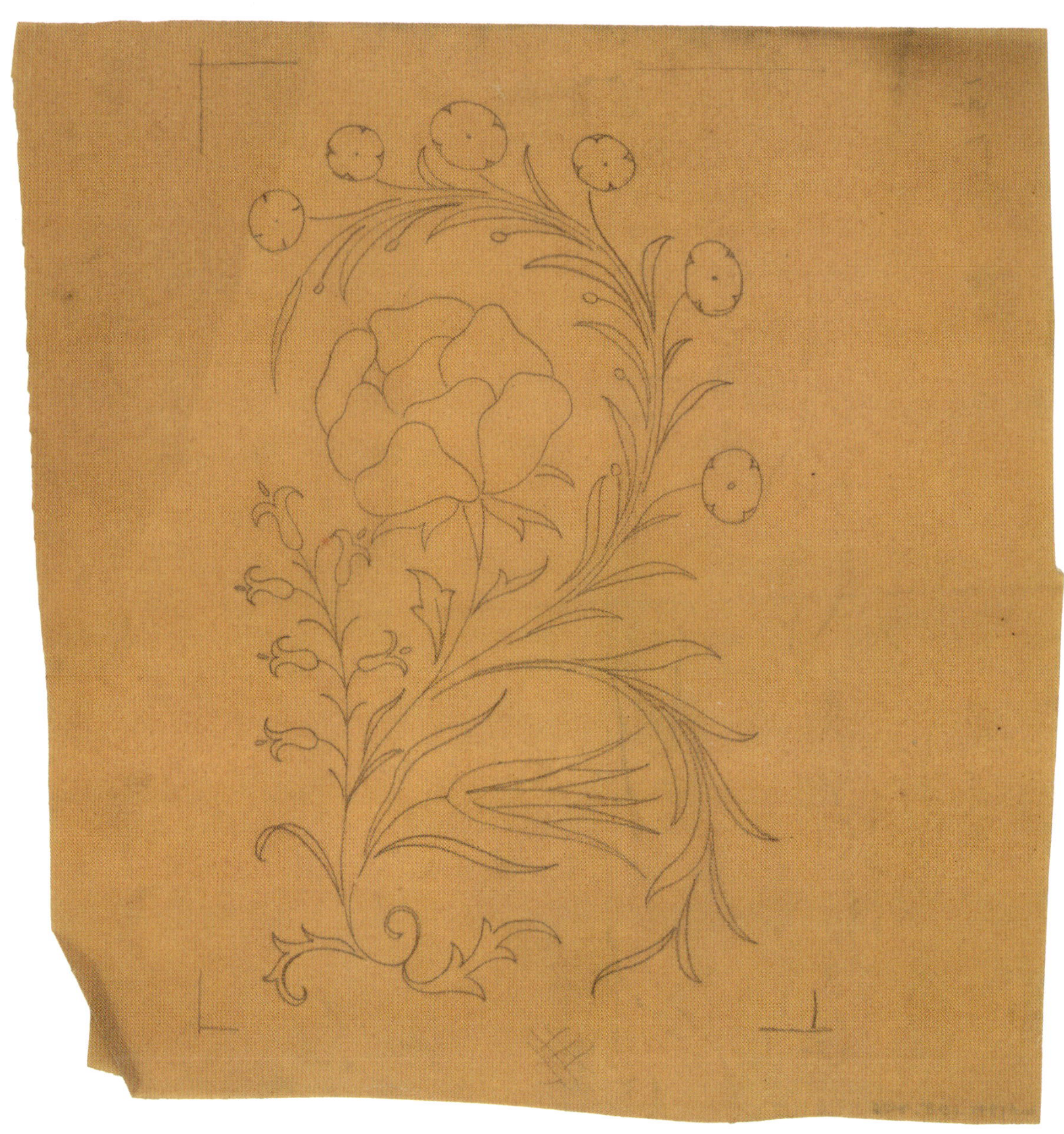

Fig.82 May Morris (1862–1938), drawing in graphite on tracing paper; pricked, 23 × 15.2 cm. Ashmolean Museum (WA1941.108.406)

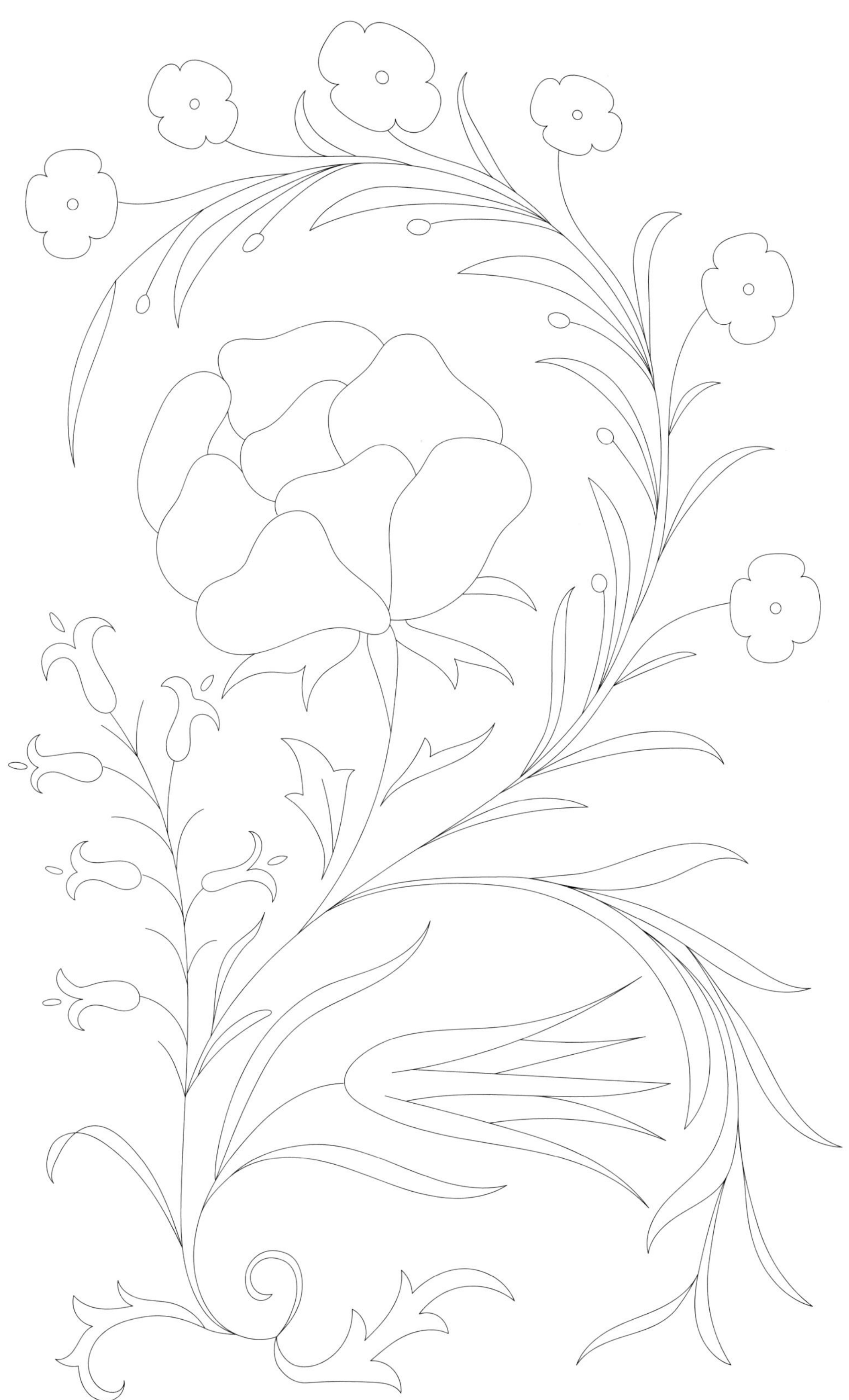

Fig.83 May Morris (1862–1938), drawing in graphite on tracing paper, 38.5 × 27.3 cm. Ashmolean Museum (WA1941.108.419)

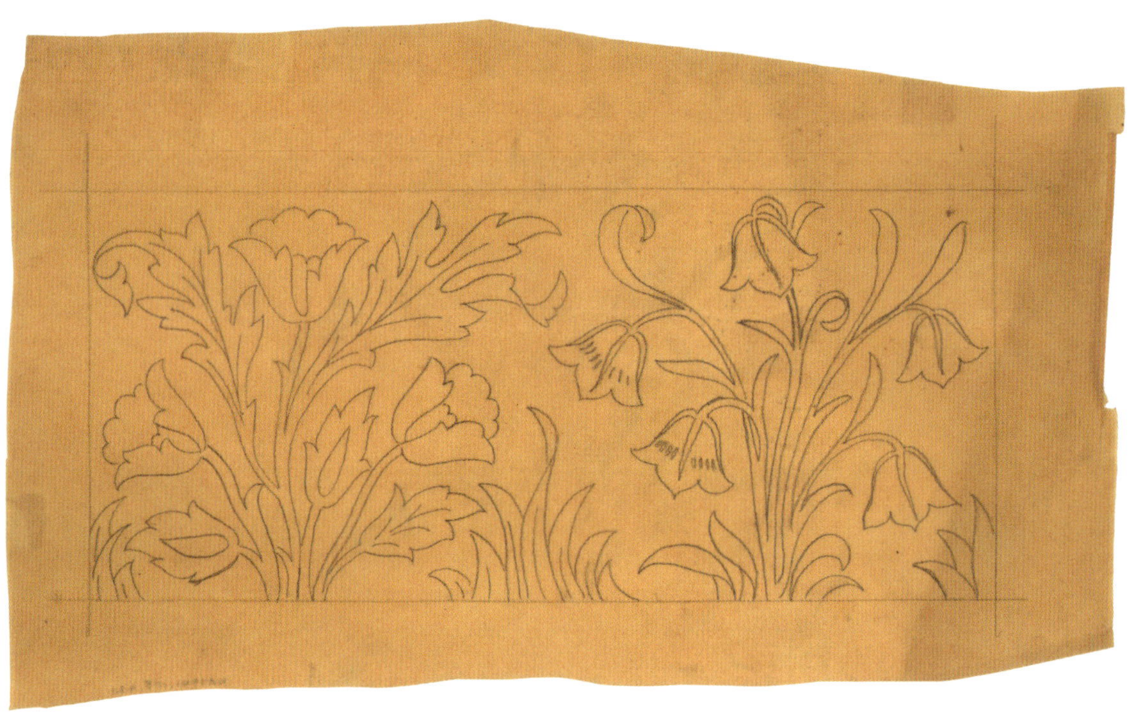

Fig.84 May Morris (1862–1938), drawing in graphite on tracing paper; pricked, 15 × 34.4 cm. Ashmolean Museum (WA1941.108.421)

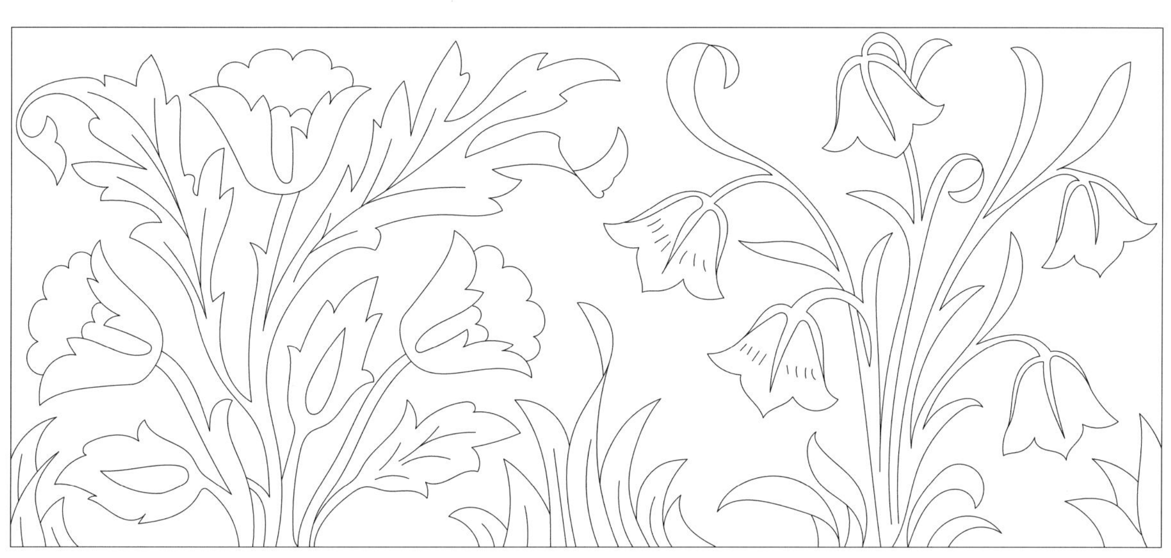

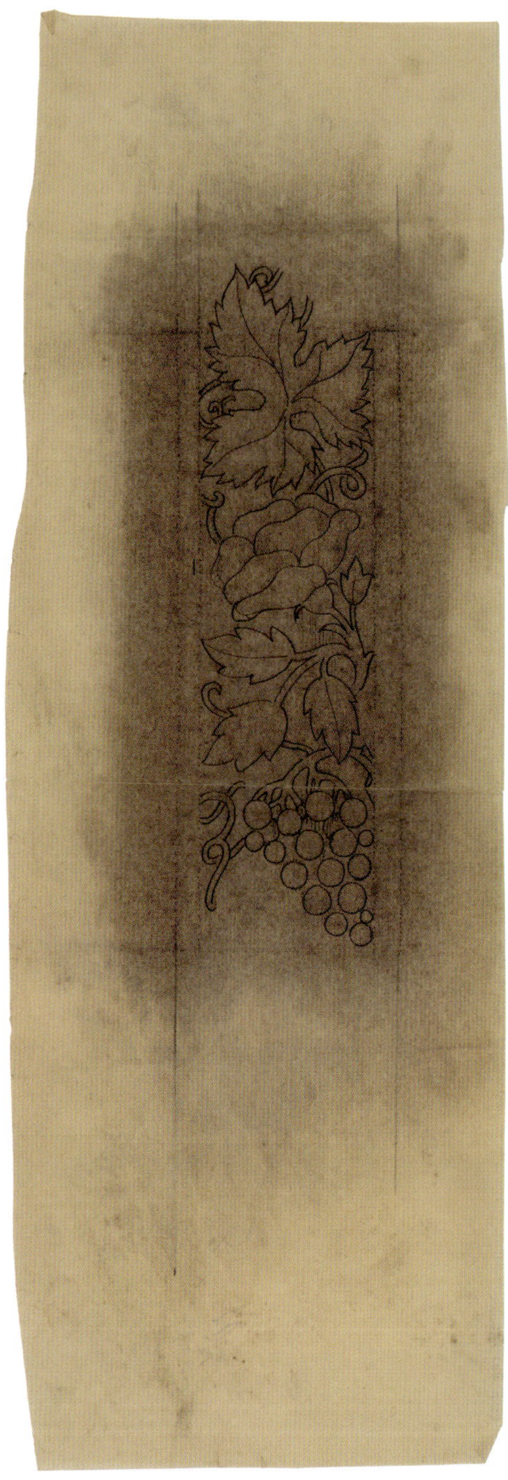

Fig.85 May Morris (1862–1938), drawing in pen and black ink on tracing paper; pricked and pounced with charcoal, 23 × 7.6 cm. Ashmolean Museum (WA1941.108.433)

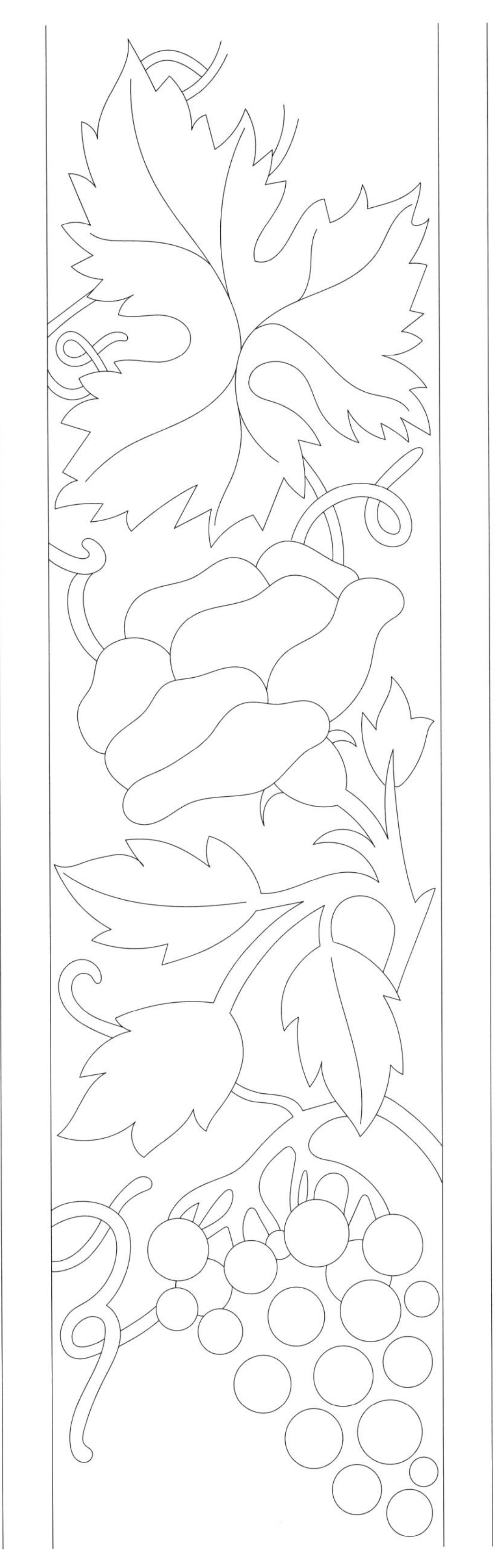

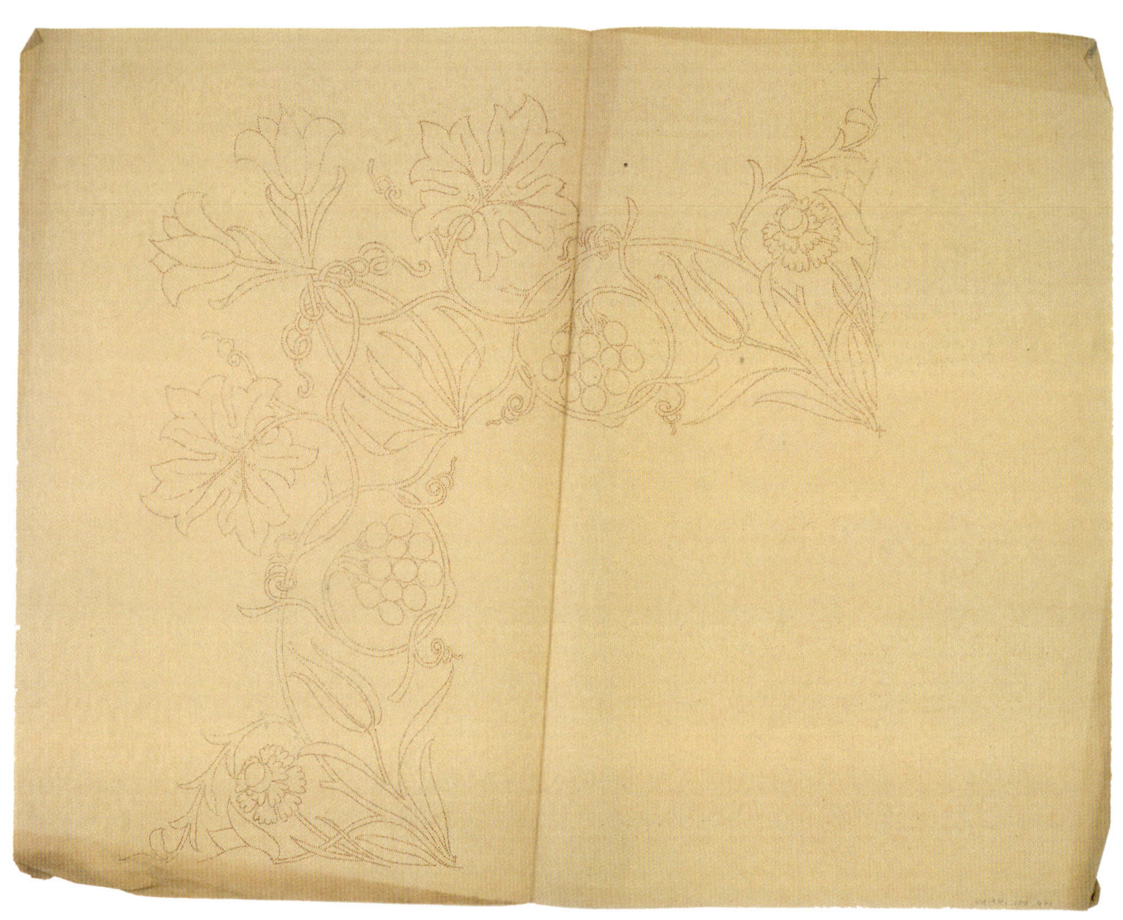

Fig.86 May Morris (1862–1938), tracing paper; pricked, 45.5 × 45.5 cm.
Ashmolean Museum (WA1941.108.441)

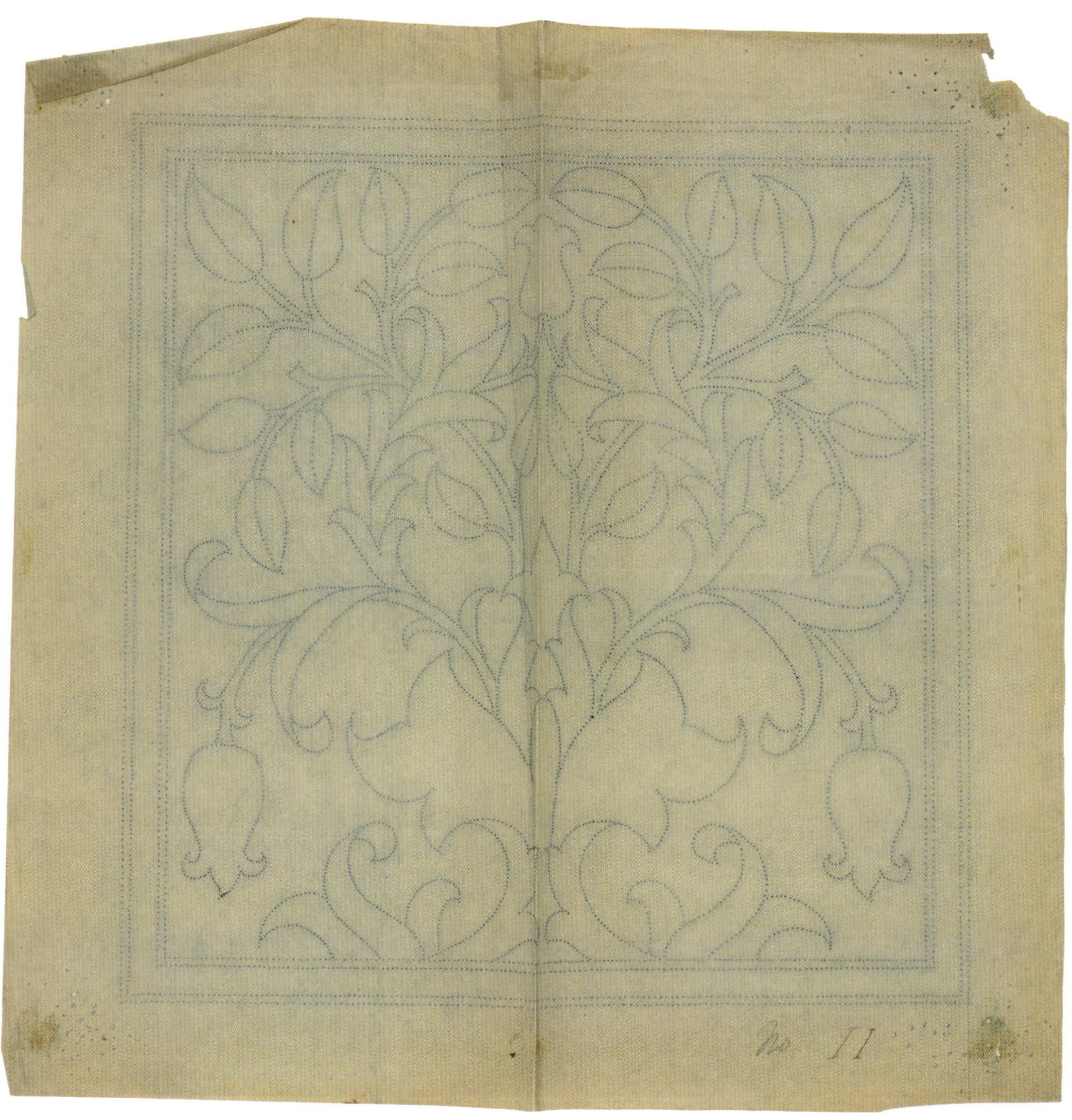

Fig.87 May Morris (1862–1938), tracing paper; pricked and pounced with blue clay powder, 39 × 38.8 cm. Ashmolean Museum (WA1941.108.450)

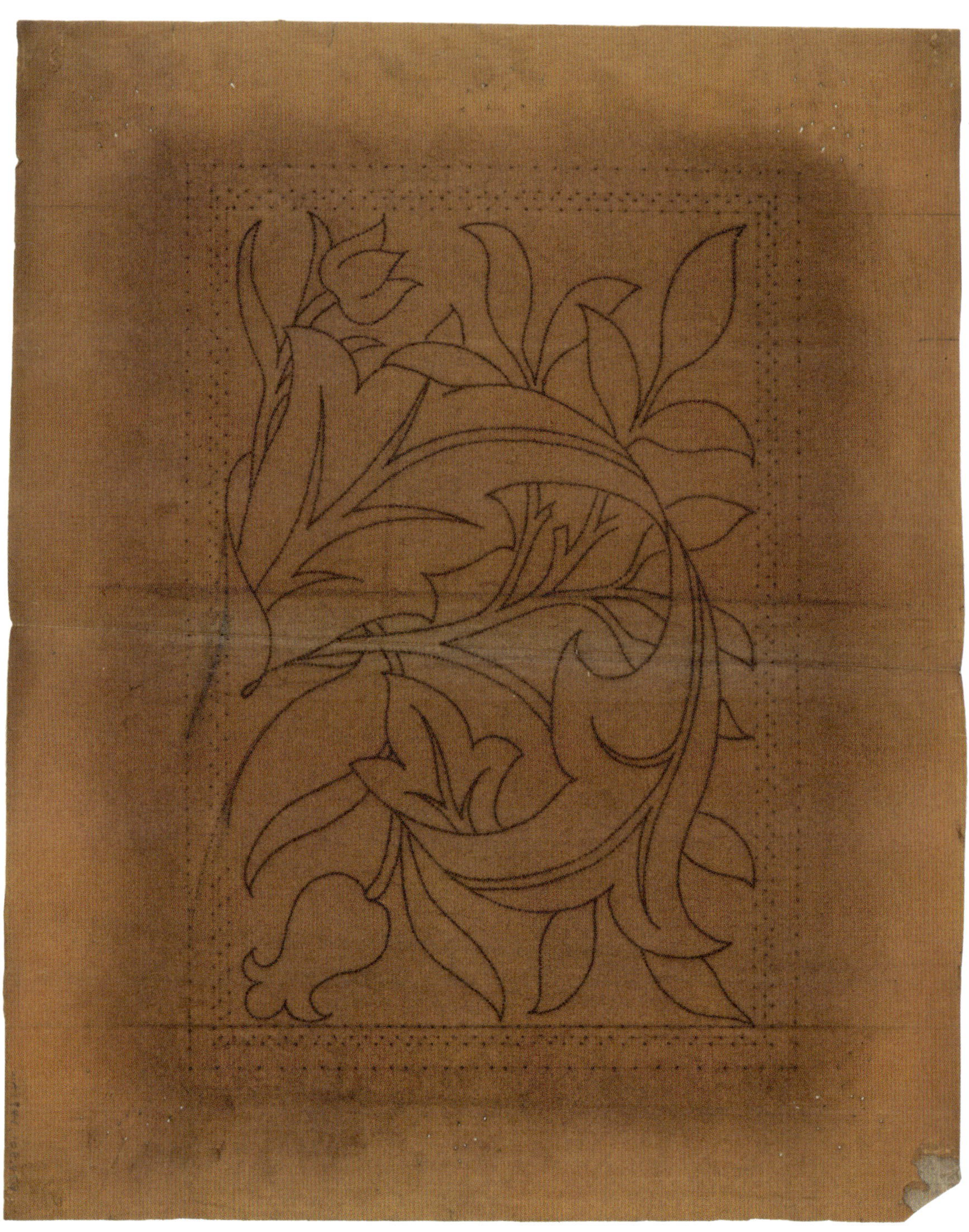

Fig.88 May Morris (1862–1938), drawing in graphite on tracing paper; pricked and pounced with charcoal, 33 × 22.8 cm. Ashmolean Museum (WA1941.108.453)

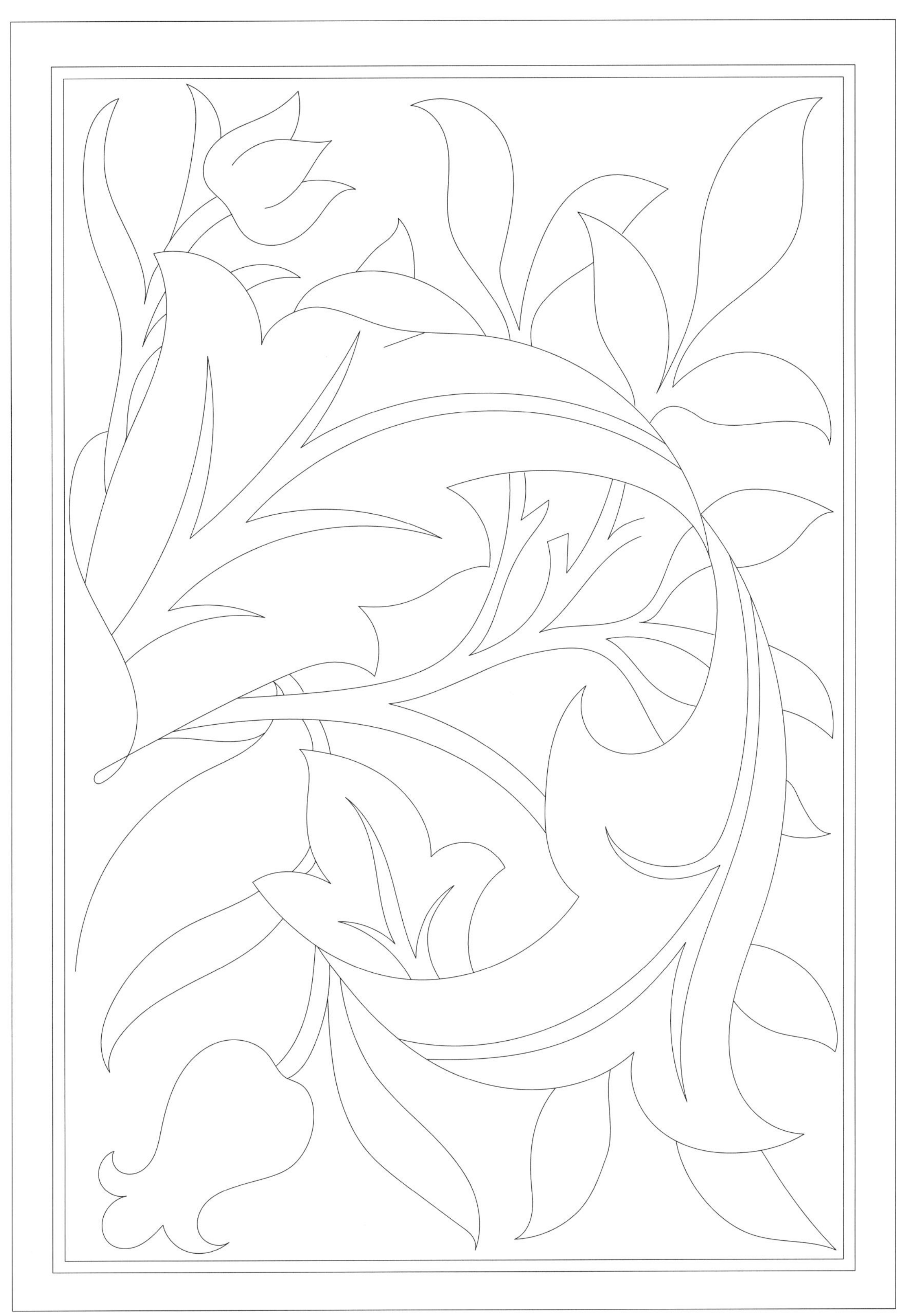

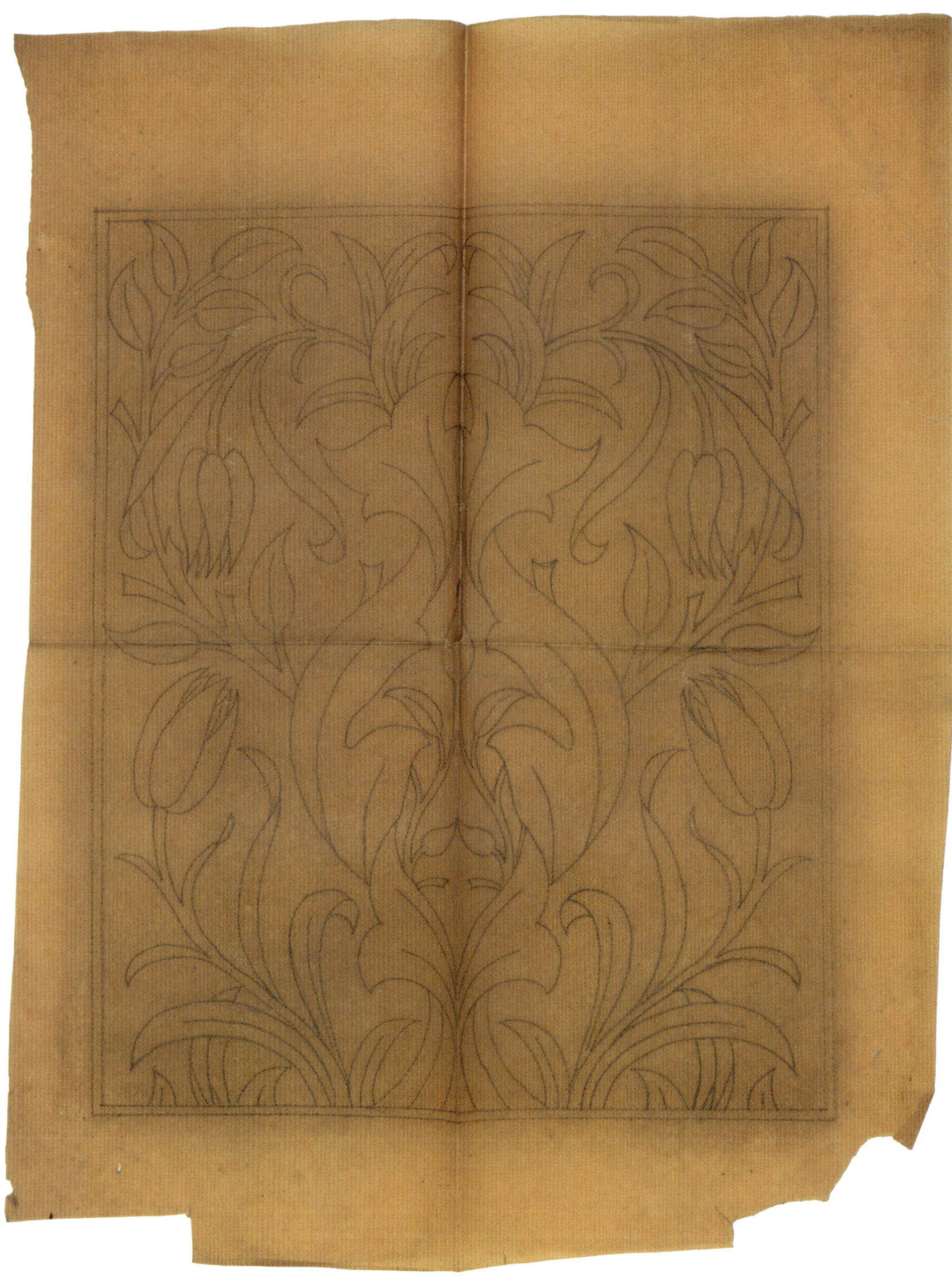

Fig.89 May Morris (1862–1938), drawing in graphite on tracing paper; pricked and pounced with charcoal, 48 × 40.8 cm. Ashmolean Museum (WA1941.108.455)

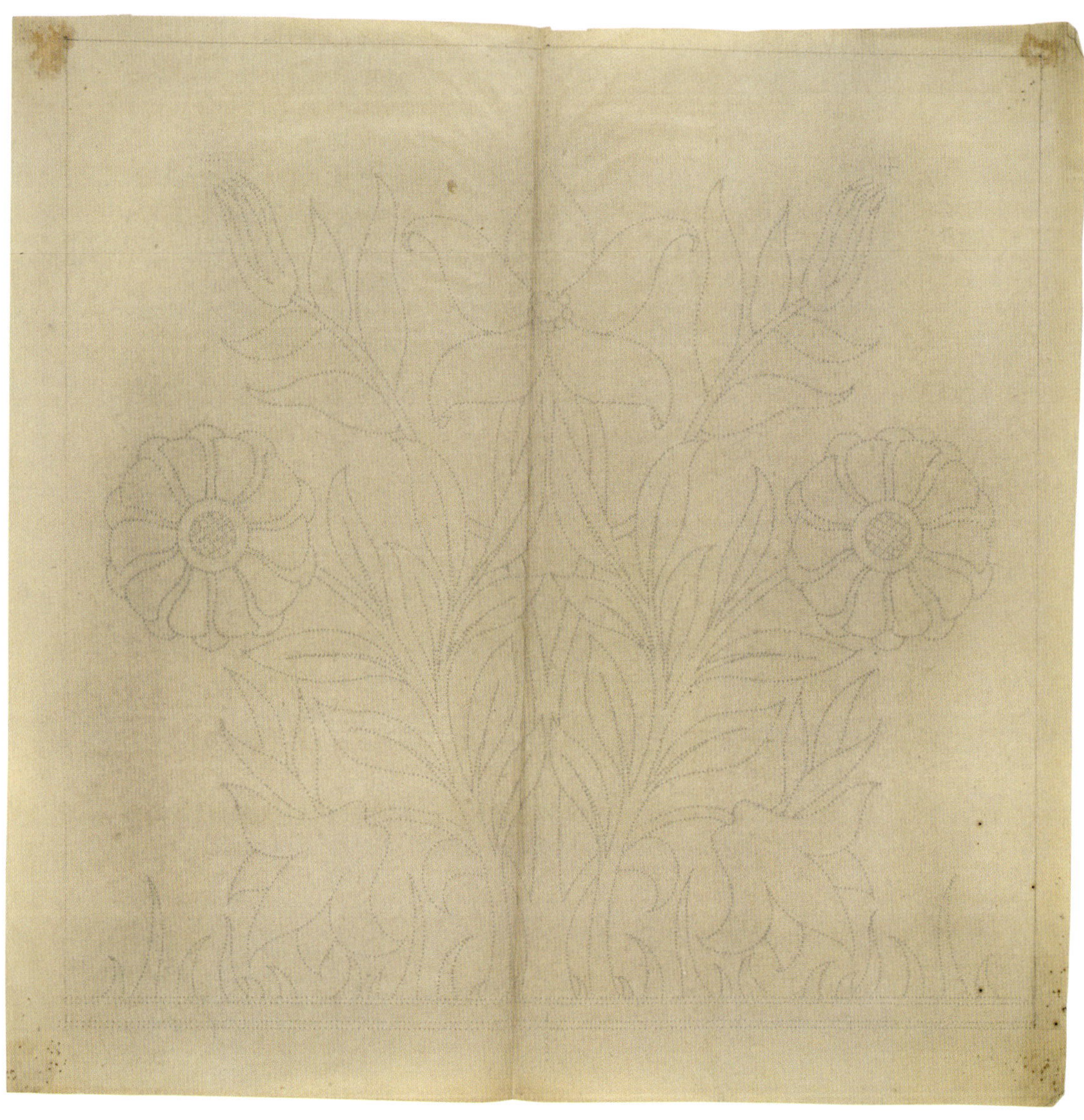

Fig.90 May Morris (1862–1938), tracing paper; pricked, 42 × 43 cm.
Ashmolean Museum (WA1941.108.458.1)

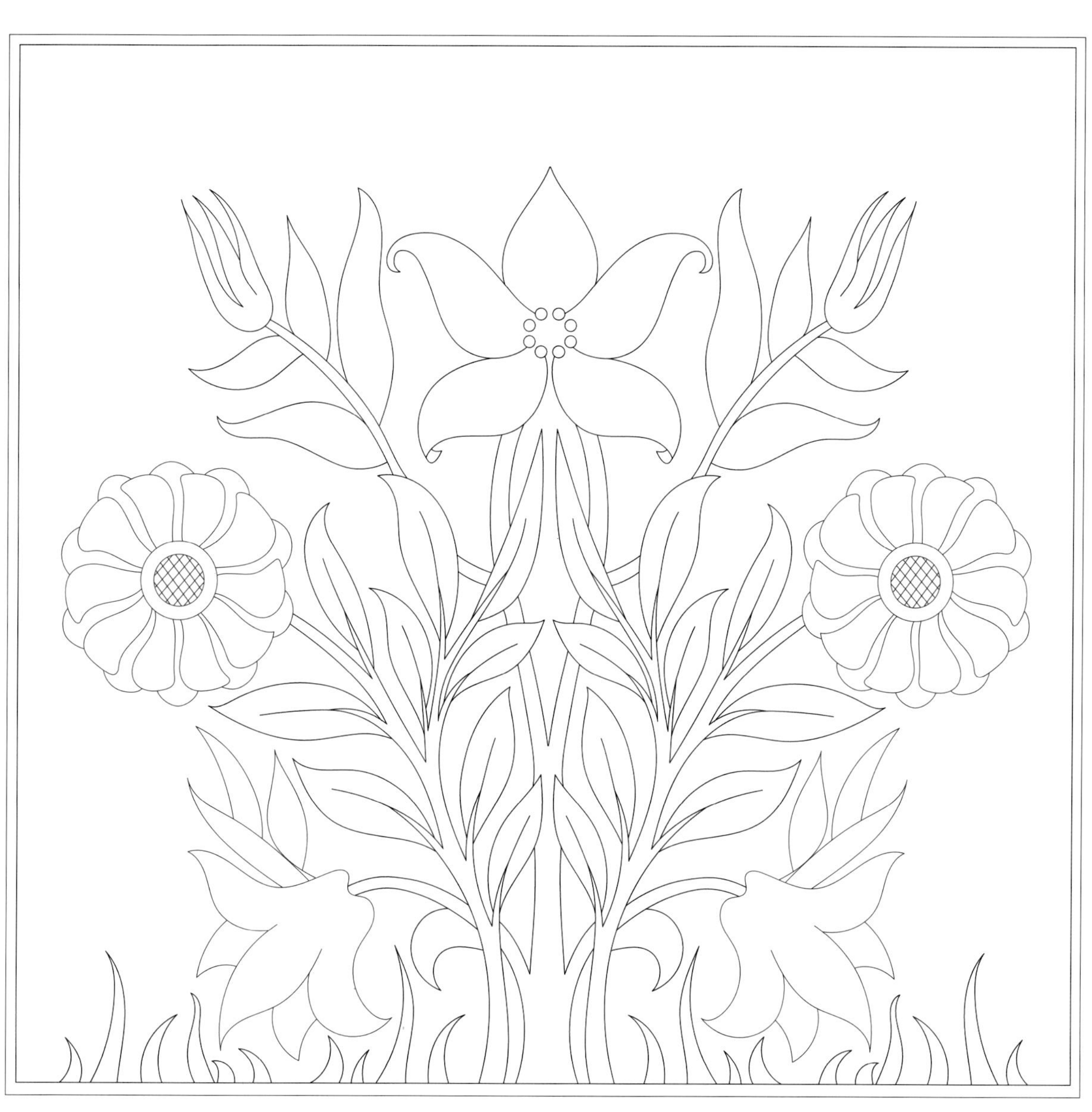

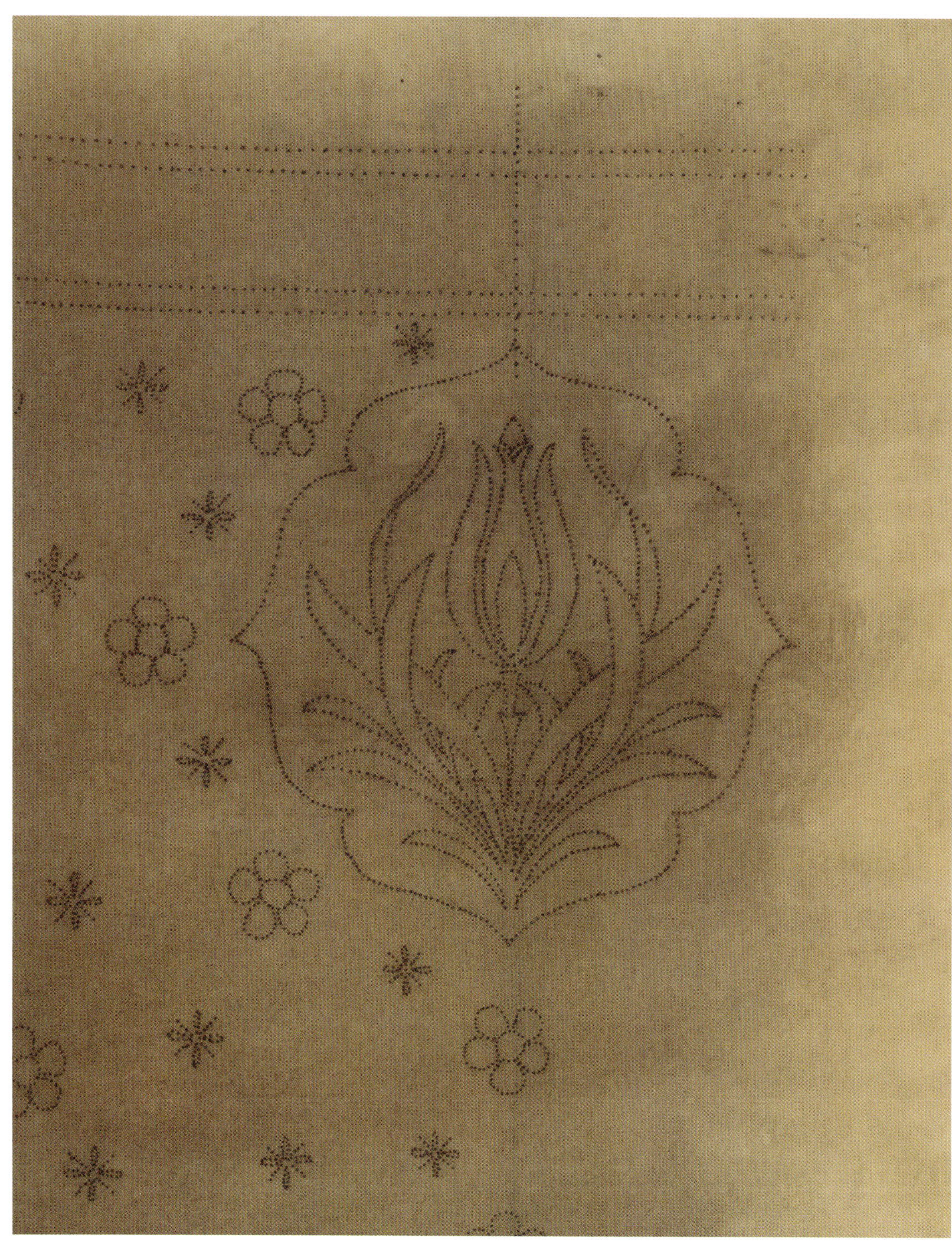

Fig.91 May Morris (1862–1938), tracing paper; pricked and pounced with charcoal, 18.5 × 18 cm. Ashmolean Museum (WA1941.108.461)

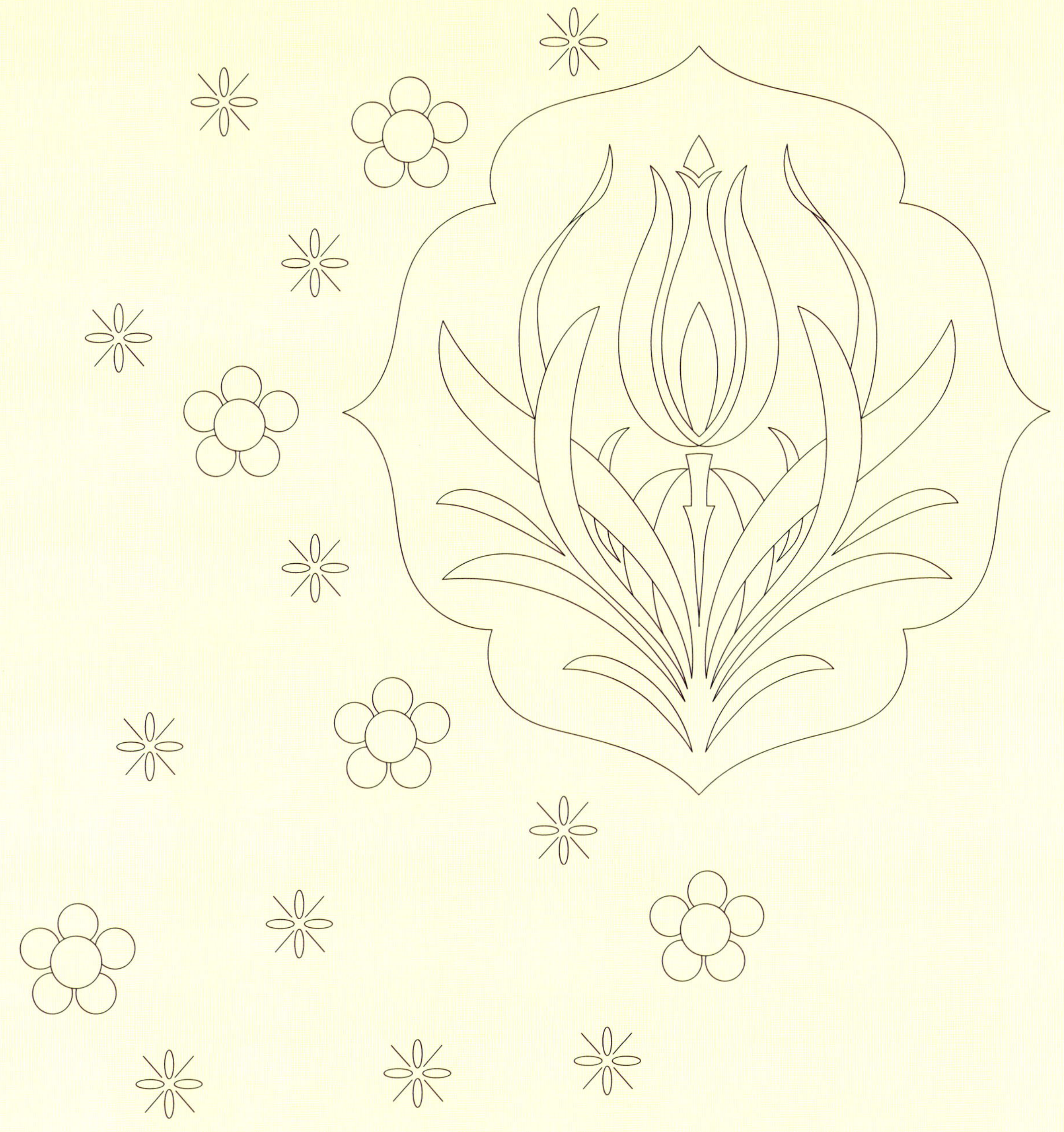

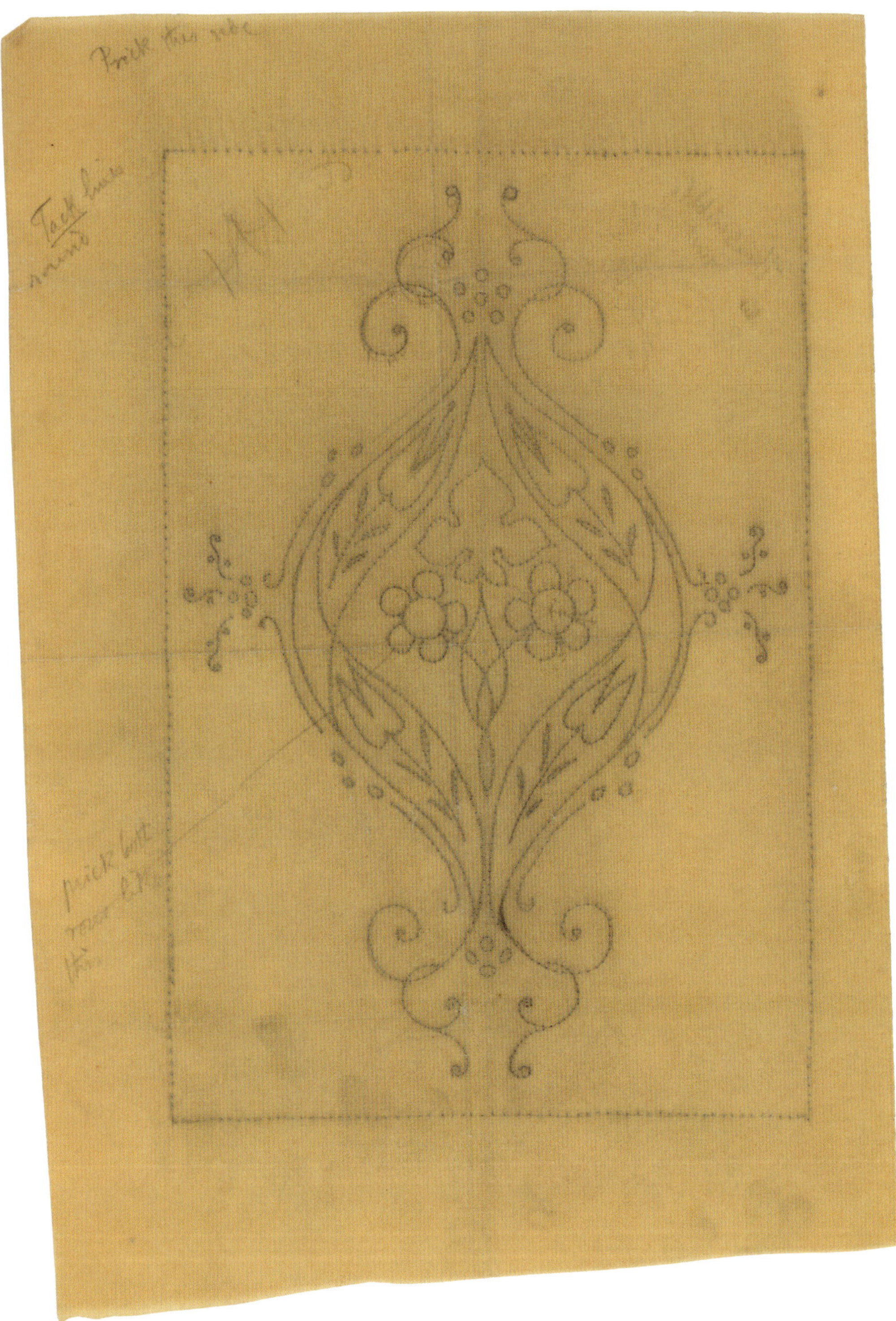

Fig.92 May Morris (1862–1938), drawing in graphite on tracing paper; pricked with some evidence of pouncing with charcoal, 21 × 14.3 cm. Ashmolean Museum (WA1941.108.462)

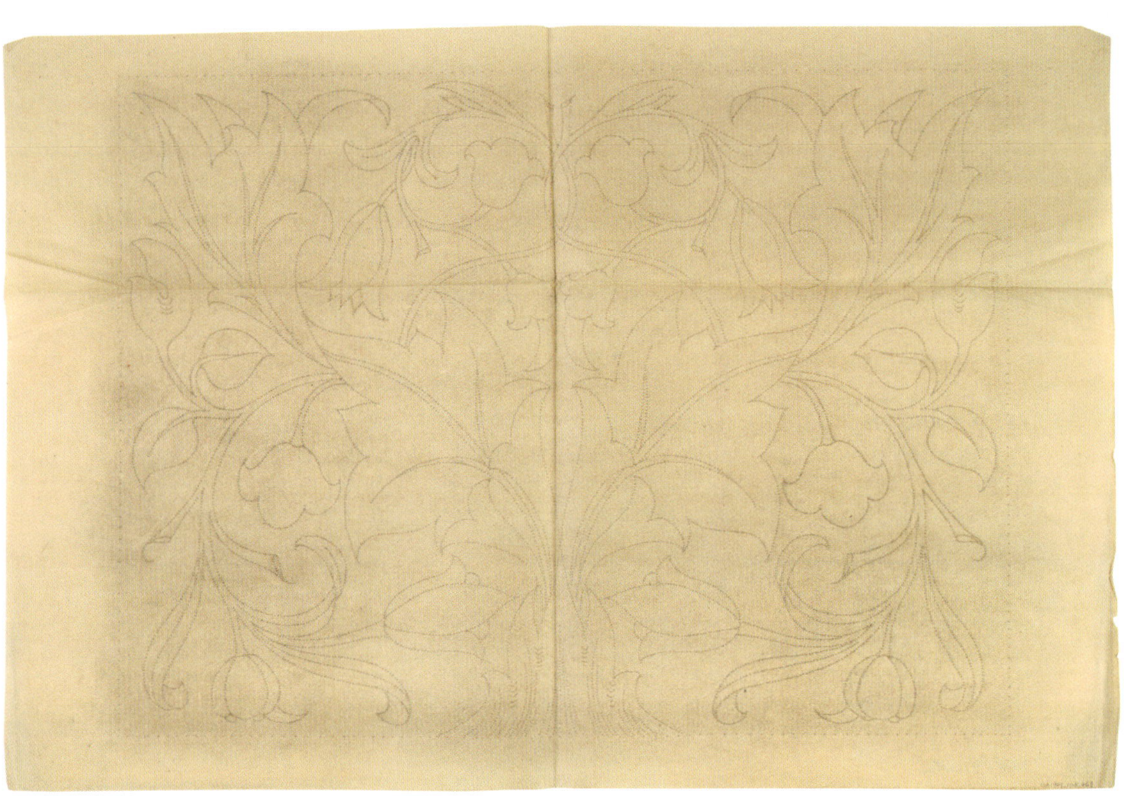

Fig.93 May Morris (1862–1938), drawing in graphite on tracing paper; pricked and pounced with charcoal, 44.2 × 61 cm. Ashmolean Museum (WA1941.108.463)

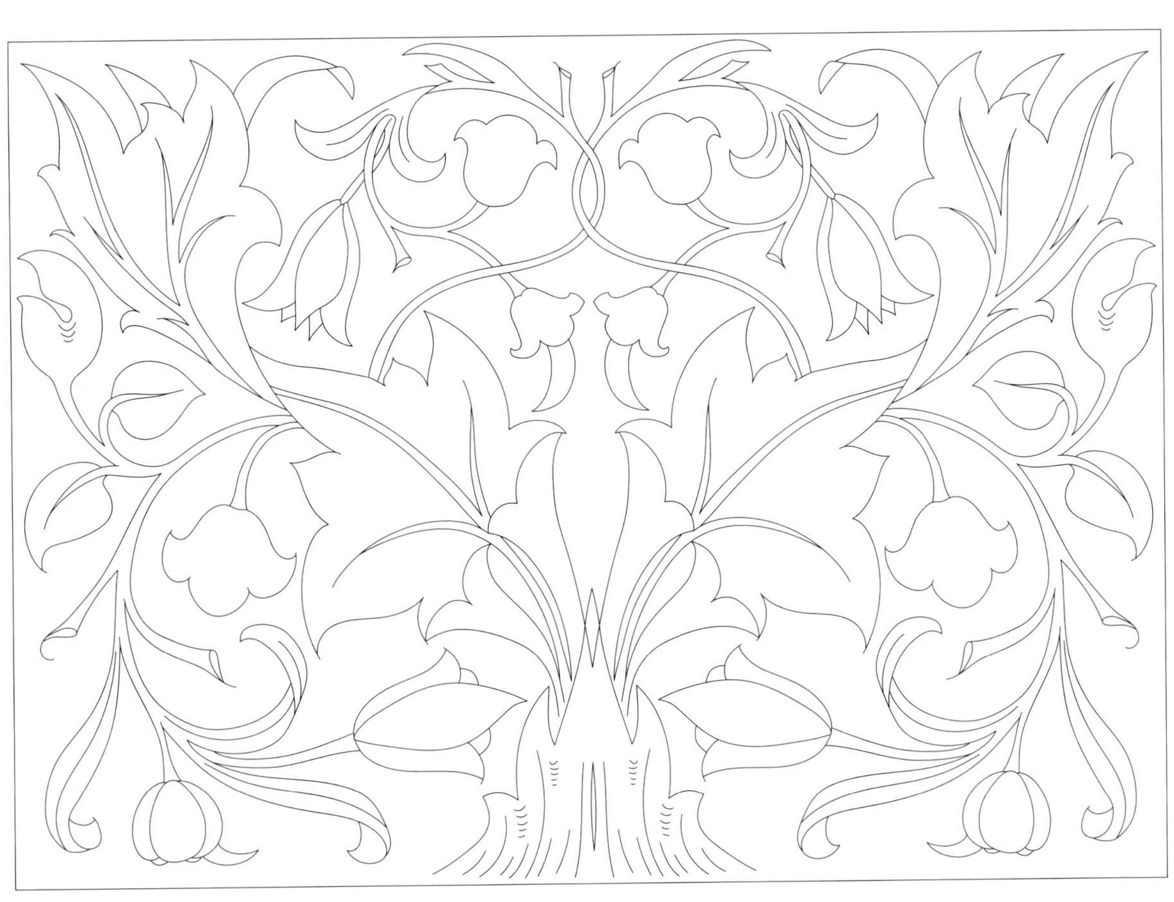

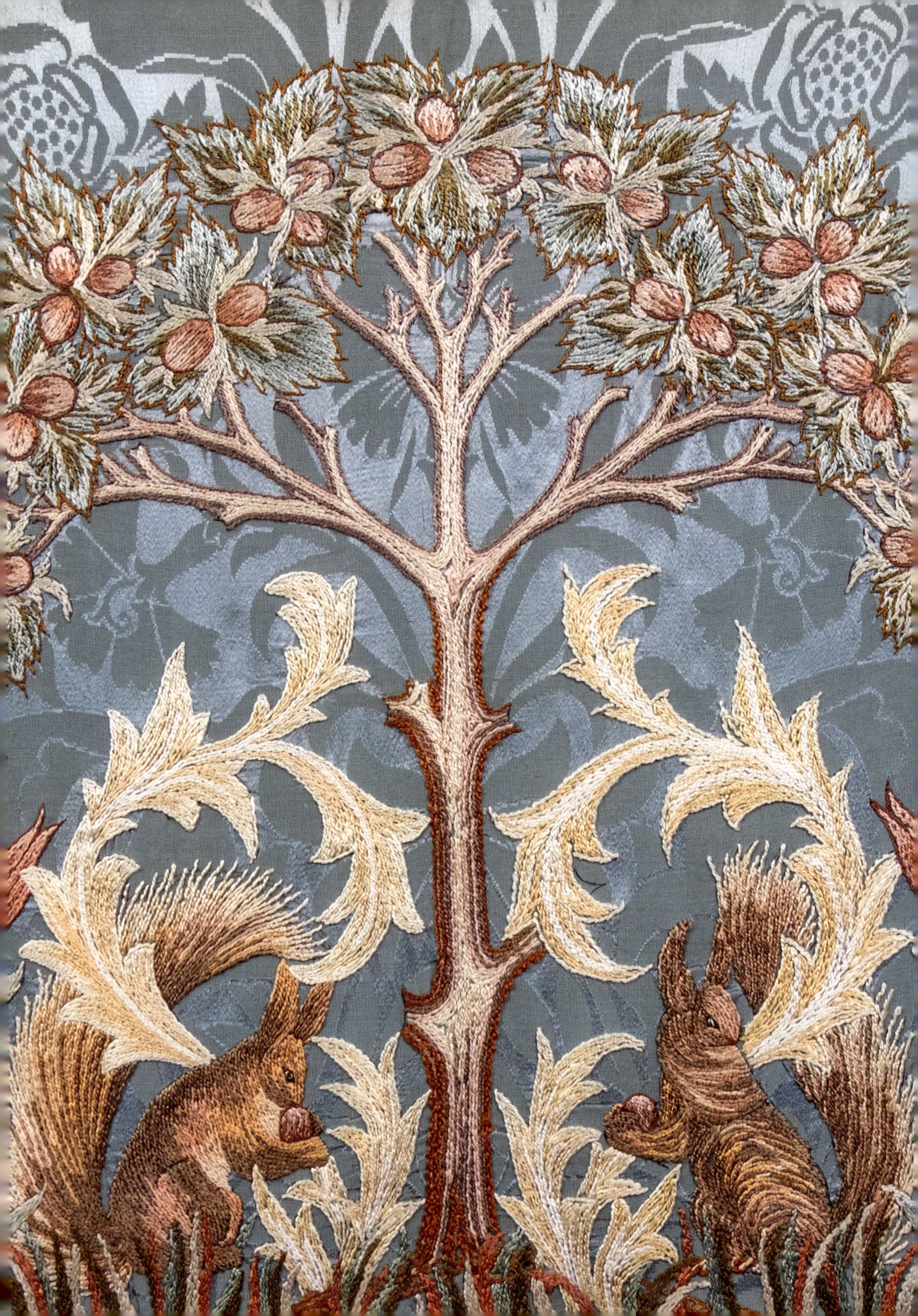

Afterword

In a letter to her American friend Margaret Peirce in January 1935, May Morris wrote:

> After the long and tiring year I think I got thoroughly run down so here I am having to "take care" which is such a nuisance. Luckily I've been able to use my eyes, so I have done a lot of reading while in bed. Now I get about a bit, and embroider a little which is pleasant (though nobody wants my work now-a-days).[1]

After the First World War, the public taste for art embroidery waned to such an extent that the RSAN dropped the word 'Art' from its title in 1922, becoming simply the Royal School of Needlework. Around the same time, May resorted to stitching canvas work owing to the high demand for petit point, even though she deplored it.

Frustrated with the neglect that May's work suffered in the years leading up to her death in October 1938, Mary Lobb outlined her companion's consummate skills in a forthright letter to the director of the Victoria and Albert Museum:

> William Morris could design embroideries but he could not embroider, anyway not as well…Mrs Morris could embroider but couldn't design. Miss Morris could and did both design as well as William Morris and embroider as well [as] any one…and her colour arrangements were unapproachable and original. To design, make and colour work which will hold its own and quite often far outstrip [others]… is what so few grasp and appreciate. They need to have their noses rubbed in it.[2]

Fortunately, in the twenty-first century, May's work is receiving the recognition it so rightly deserves. Her embroideries are much sought after in the saleroom, and her life and work are the subject of extensive study. The union of art historical knowledge and craft practice that distinguishes May as a pioneer of decorative needlework in the late nineteenth and early twentieth centuries is an inspiration for modern designers and embroiderers.

Opposite: detail of fig.21

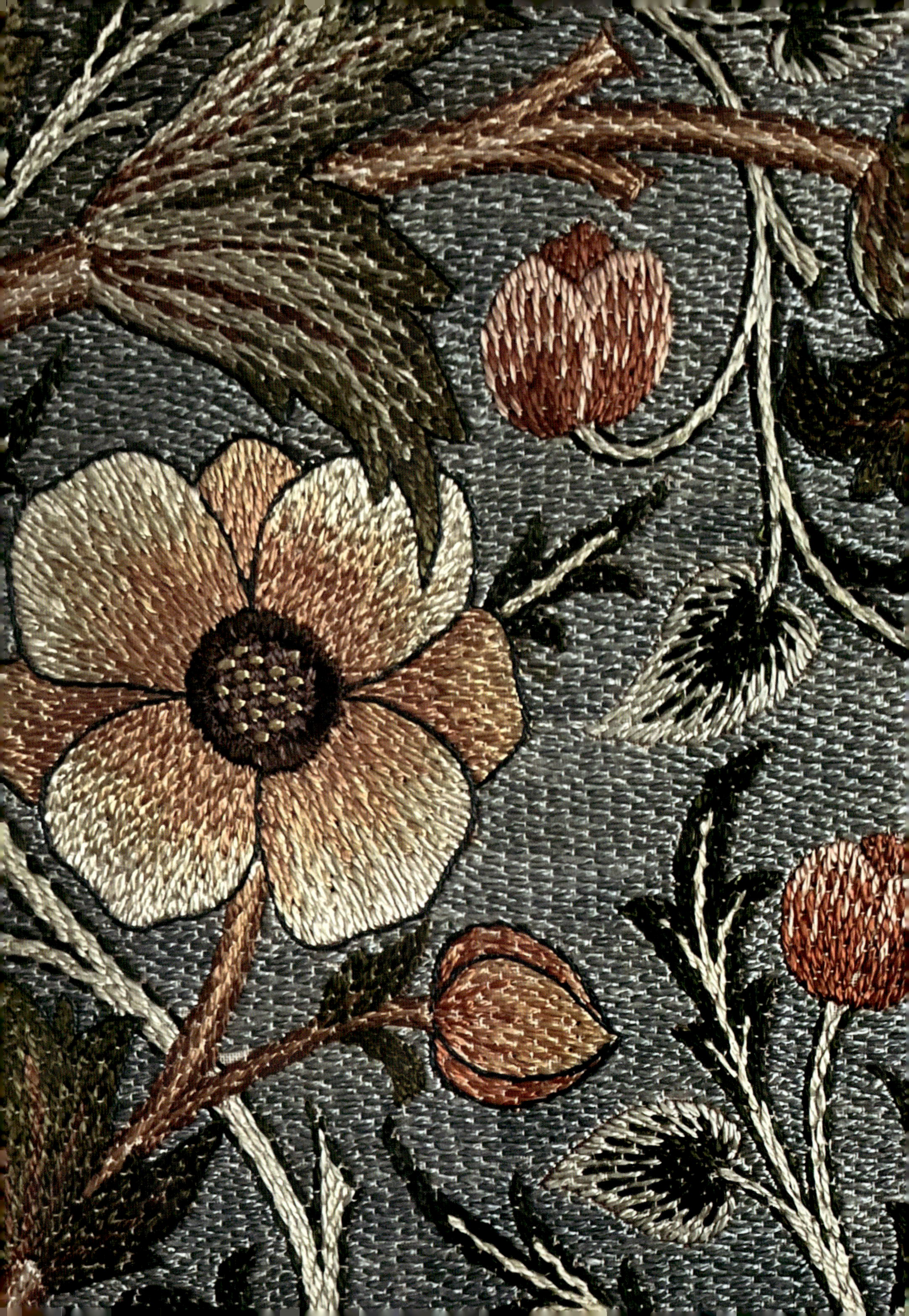

Technical samples*

These technical samples are designed to supplement the text in Chapter 2, and to give readers further insight into May Morris's working practice in relation to stitch, as set down in her manual *Decorative Needlework* and in her lecture notes.

CHAIN STITCH

When stitching in relief, May embroidered the outline in one, two or even three adjacent rows of chain stitch in contrasting colours, leaving the rest bare, except for the centre veining (**fig.94**). Occasionally, she added an inner row of decorative running stitches or filled the interior with seeding or speckling stitch (**fig.95**).

When using solid work, May filled leaves or flower petals with adjacent rows of chain stitch, beginning with the outline and working towards the centre, using a single colour or rows of contrasting shades, as in the tulips and lily in **fig.96**.

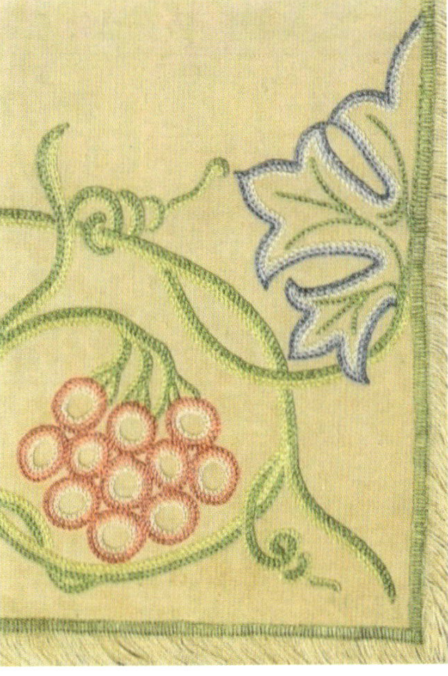

Fig.94 May Morris (1862–1938), Detail from *Vine and pinks* tray cover, 1890s, polychrome silks on linen, 86.4 × 52.1 cm, V&A, T.120–1939.

*For more information on how to work the stitches, see the Royal School of Needlework stitch bank, https://rsnstitchbank.org [20 February 2025]

Opposite: detail of fig.97

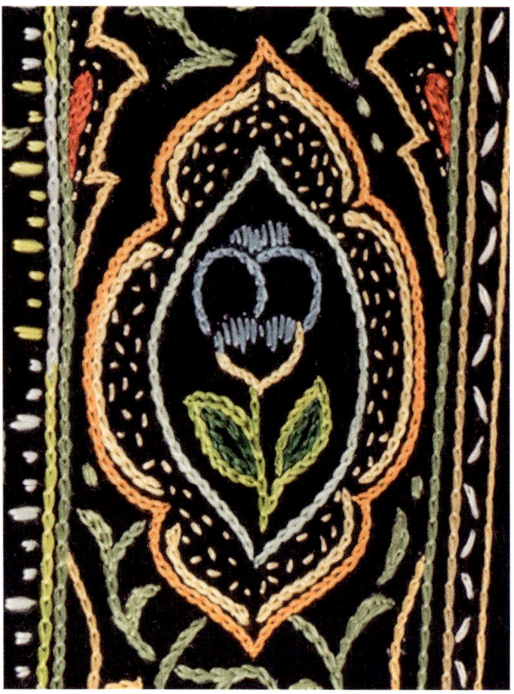

Fig.95 May Morris (1862–1938), Detail from a cloak embroidered by May Morris and Maude Deacon, *c.*1897, polychrome silks on fine wool, 123 × 297 cm. William Morris Gallery, F204.

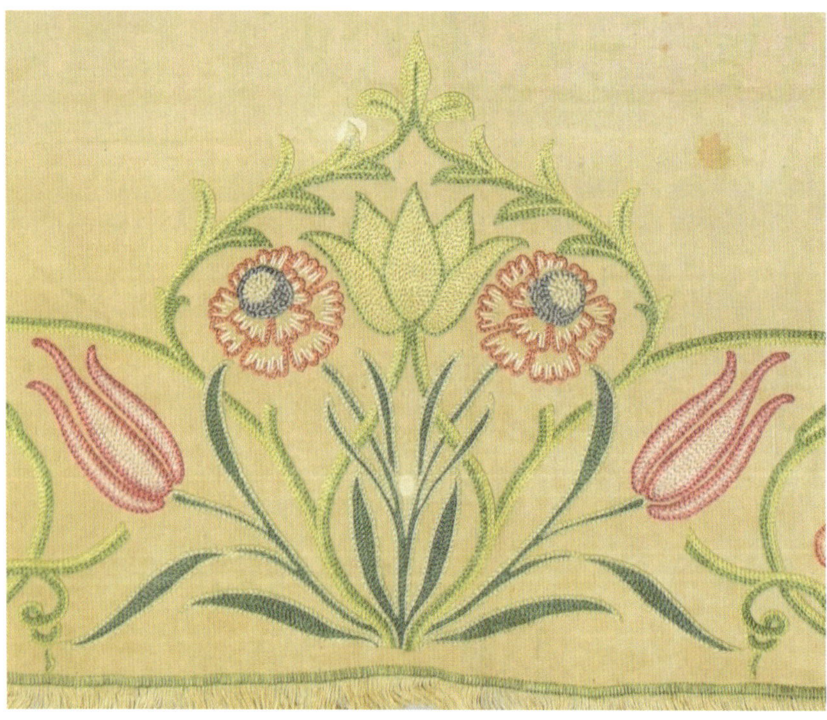

Fig.96 May Morris (1862–1938), Detail from *Vine and pinks* tray cover, 1890s, polychrome silks on linen, 86.4 × 52.1 cm, V&A, T.120–1939.

FRENCH KNOTS

May used French knots to fill flower centres; see, for example, the pinks illustrated in **fig.96**. To give texture to the surface, she recommended looping the thread several times around the needle before taking it back through the cloth, next to where it first emerged, to secure the knot.

DARNING

In the Morris & Co. kits worked in darning stitch on Manchester cloth, the rows of parallel stitches are set about one thickness of the working thread distant from one another, the needle running in and out through the material, following the line of the weft threads to create a woven surface. Only one or two warp threads of the cloth are taken up between each stitch (**fig.97**). The stitches are offset to create a brick pattern arrangement. To avoid the work becoming too regimented or machine-like, the stitches in alternate rows do not align with each other.

To work the botanical motifs in darning, the stitches run in and out through the warp and weft threads of the fabric ground, following the shape of the flower petals and leaves, and the curves of the stems. The single threads of Manchester cloth taken up between each stitch appear as vertical or horizontal cream flecks across the surface of the silk embroidery, as in the anemone petals illustrated in **fig.98**.

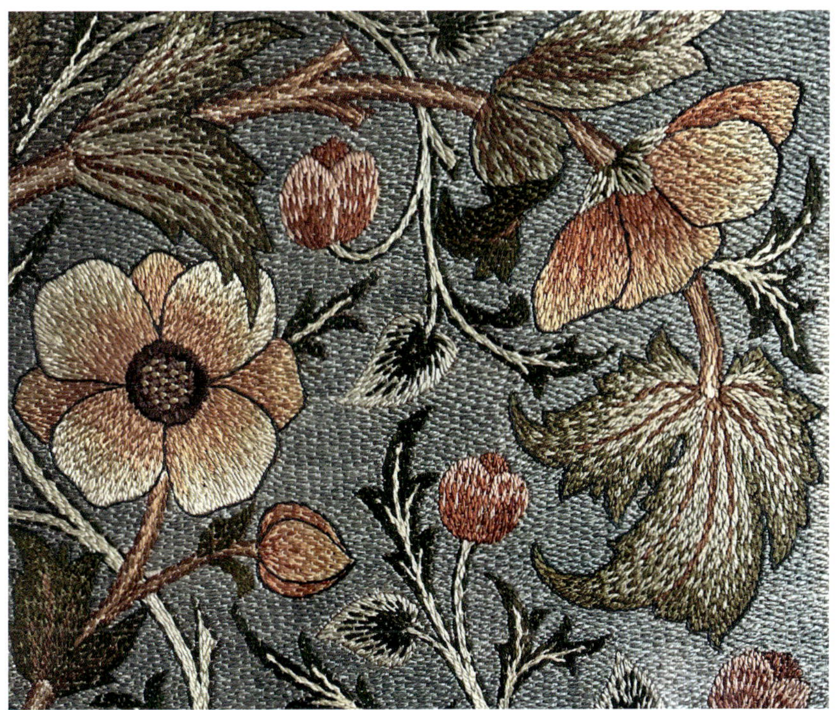

Fig.97 John Henry Dearle (1859–1932), Detail from *Anemone* screen panel, *c.*1885–90, stitched by May Morris, 1890s, polychrome silks on Manchester cloth, 132.5 × 53 cm. Private collection

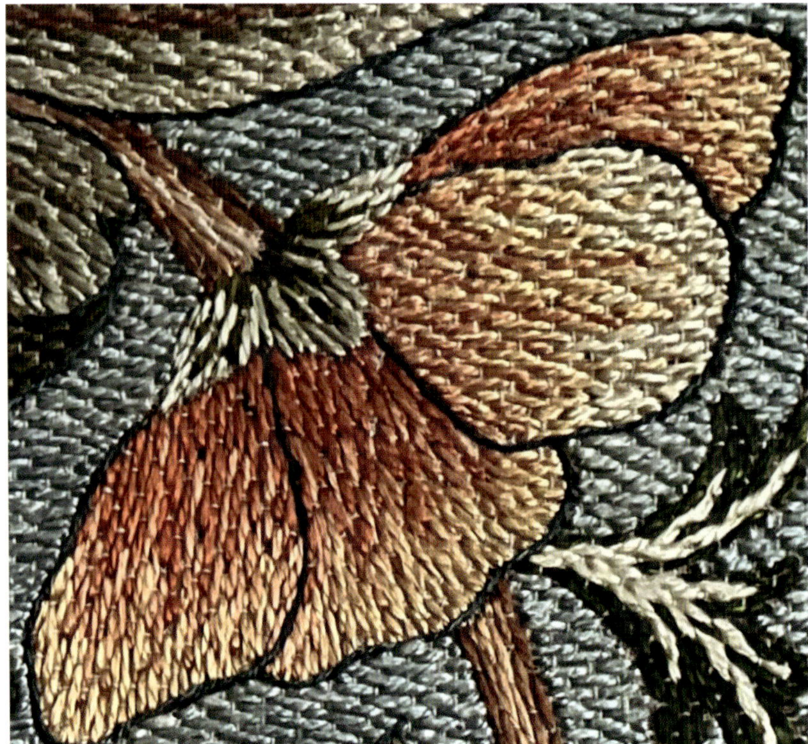

Fig.98 John Henry Dearle (1859–1932), Detail from *Anemone* screen panel, *c.*1885–90, stitched by May Morris, 1890s, polychrome silks on Manchester cloth, 132.5 × 53 cm. Private collection

STEM OR OUTLINE STITCH

Despite May describing it as 'stem', the stitch illustrated in *Decorative Needlework* is technically speaking 'outline' stitch (**fig.99**).[1] The working thread lies above or to the left of the needle to create a row of stitches that slant bottom right to top left. This seems to have been May's preferred method for working the stitch, though there are instances of her using stem, or even a combination of stem and outline stitch to create a plait effect, as in this example of a flower stem (**fig.100**).

May used outline stitch to define flowers, stems and leaves in darning work. She also utilised rows of closely worked outline stitch to fill leaves and stems, or to execute knotwork patterns (**fig.101**).

LONG & SHORT

May includes a brief section on long & short in her technical guidebook and provides a diagram showing readers how to work the first row, 'starting from the outer line, the stitches radiating slightly from the centre'. However, May's instructions are not particularly helpful when it comes to working the second row; she merely notes that it may be added 'within' in a contrasting shade, 'but for the sake of clearness it is not shown here'.[2] The answer lies in her lecture

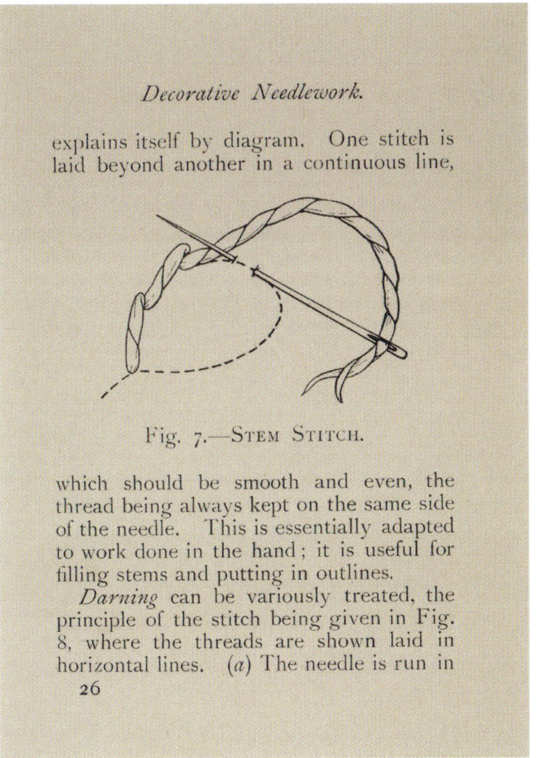

Decorative Needlework.

explains itself by diagram. One stitch is laid beyond another in a continuous line,

Fig. 7.—STEM STITCH.

which should be smooth and even, the thread being always kept on the same side of the needle. This is essentially adapted to work done in the hand; it is useful for filling stems and putting in outlines.

Darning can be variously treated, the principle of the stitch being given in Fig. 8, where the threads are shown laid in horizontal lines. (*a*) The needle is run in

26

Fig.99 May Morris (1862–1938), *Decorative Needlework* (1893), fig.7, 22.7 × 18.4 cm. Private collection

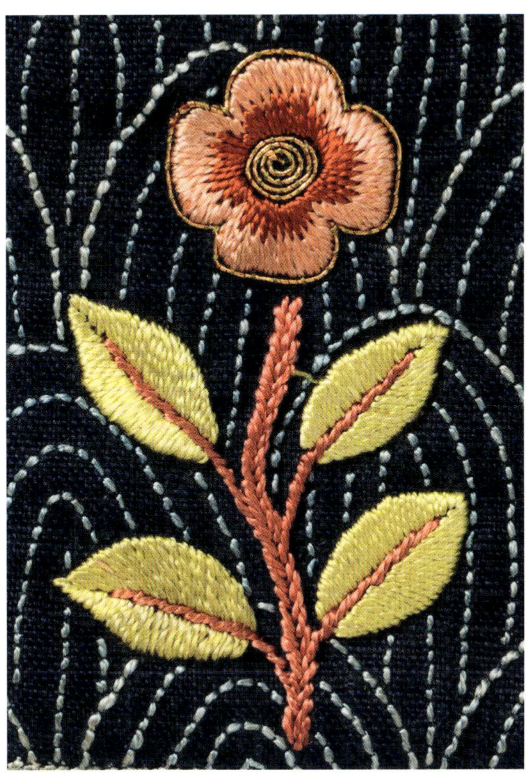

Fig.100 May Morris (1862–1938), Detail from a book bag for William Morris's medieval psalter, 1890s, stitched by May and her sister Jenny, polychrome silks and Japanese gold and indigo-dyed linen, 22.8 × 15.4 cm, William Morris Gallery, F337.

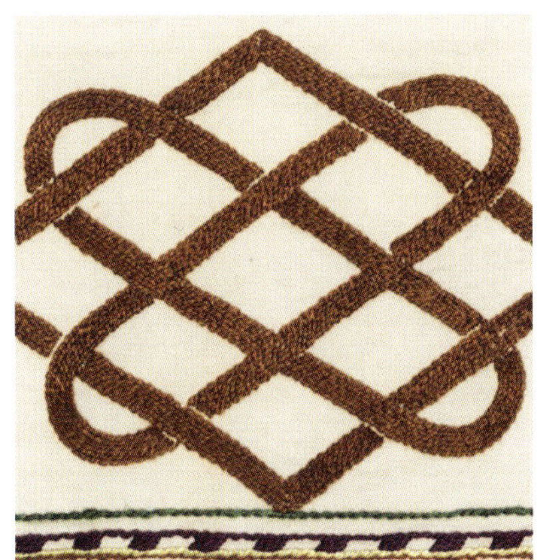

Fig.101 May Morris (1862–1938), Detail from a coverlet, 1910–3, polychrome silks on linen, 232.4 × 226.1 cm, William Morris Gallery, F203.

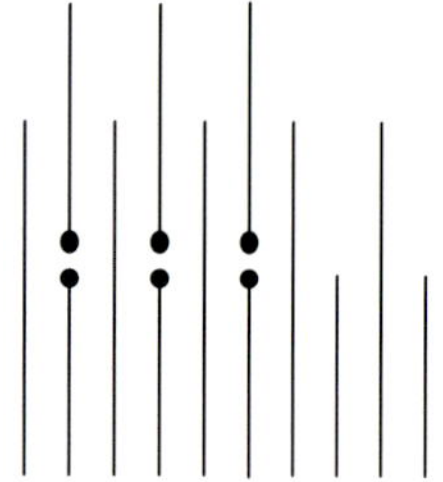

Left: fig.102 Dovetailing the stitches in long & short, taken from May Morris's lecture notes, 1899–1905, William Morris Gallery, J561iii

Below: fig.103 Three methods for working long & short, taken from May Morris's lecture notes, 1899–1905, William Morris Gallery, J561vi

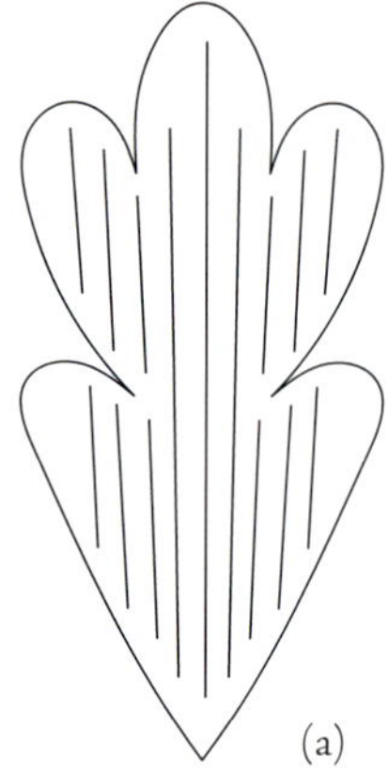

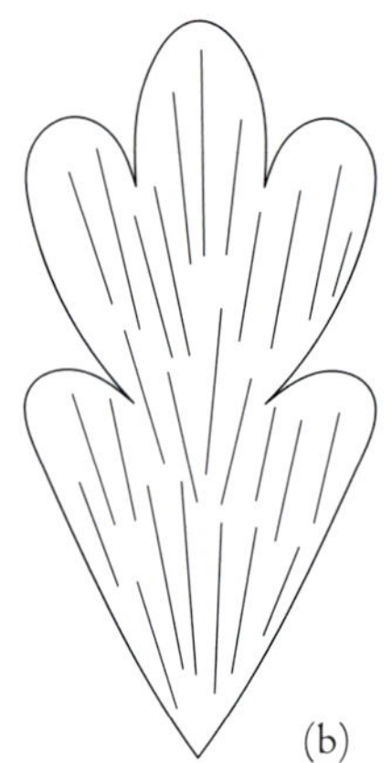

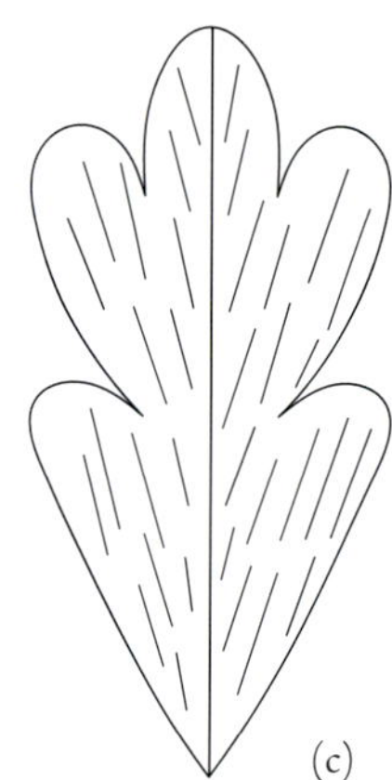

notes. In a roughly sketched diagram, the stitches are set between the ones created in the first row (**fig.102**).

There is no evidence in May's work or, for that matter, in any of the technical guidebooks or stitch primers listed in **Table 2**, of art embroiderers using a row of split stitch as a foundation for long & short to create a smooth edge around the shape. Practitioners were expected instead to place the top edge of the stitches in the first row, on the design line.

Elsewhere in her lecture notes, May sketches three different methods for shading a leaf, using long & short: a) 'tapestry' shading, in which the stitches lie parallel to each other down the length of the leaf; b) 'natural' shading, where the stitches follow the shape of the leaf; and c) again 'natural' shading, but with the stitches worked this time towards the centre vein (**fig.103**).

LAID AND COUCHED WORK

May describes two methods for working flat couching in her technical guidebook: 'The design is filled in by long threads stretching from side to side, either passing underneath and up again, as in satin-stitch, both sides similar, or the needle going down and up again on the same side as close as may be, the silk being thus all *on* the surface.'[3] The second method creates a tiny

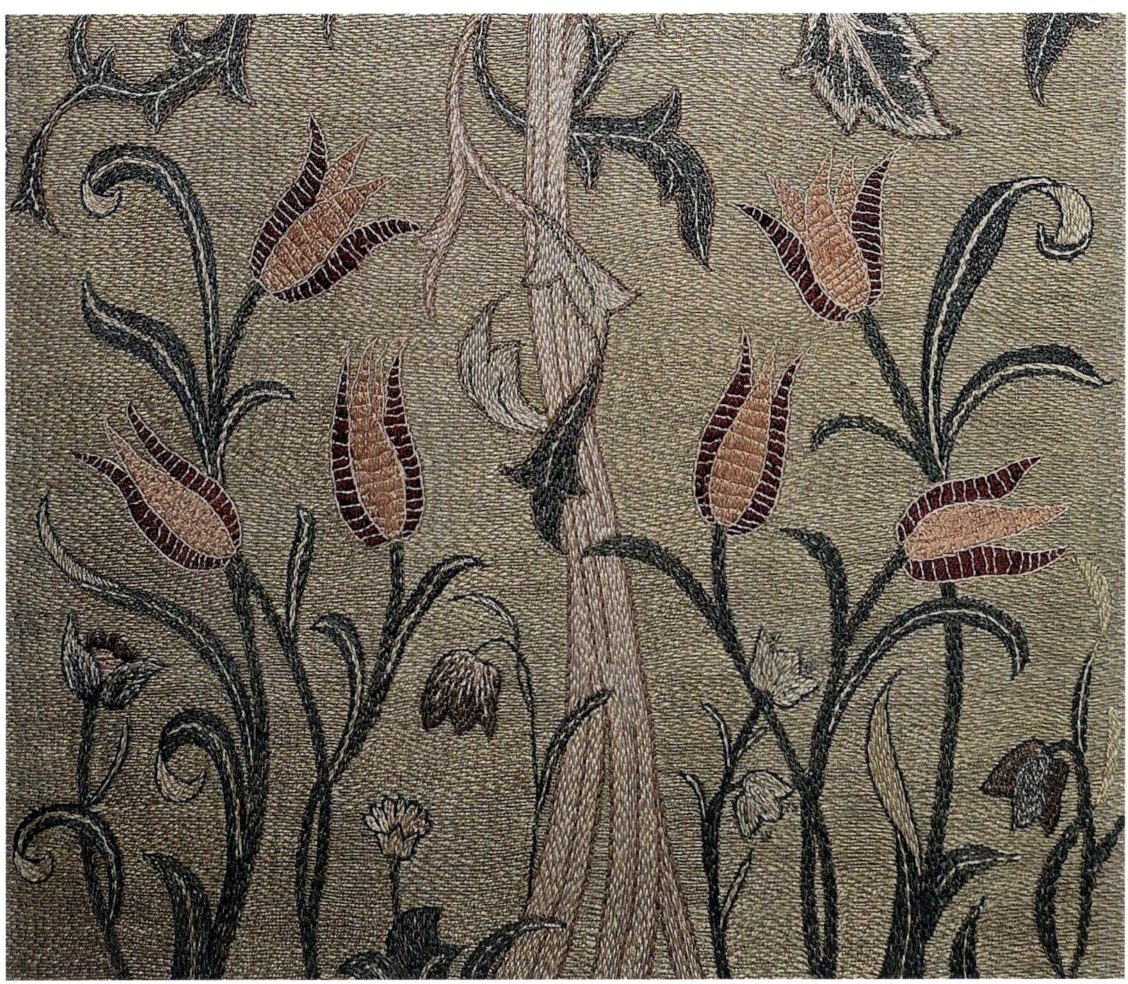

Fig.104 May Morris (1862–1938), *Rose and lattice* screen panel, *c*.1890, polychrome silks on Manchester cloth, 137.2 × 57 cm. Ashton Beer collection.

stitch on the back and is more economical when using expensive yarns. The threads couched at right angles are caught down at regular intervals with tiny stitches, offset to create a brick pattern. This method of laid and couched work is known today as Bayeux stitch, after its use in the Bayeux tapestry. There are a handful of examples in May's work, including the fritillaries in the *Spring and Summer* cabinet panel (**fig.47**), and the tulips in the *Rose and lattice* screen panel (**fig.104**).

SATIN STITCH

May's lecture notes contain further instruction on working satin stitch. In the first of two diagrams, the stitches lie at an angle of 45 degrees across the ovate leaf, known as 'slanted satin stitch', while in the second, the threads are laid in horizontal rows over padding to create a 'moulding effect' (**fig.105**).[4] May described this technique in *Decorative Needlework*, noting: 'For any articles that are expected to receive hard wear this is an excellent and enduring

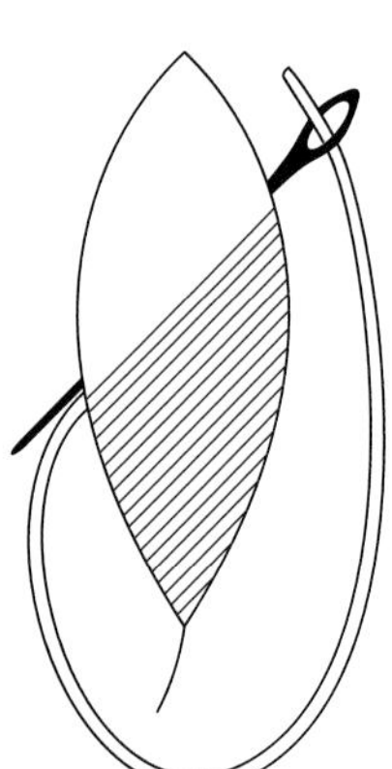

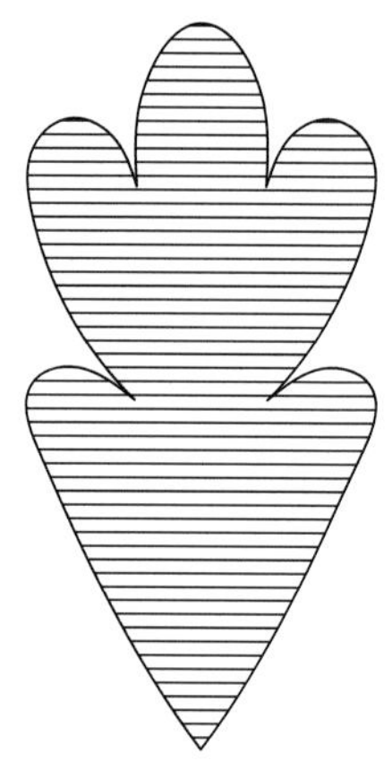

Fig.105 Directions for working satin stitch, taken from May Morris's lecture notes, 1899–1905, William Morris Gallery, J561iii

method of work: but as it is inclined to have a hard and mechanical look (particularly if it is smoothly done), the relief should be mostly flat and low.'[5] She advised readers to lay cotton or linen thread backwards and forwards across the form to be covered until the required relief is obtained, then work satin stitch at right angles to the layer of stuffing. The grapes in the border of the RSAN's embroidered replica of the *Pomona* tapestry, designed by William Morris and Burne-Jones, and worked at the School under May's direction in 1891, are padded and covered with a fine layer of silk thread so that the 'light catches the floss and makes them appear in good contrast to the rest.'[6]

Notes

INTRODUCTION

1 'Arts and Crafts at the New Gallery', *The Standard*, 3 October 1890, p.3.

CHAPTER 1: MAY MORRIS AND THE REVIVAL OF DECORATIVE NEEDLEWORK

1 Morris (1888) p.25.
2 Illustrated in Mason et al. (2017) p.151.
3 Glaister (1880) p.3.
4 Caulfeild and Saward (1882) 1, p.15.
5 For more information on Berlin wool work, see Proctor (1972); Ledbetter (2012); and Desnoyers (2019).
6 Street (1863) p.278.
7 Lockwood and Glaister (1878) p.12.
8 For more information on the early history of the South Kensington Museum, see Robertson (2004) and Bryant (2022).
9 The seventeenth-century distinction in terminology between 'needlework' (stitching through an open plain-weave linen to create a dense pattern that often covered the whole of the ground) and 'embroidery' (stitching in a variety of surface stitches on a luxurious cloth such as fine linen, silk, or velvet) did not exist in the Victorian period.
10 'Art Needlework', *The Building News*, 12 March 1875, p.283. For more information on the exhibition and its impact on the decorative arts, see Hulse (forthcoming).
11 Crane (1882) p.2.
12 Morris (1893) 'Dedicatory Note' (this author's emphasis).
13 Asphaltites, 'What is Art Needlework?', *The Queen*, 14 August 1875, p.115.
14 Masé's publication grew out of a short article entitled 'Colour and Design in Ornamental Needlework', published in *The Englishwoman's Domestic Magazine*, 21 (July 1876) pp.43, 46.
15 'Flittings', *The Englishwoman's Domestic Magazine*, 22 (May 1877) p.257.
16 'Practical Hints on the Revived Art of Crewel and Silk Embroidery', *The Queen*, 21 April 1877, p.272. The sixth edition of Turner's guide was released in 1882.
17 'Minor Notices', *The Examiner*, 9 March 1878, p.312 .
18 Proctor (2009) p.42. Wentworth Fitzwilliam and Morris Hands's publication *Jacobean Embroidery* was specifically aimed at these needlewomen.
19 'Current Literature', *The Daily News*, 16 October 1880, p.6; 'Handbook of Embroidery', *The Queen*, 7 February 1880, p.121
20 Morris (1891) pp.427–40.
21 Edwards (1975) p.104.
22 May's design recalls the embroidered binding created by her aunt Elizabeth Burden for a copy of Dante Gabriel Rossetti's *Ballads and Sonnets* (1881), National Library New Zealand, REng ROSS Ball 1881, https://natlib.govt.nz/records/21622085 [accessed 2 February 2025].
23 Masterman (1984) p.167.
24 'Books for the Boudoir', *The Westminster Gazette*, 8 June 1893, p.2.
25 'Books to Read and Books to Use', *The Yorkshire Post and Leeds Intelligencer*, 20 September 1893, p.3.
26 'The Revival of Needlework', *The Queen*, 4 March 1876, p.145.
27 Lockwood and Glaister (1878) p.8.
28 Morris (1890) p.844. See also Morris (1889) p.72; Morris (1892) p.46.
29 Day and Buckle (1900) pp.10 and 242.
30 Morris (1973) 1, pp.79 and 304.
31 Ida B. Cole, 'May Morris, Daughter of Master Craftsman', *The Woman's Magazine, The St Louis Star and Times*, 16 January 1910, p.59.
32 Lubbock (1920) 1, p.17.
33 Kelvin (1984) p.467.
34 Among the entries in the 1939 Kelmscott Manor sale catalogue (William Morris Gallery, box S4.4.8) are two old samplers (lot no.248), one stitched by Elizabeth Burden in 1850 (aged nine) and the other by her eldest sister Mary Anne Burden (1835–1849) in 1845 (aged ten).
35 Marsh and Sharp (2012) p.423.
36 Burne-Jones (1904) 1, p.273.
37 MacCarthy (1994) p.359.
38 Kelvin (1984) 1, p.561.
39 *Myra's Journal of Dress and Fashion*, 1 January 1877, p.22.
40 Parry (2013) pp.29, 31.
41 Kelvin (1984) p.465.
42 Newberry Library, Chicago, John M. Wing Collection, Wing MS ZW 845.M877, May Morris to Winifred Holiday, from Kelmscott Manor, 4 June 1928. I am grateful to Anna Mason for this reference.
43 Newberry Library, Chicago, John M. Wing Collection, Wing MS ZW 845.M877, May Morris to Winifred Holiday, from Kelmscott Manor, 24 May 1927 and 19 September 1927. I am grateful to Anna Mason for these references. For more information on

the role of Kelmscott in May's memorialisation of her father's legacy, see Dudkiewicz (2017) pp.221–25.

44 Ferry (2021) pp.130–36 and Schoeser (1998) pp.51–54 and 112–15.

45 Hulse (2014) pp.22–34.

46 Hulse (forthcoming).

47 Morris (1900) p.191.

48 Ibid.

49 Morris (1973) I, p.230.

50 Marsh (1986) pp.141–42.

51 Marsh and Sharp (2012) p.41.

52 Morris (1973) II, p.458.

53 Morris (1975) pp.159–75.

54 Textile (1884) p.366.

55 White (2017) p.57, n.3.

56 Kelmscott Manor acquisition no.KM641

57 Dickens jr, Charles, 'Art Training School', *Dickens's Dictionary of London* (1879), https://www.victorianlondon.org/education/dickens-arttrainingschool.htm [accessed 2 February 2025].

58 Cole (1888). The catalogue includes a selected list of books on making embroidery, pp.426–32.

59 Burton (1988) pp.54–55. For more information on the South Kensington system, see Frayling (1987) pp.44–64 and MacDonald (2005) pp.17–56.

60 National Art Library, V&A Special Collections: Science and Art Education: Art Examination Papers, 1878–82.

61 Textile (1884) p.365.

62 Cooper (2023) p.419.

63 Kelvin (1987) II, p.506.

CHAPTER 2: THE ELEMENTS OF ART EMBROIDERY

1 Morris (1892) p.46.

2 Morris (1890) p.844; Morris (1893) p.79.

3 Crane (1898) p.202.

4 Morris (1893) pp.5–6, 105. May's passion for medieval embroidery is discussed in Hulse (2017).

5 Sedding (1890) p.127.

6 Sedding (1890) pp.127–28. Sedding's comment refers to students and pupils from the art colleges and other institutions like the RSAN who were admitted to the South Kensington Museum on Wednesdays, Thursdays and Fridays at a weekly rate of 6d to study the collections and to use the 'Art Library and Educational Reading-room', *Catalogue of the Special Loan Exhibition of Decorative Art Needlework* (1873), back cover.

7 William Morris Gallery, Box S4.3.20.2, May Morris, 'Pattern-Designing' (1909–10) p.22. Both volumes are in the collection at Kelmscott Manor.

8 William Morris's collection of books is listed in https://williammorrislibrary.wordpress.com [accessed 8 February 2025].

9 Morris (1888) p.29.

10 Morris (1893) pp.6, 10.

11 Sedding (1890) p.125; Image (1890) p.132.

12 Image (1890) p.132.

13 Hulse (forthcoming).

14 Sedding (1890) pp.124–25.

15 Burges (1862) p.254.

16 Lockwood and Glaister (1878) p.73.

17 Quoted in Bain (2019) p.31.

18 May's collection of Islamic textiles is discussed in Cooper (2024).

19 Sedding (1890) p.127.

20 Morris (1881) p.409.

21 Redgrave (1876) p.21.

22 Ibid. pp.165–67.

23 Morris (1893) p.84.

24 National Gallery of Canada Library, Douglas Schoenherr Donation, May Morris to Margaret Peirce, 14 December 1931, from Kelmscott Manor. I am grateful to Anna Mason for this reference.

25 Morris (1893) p.84.

26 Asphaltites, 'What is Art Needlework?', *The Queen*, 14 August 1875, p.115.

27 Jones (1856) 'Leaves and Flowers from Nature', p.2.

28 Alford (2025) pp.144–47.

29 Morris (1893) pp.82–83.

30 Christie (1906) p.58.

31 Ibid. pp.58 and 60.

32 Morris (1894) p.245; Morris (1905) pp.278 and 283

33 The bedcover is illustrated in Mason et al. (2017) pp.102–03.

34 Morris (1893) p.6.

35 Paulson Townsend (1899) p.18.

36 William Morris Gallery J561vii. May reiterated this point in her lecture 'Pattern-Designing', William Morris Gallery, Box S4.3.20.2, pp.14–15.

37 Alford (1886) p.71.

38 Morris (1893) p.90.

39 Lockwood and Glaister (1878) pp.16–17.

40 Bisgrove (2008) pp.70–83, 128–39.

41 Lockwood and Glaister (1878) p.25.

42 Asphaltites, 'What is Art Needlework?', *The Queen*, 14 August 1875. p.115.

43 Ibid.

44 Morris (1893) p.30.

45 Ibid. pp.30, 114, 120.

46 Asphaltites, 'What is Art Needlework?', *The Queen*, 14 August 1875, p.115.

47 Crane (1882) p.76. For more information on the development of synthetic dyes, see Winterbottom (2023) pp.87–101.

48 Morris (1890) p.104.

49 Wardle (1879) p.513.

50 Higgin (1880) p.7.

51 For Wardle's experiments with dyeing, see King (2009).
52 Pearsall (1880s).
53 William Morris (1889) pp.56–67; Morris (1973) 1, p.304.
54 Morris (1890) pp.101–04.
55 Ibid. pp.106–07.
56 Morris (1962) p.124.
57 Glaister (1880) p.2.
58 Lockwood and Glaister (1878) p.30.
59 Morris (1890) pp.100–101.
60 Masters (1892) p.59. She was a regular contributor to *The Queen* and *Cassell's Family Magazine*.
61 Christie (1906) p.45.
62 Morris (1890) pp.92–93.
63 Masters (1892) p.52.
64 Higgin (1880) pp.11–12; Masters (1892) p.59; Christie (1906) p.47. For more information on the Decorative Needlework Society, see Hulse (forthcoming).
65 Morris (1894) p.74.
66 Ibid.; Higgin (1880) p.12.
67 Morris (1890) p.97.
68 'The Langdale Linen Industry', *The Queen*, 13 September 1902, p.413.
69 Fleming (1889) pp.521–27; Fleming (1889) pp.37–38; Russell (1897) pp.329–32; Pricket (1985) pp.9–12.
70 Ruskin Museum, Coniston, WDB73/1, Langdale order book, entries dated 11, 18 & 21 March; 4 & 13 September; 16 October. The corresponding postage for orders, letters and samples can be found in the Langdale account book, WDB73/2, in the Kendal Archive Centre.
71 Mason et al. (2017) p.104; Carruthers (2017) pp.121–22.
72 Old Bleach linen company advertisement, *The Queen*, 19 May 1906, p.4.
73 Masé (1877) p.26; Higgin (1880) pp.12–13; Downing (2021) p.78; Edwards (2007) p.27.
74 Illustrated in Mason et al. (2017) p.150.
75 Morris (1890) pp.97–98.
76 Masé (1877) p.27; Edwards (2007) pp.190–91.
77 Orrinsmith (1878) pp.73 and 77.
78 Morris (1890) p.99. For more information on the embroidered furnishings at Red House, see Wild (2018) pp.89–105.
79 Morris (1890) pp.98–99.
80 Edwards (2007) p.54.
81 Masé (1877) p.27.
82 Mason et al. (2017) pp.68–71.
83 Masters (1892) p.61.
84 Higgin (1880) p.15.
85 Morris & Co. (*c*.1912).
86 Morris (1890) p.93.
87 Townend (1909) p.22.
88 Morris & Co. (*c*.1912); Morris (1890) p.93.
89 Edwards (2007) pp.99–100, illustrated in Mason et al. (2017) p.79.
90 Turner (1890) pp.88–89.
91 Higgin (1880) pp.3–4.
92 Morris & Co. (*c*.1912).
93 Morris (1890) p.94.
94 Ibid.
95 Masters (1892) p.66.
96 Morris (1890) p.94.
97 Higgin (1880) p.6.
98 'Liberty Art' advertisement, *The Queen*, 2 October 1886.
99 Ridsdale (1894) Introduction.
100 Kelvin (1984) pp.417–18.
101 Morris & Co. (*c*.1912).
102 Ibid.
103 Morris (1890) p.95.
104 The V&A hanging is illustrated in Mason et al. (2017) p.111. The Art Institute of Chicago *Lotus* panel is one of a set of four made by the Chicago Society of Decorative Art in 1888 for the parlour of Frances Glessner's house on Prairie Avenue.
105 National Art Library, MSL/1939/2636, nos 1995, 2054 and 2285. For more information on the Embroidery Day Book, see Lister and Faurby (2017) pp.73–86.
106 Turner (1877) p.13.
107 Adams & Co. advertisement, *The Queen*, 8 May 1875, p.287.
108 Dolby (1867) p.158; Pearsall (1880s).
109 Hulse (forthcoming).
110 Dolby (1867) pp.136–37; Higgin (1880) pp.8–9; Kramer (2009–10) pp.19–27.
111 Marsh and Sharp (2012) p.422.
112 Kramer (2009–10) p.22.
113 Morris (1890) pp.95–96.
114 Morris (1895) p.394.
115 Masters (1892) p.67.
116 Morris (1890) pp.92–93; Morris (1893) p.25.
117 Sketchley (1907) pp.323–25.
118 Sedding (1890) p.122.
119 Ferry (2021) pp.130–36; Schoeser (1998) pp.112–15; Hulse (forthcoming).
120 Marsh and Sharp (2012) p.423.
121 Rock (1870) pp.xcii–civ; Coatsworth (2016) pp.43–67
122 Long & short and stem stitch were also known as 'embroidery' or 'feather stitch', and 'Kensington' or 'crewel stitch' respectively. The term 'Kensington' was coined in the 1870s in deference to the RSAN, situated in the heart of South Kensington.
123 Masters (1899) pp.1–2.
124 Day (1900) pp.8–9.
125 Cole (1886) p.966; Cole (1890) pp.108–21.
126 Masters (1899) p.2.
127 Paulson Townsend (1899) p.86, plates 41, 59–60.
128 Glaister (1880) p.28.

129 Morris (1913) p.clxii; Morris (1893) pp.78–79.
130 Coatsworth (2014) pp.169–70; Christie (1906) p.75.
131 Morris & Co. (*c*.1912); Morris (1893) p.29.
132 Kelvin (1984) p.387.
133 Ellis and Wearden (2001) pp.135–37.
134 William Morris Gallery, May Morris lecture notes, J561i. For more information on her teaching appointments, see Bratt-Wyton (2017) pp.130–40.
135 William Morris Gallery, May Morris lecture notes, J561i.
136 Morris (1893) pp.28–29.
137 Masters (1892) p.57.
138 William Morris Gallery May Morris lecture notes, J561iii.
139 Masters (1899) p.21.
140 Day (1900) pp.100, 103; Townend (1909) p.36.
141 Morris (1893) p.42.
142 Higgin (1880) p.27; Masters (1899) p.7.
143 Morris (1888) p.25; see also Morris (1893) p.17.
144 'Art Needlework I', *The Magazine of Art*, 3 (1880–81) p.79.
145 Morris (1894) p.3.
146 She may have had in mind a quilt with scenes from the Old Testament, which her father had advised the Museum to purchase two years earlier (V&A, 616–1886). William Morris wrongly attributed this object to Goa; it has since been identified as Bengali.
147 Morris (1888) pp.27–28; Cooper (2024) pp.110–13.
148 Morris (1888) p.26; Morris (1902) pp.19–20; William Morris Gallery, May Morris lecture notes, J561iv.
149 Mason (2017) pp.182–83.
150 Morris's design for a card case, made for Mrs Joanna Hawker, also contains advice on the choice of stitch, see Ashmolean Museum, WA1941.108.39.
151 Morris (1893) pp.46–47.
152 Morris (1913) p.clxx. The panel may have been designed by the architect Philip Webb (1831–1915); illustrated in Mason et al. (2017) p.126.
153 Manning (1980) p.19.
154 *Arts & Crafts Exhibition Society Catalogue of the Thirteenth Exhibition* (1926) p.65, nos 218(n) and 218(p). Morris's sketchbook of canvas work designs in graphite and watercolour on squared paper is in the collection at Kelmscott Manor, KM613.
155 The Gallery owns a second bag with the initial 'M' set within an Anglo-Saxon-style roundel, *c*.1932, William Morris Gallery, F338.
156 National Gallery of Canada Library and Archives, Douglas Schoenherr Donation, May Morris to Margaret Peirce, 14 December 1931, from Kelmscott Manor. I am grateful to Anna Mason for this reference.
157 Fielding (1968) p.3.
158 Morris (1913) p.clxii.

CHAPTER 3: FROM SKETCH TO FINISHED PATTERN

1 Palmer (2018) p.123. The purchase also included various drawings by Edward Burne-Jones.
2 Masé (1877) p.36.
3 Ibid. pp.38–39.
4 For more information on Briggs transfer papers, see Proctor (2009) pp.6–12.
5 Higgin (1880) p.vi. The French experimented with using pounce made of coloured resin that was rubbed over pricked patterns and heated with an iron, but the technique was found to be unsuccessful; Edward Tattersall to Victoria Welby, The English Church Rooms, 10 October 1873, Hulse (forthcoming).
6 See, for example, 'Home taught copying of designs', *The Queen*, 30 April 1887, p.543.
7 Ibid.
8 There is also a note warning the worker pricking the design to ignore a scribble top left.
9 Masé (1877) p.37.
10 Morris & Co. (*c*.1912). The catalogue contains designs by William and May Morris as well as John Henry Dearle (1859–1932), who became head designer at Morris & Co. in 1890 and Artistic Director in 1896.
11 National Art Library, MSL/1939/2636; Lister and Faurby (2017) pp.73–86.
12 Jessica Roberson, 'Pens and Needles: Reviving Book-Embroidery in Victorian England', https://publicdomainreview.org/essay/pens-and-needles-reviving-book-embroidery-in-victorian-england/#fn6 [accessed 10 February 2025].
13 Brassington (1894), p.167.
14 The Bancroft Library, Berkeley, T.J. Cobden-Sanderson Papers, BANC MSS 2011/260, May Morris to Frederick Ellis, 7 October 1890. I am grateful to Anna Mason for this reference. The book cover was one of six listed in the Kelmscott Manor sale in 1939 and was purchased by May's cousin, Dr Una Fielding (no.168).
15 Mason (2017) pp.152–73.
16 Nahum (1976) p.56. I am grateful to Caroline Palmer for identifying the monogram.
17 Several volumes of Rossetti's poems are listed in the catalogue of William Morris's library, including Jane Morris's copy of *Ballads and Sonnets*, https://williammorrislibrary.wordpress.com/2015/09/23/¶-rossetti-ballads-and-sonnets-1881/ [accessed 8 February 2025]. For Rossetti's offer to send Jane a gift of his 'new book', see Marsh and Sharp (2012), p.120; Faulkner (2014) p.62.
18 Illustrated in Mason et al. (2017) pp.160–61.
19 University of St Andrews, Lib Z232.M87N4. The slipcover is discussed in https://university-collections.wp.st-andrews.ac.uk/2012/02/08/52-weeks-of-fantastic-bindings-

week-35-a-20th-century-embroidered-binding-possibly-by-may-morris/ [accessed 10 February 2025]. For more information on the Culmers, see Bain (2017), pp.42–55; 'Death of Mrs A. M. Culmer', *Faversham and North East Kent News*, 1st December 1939, p.4.

20 Illustrated in Mason et al. (2017) p.92.

21 Scrapbooking was a popular pastime among middle- and upper-class women in nineteenth-century Britain.

22 MSL/1939/2636, nos.1557, 1629, 1832 and 2066.

23 Lyon and Turnbull (2024) lot no.240.

24 Morris (1893) p.99.

25 MSL/1939/2636, Helena Wolfe to Mrs Sparling [May Morris], Grand Pump Room Hotel Bath, 14 February 1893, glued to one of the blank pages at the end of the Embroidery Day Book.

26 MSL/1939/2636, nos.1486, 1490, 1507, 1568 and 1637.

27 MSL/1939/2636, no.1681.

28 Morris (1890) p.844.

29 The pattern for this design is in the Ashmolean collection, WA1941.108.466.

30 The William Morris Society, WMS–D55 and D80; Elletson (2025) pp.16–17.

31 Lyon and Turnbull (2024) lot. no.229.

32 A second copy of the tracing, pricked and pounced with charcoal, can be found in the Ashmolean collection, WA1941.108.458.2.

33 MSL/1939/2636, nos.1459, 1487, 1498–99 and 1525.

34 MSL/1939/2636, no.1813.

35 Charterhouse Auctioneers (2025) lot no.118. The mirror frame is inscribed 'Mrs Hawker, Gate House, Framfield'. May also designed a card case for Joanna Hawker in September 1896, MSL/1939/2636, no.2280, price £1. The corresponding pattern in the Ashmolean (WA1941.108.39) is a rare survival among May's designs in providing instructions on colouring and stitching.

36 MSL/1939/2636, nos.1489, 1691, 1693, 1961, 1973–74 and 2251.

37 Sketchley (1907) pp.323–24.

38 Two copies of wood sorrel exist: one on lined paper (WA1941.108.90) and the other on tracing paper (WA1941.108.78).

39 Higgin (1880) p.63 and plate 6. May bequeathed the original design to the V&A, E.41–1940.

40 University of Iowa Redpath Chautauqua Collection MSC0150, *Mary Elliott Hobbs*; D. N. K., 'May Elliott Hobbs' (1956) p.8. For the quilt, see Haslam (2016) pp.2–5; *idem* (2017) pp.200–01; illustrated in Mason et al. (2017) pp.118–19.

41 The construction of the sofa back is sketched on a design for a primrose, WA1941.108.72, drawn on the same paper as the other floral motifs, but not included in this project. The finished embroidery measures 40 × 157 cm.

42 Roberson (2017) pp.18–19.

43 Morris & Co. (*c*.1912).

44 MSL/1939/2636, no.1736, April 1894.

45 Morris (1892) p.946.

46 Conroy (2025) pp.152–55.

47 Illustrated in Mason et al. (2017) p.186.

48 V&A Archive, Nominal file MA/1/M2833 1914–54, extract from the will of May Morris, 'a silver topped bag designed by my late father and worked by my late mother'.

49 Morris (1895) p.387. See also 'Embellished textile purses in the French 14th century', https://cottesimple.com/articles/aumonieres/ [accessed 10 February 2025].

50 'London and Paris Fashions', *The Queen*, 19 December 1863, p.411.

51 Morris (1890) p.844.

52 MSL/1939/2636, nos.1356–58. The Art Gallery of South Australia contains several embroideries made by members of the Barr Smith family, to May's designs.

53 MSL/1939/2636, no.2064.

54 MSL/1939/2636, nos.1899, 2131 and 2285.

AFTERWORD

1 National Gallery of Canada Library and Archives, Douglas Schoenherr Donation, May Morris to Margaret Peirce, 24 January 1935, from Kelmscott Manor. I am grateful to Anna Mason for this reference.

2 Quoted in Parry (1996) p.59.

TECHNICAL SAMPLES

1 Morris (1893) p.26.

2 Morris (1893) pp.41–42.

3 Morris (1893) p.49.

4 William Morris Gallery, May Morris lecture notes, J561iii.

5 Morris (1893) p.25.

6 Paulson Townsend (1899) p.41. *Pomona* is illustrated in Mason et al. (2017) p.59.

Bibliography

MANUSCRIPTS

Kendal Archive Centre, Cumbria, WDB73/2, Langdale account book

National Art Library, London, MSL/1939/2636, Morris & Co. Embroidery Day Book, May 1892–November 1896

National Gallery of Canada Library, Ottawa, Douglas Schoenherr Donation, May Morris to Margaret Peirce, 14 December 1931, from Kelmscott Manor

Newberry Library, Chicago, John M. Wing Collection, Wing MS ZW 845.M877, May Morris to Winifred Holiday, from Kelmscott Manor, 24 May 1927, 19 September 1927 and 4 June 1928

Ruskin Museum, Coniston, WDB73/1, Langdale order book

Society of Antiquaries of London, Kelmscott Manor, KM613, May Morris, Sketchbook of canvas work designs, *c.*1910s–20s

The Bancroft Library, Berkeley, T.J. Cobden-Sanderson Papers, BANC MSS 2011/260, May Morris to Frederick Ellis, 7 October 1890

University of Iowa, Redpath Chautauqua Collection, MSC0150, *Mary Elliott Hobbs*

Victoria and Albert Museum, London, V&A Archive, nominal file MA/1/M2833 1914–54, May Morris

William Morris Gallery, London, J561, May Morris, Lecture notes, 1899–1905

William Morris Gallery, London, Box S4.3.20.2 'May Morris, 'Pattern-Designing', 1909–10

PRINTED SOURCES

Adams & Co. advertisement, *The Queen*, 8 May 1875, p.287

Alford, Lady Marian, *Needlework as Art* (London, 1886)

Alford, Sarah, *Art Botany in British Design Reform, 1835–1865* (London, 2025)

Amyot, Thomas, 'A Transcript of two Rolls, containing an Inventory of Effects formerly belonging to Sir John Fastoffe', *Archaeologia*, 21 (1827) pp.232–79

Art Examination Papers, 1878–82, National Art Library, London, Special Collections: Science and Art Education Collection

'Art Needlework', *The Building News*, 12 March 1875, p.283

'Art Needlework I', *The Magazine of Art*, 3 (1880–81) pp.76–79

'Arts and Crafts at the New Gallery', *The Standard*, 3 October 1890, p.3

Arts & Crafts Exhibition Society Catalogue of the Thirteenth Exhibition (1926)

Asphaltites, 'What is Art Needlework?', *The Queen*, 14 August 1875, p.115

Bain, Rowan, 'A tale of two sisters: May and Jenny Morris', in ed. Lynn Hulse, *May Morris: Art & Life* (London, 2017) pp.42–55

Bain, Rowan, *William Morris's Flowers* (London, 2019)

Bisgrove, Richard, *William Robinson: The Wild Gardener* (London, 2008)

'Books for the Boudoir', *The Westminster Gazette*, 8 June 1893, p.2

'Books to Read and Books to Use', *The Yorkshire Post and Leeds Intelligencer*, 20 September 1893, p.3

Brassington, William Salt, *A History of the Art of Bookbinding* (London, 1894)

Bratt-Wyton, Helen, 'May Morris: Special Teacher of Needlework at the Birmingham School of Art, 1899–1902', in ed. Lynn Hulse, *May Morris: Art & Life* (London, 2017) pp.130–40

Bryant, Julius, *Enriching the V&A: A Collection of Collections, 1862–1914* (London, 2022)

Burges, William, 'The Japanese Court at the International Exhibition', *The Gentleman's Magazine*, 213 (1862) pp.243–54

Burne-Jones, Georgiana, *Memorials*, 2 vols (London, 1904)

Burton, Anthony, 'Redgrave as Art Educator, Museum Official and Design Theorist', in eds. Susan P. Casteras and Ronald Parkinson, *Richard Redgrave 1804–1888* (New Haven and London, 1988) pp.48–70

Carruthers, Annette, 'Darning, dyeing and embroidery: May Morris at Melsetter', in ed. Lynn Hulse, *May Morris: Art & Life* (London, 2017) pp.111–29
Catalogue of the Special Loan Exhibition of Decorative Art Needlework made before 1800 (London, 1873)
Caulfeild, S. F. A., and Blanche C. Saward, *The Dictionary of Needlework*, 6 vols (London, 1882)
Charterhouse Auctioneers, *Textiles and the Contents of a Seamstress Studio*, 2 January 2025
Coatsworth, Elizabeth, '"A formidable undertaking": Mrs A. G. I. Christie and *English Medieval Embroidery*', in eds. Robin Netherton and Gale R. Owen-Crocker, *Medieval Clothing and Textiles*, 10 (Woodbridge, 2014) pp.165–93
Coatsworth, Elizabeth, 'Opus What? The Textual History of Medieval Embroidery Terms and Their Relationship to the Surviving Embroideries *c.*800–1400', in eds. Maren Clegg Hyer and Jill Frederick, *Textiles, Text, Intertext Essays in Honour of Gale R. Owen-Crocker* (Woodbridge, 2016) pp.43–67
Christie, Grace, *Embroidery and Tapestry Weaving* (London, 1906)
Cole, A. S., 'The Arts of Tapestry-Making and Embroidery, Lecture III', *Journal of the Society of Arts*, 34 (20 August 1886) pp.963–67
Cole, Alan S., *A Descriptive Catalogue of the Collections of Tapestry and Embroidery in the South Kensington Museum* (London, 1888)
Cole, A. S., 'Stitches and Mechanism', *Arts and Crafts Exhibition Society: Catalogue of the Third Exhibition* (1890) pp.108–121
Cole, Ida, B., 'May Morris, Daughter of Master Craftsman', *The Woman's Magazine, The St Louis Star and Times*, 16 January 1910, p.59
Conroy, Rachel, *Women Artists & Designers at the National Trust* (Swindon, 2025)
Cooper, Thomas, 'A "Morris Room" in Cardiff: Mary Lobb and the National Museum of Wales', *The Burlington Magazine*, 165 (April 2023) pp.148–21
Cooper, Thomas, 'May Morris as Collector and Donor of Textiles from the Islamic World', in ed. Rowan Bain, *Tulips and Peacocks: William Morris and Art from the Islamic World* (London and New Haven, 2024) pp.110–23
'Colour and Design in Ornamental Needlework', *The Englishwoman's Domestic Magazine*, 21 (July 1876) pp.43, 46
Crane, Lucy, *Art and the Formation of Taste* (London, 1882)
Crane, Walter, 'Needlework as a Mode of Artistic Expression', *The Magazine of Art*, 22 (1898) pp.144–48 and 197–202
'Current Literature', *The Daily News*, 16 October 1880, p.6
Day, Lewis Foreman, and Mary Buckle, *Art in Needlework: A Book about Embroidery* (London, 1900)
'Death of Mrs A. M. Culmer', *Faversham and North East Kent News*, 1st December 1939, p.4
Desnoyers, Rosika, *Pictorial Embroidery in England: A Critical History of Needlepainting and Berlin Work* (London, 2019)
Dolby, Anastasia, *Church Embroidery Ancient and Modern* (London, 1867)
Downing, Sarah Jane, 'Textile Towns: Manchester Cottonopolis', *Selvedge*, 100 (April 2021) pp.100–101
Dudkiewicz, Julia, 'Memorialising her father's legacy: May Morris as curator and gatekeeper of William Morris's estate and the role of Kelmscott', in ed. Lynn Hulse, *May Morris: Art & Life* (London, 2017) pp.209–35
Edwards, Clive, *Encyclopedia of Furnishing Textiles, Floorcoverings and Home Furnishing Practices, 1200–1950* (Aldershot, 2007)
Edwards, Joan, 'May Morris, embroiderer 1862–1938', *Embroidery*, 26/2 (Winter 1975) pp.104–105 and 120
Elletson, Helen, 'New acquisition: exquisite embroidery by May Morris', *The William Morris Society Magazine* (Spring 2025) pp.16–17
Ellis, Marianne and Jennifer Wearden, *Ottoman Embroidery* (London, 2001)
Faulkner, Peter, 'Jane Morris and her Male Correspondents', *The Journal of William Morris Studies*, 20/4 (Summer 2014) pp.60–78
Ferry, Kathryn, *The Old Convent East Grinstead* (East Grinstead, 2021)
Fielding, Una, 'Memories of May Morris: 1923–1938', *The Journal of William Morris Studies*, 2/3 (Winter 1968) pp.2–5
Fleming, Albert, 'Revival of Hand Spinning and Weaving in Westmoreland', *The Century Illustrated Monthly Magazine*, 37 (new series 15) (February 1889) pp.521–27
Fleming, Albert, 'Langdale Linen Industry', *Ruskin Reading Guild Journal*, ½ (February 1889) pp.37–38
'Flittings', *The Englishwoman's Domestic Magazine*, 22 (May 1877) p.257

Frayling, Christopher, *The Royal College of Art: One Hundred & Fifty Years of Art & Design* (London, 1987)
Glaister, Elizabeth, *Needlework*, Art at Home Series (London, 1880)
'Handbook of Embroidery', *The Queen*, 7 February 1880, p.121
Haslam, Kathy, 'The Homestead and the Forest cot quilt', *The William Morris Society Magazine* (Spring 2016) pp.2–5
Haslam, Kathy, 'Our beloved Oxfordshire Home: May Morris and Kelmscott', in ed. Lynn Hulse, *May Morris: Art & Life* (London, 2017) pp.191–208
Higgin, Letitia, *Handbook of Embroidery*, ed. Lady Marian Alford (London, 1880)
'Home taught copying of designs', *The Queen*, 30 April 1887, p.543
Hulse, Lynn, 'Elizabeth Burden and the Royal School of Needlework', *The Journal of William Morris Studies*, 21/1 (Winter 2014) pp.22–34
Hulse, Lynn, '"When needlework was at its very finest": *Opus Anglicanum* and its influence on the work of May Morris', in ed. Lynn Hulse, *May Morris: Art & Life* (London, 2017) pp.87–110
Hulse, Lynn, *Reviving the Art of Embroidery: Lady Victoria Welby and the Founding of the Royal School of Needlework* (forthcoming)
Image, Selwyn, 'Of Designing for the Art of Embroidery', *Arts and Crafts Exhibition Society Catalogue of the Third Exhibition* (London, 1890) pp.128–33
Jones, Owen, *The Grammar of Ornament* (London, 1856)
K., D. N., 'May Elliott Hobbs', *Journal of the English Folk Dance and Song Society*, 8/1 (1956) p.8
Kelvin, Norman, ed., *The Collected Letters of William Morris*, I, 1848–1880 (Princeton, 1984)
Kelvin, Norman, ed., *The Collected Letters of William Morris*, II, 1885–1888 (Princeton, 1987)
King, Brenda M., *Dye, Print, Stitch: Textiles by Thomas and Elizabeth Wardle* (Macclesfield, 2009)
Kramer, Elizabeth, 'Japanese Inspiration and the "Art" of Victorian Art Embroidery', *Text*, 37 (2009–2010) pp.19–27
Ledbetter, Kathryn, *Victorian Needlework* (Santa Barbara, 2012)
'Liberty Art' advertisement, *The Queen*, 2 October 1886
Lister, Jenny, and Hannah Faurby, 'Apple Tree to Vine Leaf: the Morris & Co. embroidery day book, 1892–1896', in ed. Lynn Hulse, *May Morris: Art & Life* (London, 2017) pp.73–86
Lockwood, M. S., and Elizabeth Glaister, *Art Embroidery: A Treatise on the Revived Practice of Decorative Needlework* (London, 1878)
'London and Paris Fashions', *The Queen*, 19 December 1863, p.411
Lubbock, Percy, ed., *The Letters of Henry James*, I (New York, 1920)
Lyon and Turnbull Edinburgh, *Design since 1860*, sale cat. (16 October 2024)
MacCarthy, Fiona, *William Morris* (London, 1994)
Macdonald, Stuart, *A Century of Art Education: From Arts and Crafts to Conceptual Art* (Cambridge, 2005)
Manning, Elfrida, 'A visit to May Morris, 1925', *The Journal of William Morris Studies*, 4/2 (Summer 1980) pp.18–19
Marsh, Jan, *Jane and May Morris: A Biographical Study 1839–1938* (London, 1986)
Marsh, Jan, and Frank C. Sharp, eds., *The Collected Letters of Jane Morris* (Woodbridge, 2012)
Masé, E., *Art Needlework: A Guide to Embroidery in Crewels, Silks, Appliqué, etc.* (London, 1877)
Mason, Anna, Jan Marsh, Jenny Lister, Rowan Bain and Hannah Faurby, *May Morris Arts & Crafts Designer* (London, 2017)
Mason, Anna, 'Book Covers and Designs', in Anna Mason, Jan Marsh, Jenny Lister, Rowan Bain and Hannah Faurby, *May Morris Arts & Crafts Designer* (London, 2017) pp.152–73
Masterman, Elizabeth, 'May Morris: Some notes for book collectors', *The Book Collector*, 13/2 (Summer 1984) pp.163–78
Masters, Ellen T., *The Gentlewoman's Book of Art Needlework* (London, 1892)
Masters, Ellen T., *The Book of Stitches* (London, 1899)
'Minor Notices', *The Examiner*, 9 March 1878, p.312
Morris & Co., *Embroidery work* catalogue (London, c.1912)
Morris, Barbara, *Victorian Embroidery* (London, 1962)
Morris, Barbara, 'William Morris and the South Kensington Museum', *Victorian Poetry*, 13/3–4 (1975) pp.159–75
Morris, May, 'Chain-Stitch Embroidery', *The Century Guild Hobby Horse*, 3 (1888) pp.24–29
Morris, May, 'Of Embroidery', *Arts and Crafts Exhibition Society: Catalogue of the Second Exhibition* (London, 1889) pp.68–74

Morris, May, 'Of Materials' and 'Of Colours and Colouring', *Arts and Crafts Exhibition Society: Catalogue of the Third Exhibition* (London, 1890) pp.92–107

Morris, May, 'Design in Embroidery', *The Queen, The Lady's Newspaper*, 6 December 1890, p.844

Morris, May, 'How to Make the Home Pretty', *Hughes's Domestic Economy* (London, 1891) pp.427–40

Morris, May, 'Embroidery', in A. H. Mackmurdo, *Plain Handicrafts, being Essays by Artists Setting Forth the Principles of Design & Established Methods of Workmanship* (London, 1892) pp.46–56

Morris, May, 'Embroidered Sleeves', *The Queen, The Lady's Newspaper*, 3 December 1892, pp.946–47

Morris, May, *Decorative Needlework* (London, 1893)

Morris, May, 'Of Church Embroidery, I', *The Building News*, 65/2023 (13 October 1893) pp.465–66

Morris, May, 'Of Church Embroidery, VII: Figure Work', *The Building News*, 66/2035 (5 January 1894) pp.3–4

Morris, May, 'Of Church Embroidery, VIII: White Linen Work', *The Building News*, 75/2037 (19 January 1894) pp.73–74

Morris, May, 'Of Church Embroidery, X: Design', *The Building News*, 66/2042 (23 February 1894) pp.245–46

Morris, May, 'Mediæval Embroidery', *Journal of the Society for Arts*, 43/2207 (8 March 1895) pp.384–96

Morris, May, 'Decorative Needlework', *Women in Professions being the Professional Section of The International Congress of Women, London, July 1899*, ed. The Countess of Aberdeen (London, 1900) pp.191–94

Morris, May, 'Line Embroidery', *The Art Workers' Quarterly*, 1/4 (October 1902) pp.117–21

Morris, May, 'Opus Anglicanum – The Syon Cope', *The Burlington Magazine*, 6/22 (January 1905) pp.278–85

Morris, May, 'Embroidery' in Board of Trade, *Ghent International Exhibition 1913: Catalogue of the British Arts and Crafts Section* (London, 1913) pp.clxii–clxxvii

Morris, May, *The Introductions to The Collected Works of William Morris*, 2 vols (New York, 1973)

Morris, William, 'Some Hints on Pattern-Designing', *The Architect*, 26 (1881) pp.391–94 and 408–10

Morris, William, 'Textiles', *Arts and Crafts Essays* (London, 1893) pp.22–38

Myra's Journal of Dress and Fashion, 1 January 1877, p.22

Nahum, Peter, *Monograms of Victorian and Edwardian Artists* (London, 1976)

Old Bleach Linen Company advertisement, *The Queen*, 19 May 1906, p.4

Orrinsmith, Mrs Lucy, *The Drawing Room: its Decorations and Furniture* (London, 1878)

Palmer, Caroline, 'Picking up the Thread', *The Decorative Arts Society Journal*, 42 (2018) pp.122–41

Parry, Linda, 'May Morris, embroidery and Kelmscott', in ed. Linda Parry, *William Morris: Art and Kelmscott* (Woodbridge, 1996) pp.57–68

Parry, Linda, *William Morris Textiles* (London, 2013)

Paulson Townsend, W. G., *Embroidery: or The Craft of the Needle* (London & New York, 1899)

Pearsall's Eastern Dyes card no. 2 (London, 1880s)

'Practical Hints on the Revived Art of Crewel and Silk Embroidery', *The Queen*, 21 April 1877, p.272

Pricket, Elizabeth, *Ruskin Lace & Linen Work* (London, 1985)

Proctor, Molly G., *Victorian Canvas Work: Berlin Wool Work* (London, 1972)

Proctor, Molly G., *Art Needlework and Embroidery Transfers 1870–1970* (Wimborne, 2009)

Redgrave, Richard, *A Manual of Design* (London, 1876)

Ridsdale, Audrey, *Designs for Church Embroidery* (London, 1894)

Roberson, Sally, 'Underneath the living flowers', *The William Morris Society Magazine* (Summer 2017) pp.18–19

Robertson, Bruce, 'The South Kensington Museum in context: an alternative history', *Museum and Society*, 2/1 (March 2004) pp.1–14

Rock, Daniel *South Kensington Museum Textile Fabrics; A Descriptive Catalogue* (London, 1870)

Russell, Barbara, 'The Langdale Linen Industry', *The Art Journal*, 59 (1987) pp.329–32

Sale of a Large Portion of the Furnishings and Effects Removed from Kelmscott Manor, The Home of William Morris (July 1939)

Schoeser, Mary, *English Church Embroidery 1833–1953* (London, 1998)

Sedding, John Dando, 'Of Design', *Arts and Crafts Exhibition Society Catalogue of the Third Exhibition* (London, 1890) pp.122–27

Sketchley, R. E. D., 'Some Modern Embroideries', *The Art Journal* (1907) pp.321–26

Street, George Edmund, 'On Mediæval Embroidery', *The Ecclesiologist*, 24/157, new series 21/122 (October 1863) pp.255–80

Textile, 'National Art Education. By a Designer', *The Art Journal* (1884) pp.165–67

The Fourth Book of Hows, or How to Work Embroidery Stitches (Manchester, 1904)

'The Langdale Linen Industry', *The Queen*, 13 September 1902, p.413

'The Revival of Needlework', *The Queen*, 4 March 1876, pp.145–46

Townend, Mrs B., *Talks on Art Needlework* (London & Glasgow, 1909)

Townend, Mrs B., *Art Needlework Made Easy* (London, 1911)

Turner, Mary E., 'Of Modern Embroidery', *Arts and Crafts Exhibition Society: Catalogue of the Third Exhibition* (London, 1890) pp.85–92

Turner, M. A., *Practical Hints on the Revived Art of Crewel & Silk Embroidery* (London, 1877)

Wardle, Thomas, 'On the Wilds Silks of India, Principally Tusser', *Journal of the Society of Arts*, 26/1333 (9 May 1879) pp.499–513

White, Catherine, 'Decorative Needlework: May Morris and her embroiderers', in ed. Lynn Hulse, *May Morris: Art & Life* (London, 2017) pp.56–72

Wild, Tessa, *William Morris and his Palace of Art: Interiors and Design at Red House* (London, 2018)

Winterbottom, Matthew, '"The Triumph of Colour": the Synthetic Colour Revolution', in eds. Charlotte Ribeyrol, Matthew Winterbottom and Madeline Hewitson, *Colour Revolution: Victorian Art, Fashion & Design* (Oxford, 2023) pp.87–101

Fitzwilliam, Ada and A. F. Morris Hands, *Jacobean Embroidery: Its Forms and Fillings Including Late Tudor* (London, 1912)

WEBSITES

Dickens jr, Charles, 'Art Training School', *Dickens's Dictionary of London* (1879), https://www.victorianlondon.org/education/dickens-arttrainingschool.htm [accessed 2 February 2025]

'Embellished textile purses in the French 14th century', https://cottesimple.com/articles/aumonieres/ [accessed 2 February 2025]

National Library New Zealand, REng ROSS Ball 1881, Dante Gabriel Rossetti, *Ballads and Sonnets* (1881), https://natlib.govt.nz/records/21622085 [accessed 2 February 2025]

Roberson, Jessica, 'Pens and Needles: Revving Book-Embroidery in Victorian England', https://publicdomainreview.org/essay/pens-and-needles-reviving-book-embroidery-in-victorian-england/#fn6 [accessed 20 February 2025]

https://rsnstitchbank.org [accessed 20 February 2025]

https://university-collections.wp.st-andrews.ac.uk/2012/02/08/52-weeks-of-fantastic-bindings-week-35-a-20th-century-embroidered-binding-possibly-by-may-morris/ [accessed 10 February 2025]

https://williammorrislibrary.wordpress.com [accessed 8 February 2025]

Opposite: detail of fig.21

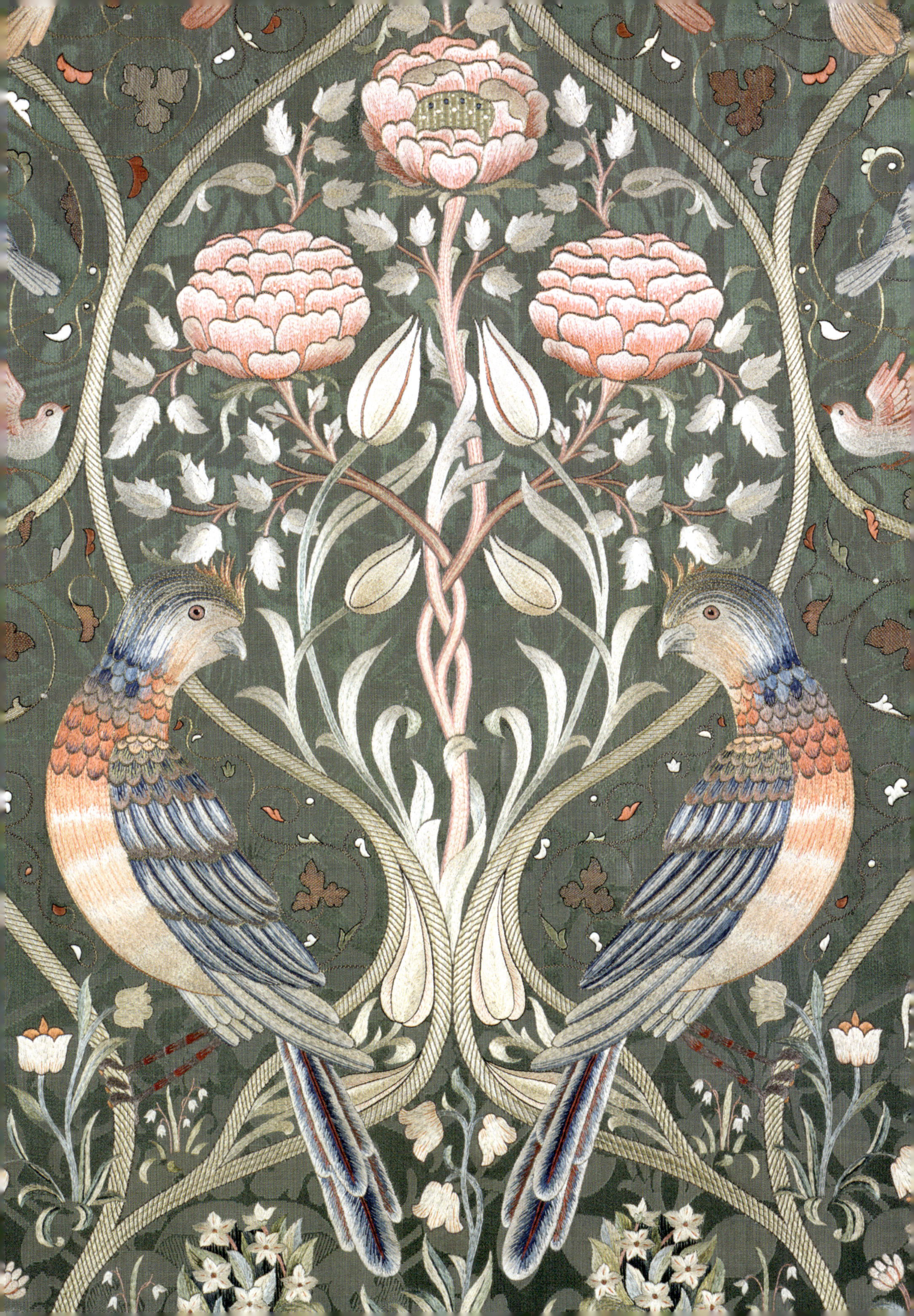

Image credits

Fig.1	Library of Congress, Rare Book and Special Collections Division. https://lccn.loc.gov/2014683895
Fig.2	© William Morris Gallery, London Borough of Waltham Forest
Fig.7	© William Morris Gallery, London Borough of Waltham Forest Photograph © Paul Tucker
Fig.8	© William Morris Gallery, London Borough of Waltham Forest
Fig.9	Library of Congress, Rare Book and Special Collections Division https://www.loc.gov/item/44028884/
Fig.10	Public Domain Mark. Source: Wellcome Collection
Fig.12	Photograph © Paul Reeves
Fig.13	© Victoria and Albert Museum, London
Fig.14	Photograph by Birmingham Museums Trust, licensed under Creative Commons Zero
Fig.20	Photograph © Paul Reeves
Fig.21	© William Morris Gallery, London Borough of Waltham Forest. Photograph © Paul Reeves
Fig.22	Photograph: Victoria and Albert Museum, London
Fig.25	© Society of Antiquaries of London (Kelmscott Manor)/ V&A
Fig.26	© Victoria and Albert Museum, London
Fig.28	Photograph © Paul Reeves
Fig.30	© Victoria and Albert Museum, London
Fig.32	© William Morris Gallery, London Borough of Waltham Forest
Fig.34	Photograph: © Lyon & Turnbull
Fig.35	The Metropolitan Museum of Art, New York, Rogers Fund, 1972
Fig.38	© William Morris Gallery, London Borough of Waltham Forest
Fig.42	Photograph © Lynn Hulse
Fig.44	© William Morris Gallery, London Borough of Waltham Forest
Fig.47	Photograph © Lynn Hulse
Fig.48	© William Morris Gallery, London Borough of Waltham Forest
Fig.55	Photograph © Lyon and Turnbull
Fig.57	© William Morris Gallery, London Borough of Waltham Forest
Fig.58	Photograph © Paul Reeves
Fig.60	© Victoria and Albert Museum, London
Fig.62	Photograph © Lynn Hulse
Fig.63	The Metropolitan Museum of Art, New York, Rogers Fund, 1928
Fig.64	© William Morris Gallery, London Borough of Waltham Forest
Fig.65	Wightwick Manor © National Trust / Sophia Farley and Claire Reeves
Fig.67	© Victoria and Albert Museum, London
Fig.94	© Victoria and Albert Museum, London
Fig.95	© William Morris Gallery, London Borough of Waltham Forest
Fig.96	© Victoria and Albert Museum, London
Fig.100	© William Morris Gallery, London Borough of Waltham Forest
Fig.101	© William Morris Gallery, London Borough of Waltham Forest
Fig.104	Photograph © Paul Reeves